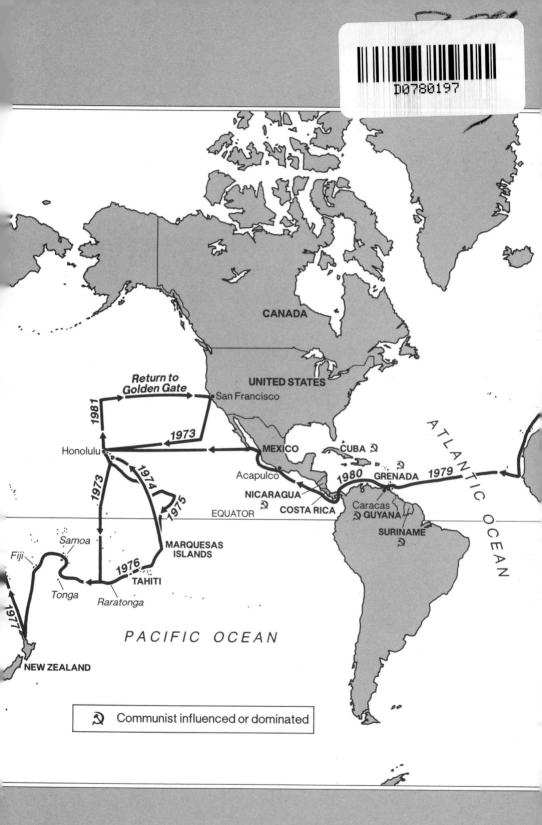

CANADA

UNITED STATES

Return to Golden Gate

1981

San Francisco

1973

Honolulu

1973   1974   1975

MEXICO   CUBA 🪓

Acapulco

1980   GRENADA   1979

NICARAGUA 🪓

COSTA RICA

Caracas 🪓

GUYANA 🪓

SURINAME 🪓

EQUATOR

Samoa   MARQUESAS ISLANDS

Fiji

1976   TAHITI

Tonga   Raratonga

1977

PACIFIC OCEAN

ATLANTIC OCEAN

NEW ZEALAND

🪓 Communist influenced or dominated

VOYAGE

OF

COMMITMENT

Morning Star Around the World

November 28, 1983

To our good friends Jack and Audrey

with all best wishes

Ray Truscell

VOYAGE
OF
COMMITMENT

Morning Star Around the World

by Raymond F. Triplett

DODD, MEAD & COMPANY
NEW YORK

Text design: LEVAVI & LEVAVI

1   2   3   4   5   6   7   8   9   10

Library of Congress Cataloging in Publication Data
Triplett, Raymond F.
    Voyage of commitment.

    1. Triplett, Raymond F.   2. Morning Star (Ketch)
3. Voyages around the world--1951-   . I. Title.
G440.T83   1983   910.4'1   82–19949
ISBN 0–396–08123–1

This book is dedicated to Shirley—

The most courageous human being I have ever known—
my wife and first mate of forty-one years.

*"Everything can be found at sea
According to the spirit of your Quest."*
JOSEPH CONRAD

CONTENTS

ACKNOWLEDGMENTS

Special acknowledgment to Natalie H. Stotz, Bud and Ann Alvernaz, Jeff and Marge Jefferson, John F. Hopkins, Marshall Wolper, Edward Dodd, Allen Klots, and to all of the many people in all parts of the world whose kindness, encouragement, help, and prayers made this voyage and book possible.

The Track of the Ketch
<u>Morning Star</u>

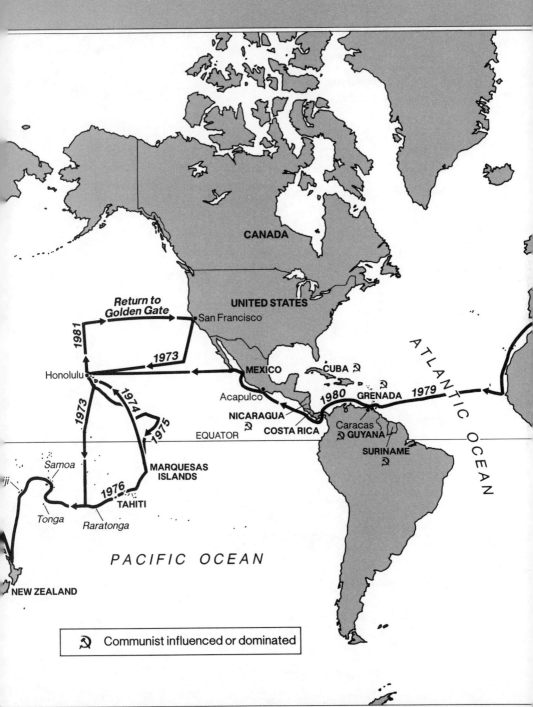

CANADA

UNITED STATES

Return to
Golden Gate
San Francisco

1981

1973

Honolulu

1973

1974

1975

MEXICO

CUBA ☭

Acapulco

1980   GRENADA ☭   1979

ATLANTIC OCEAN

NICARAGUA ☭
COSTA RICA

Caracas
☭ GUYANA

SURINAME ☭

EQUATOR

Samoa

Fiji

Tonga

Raratonga

1976

TAHITI

MARQUESAS
ISLANDS

PACIFIC OCEAN

NEW ZEALAND

☭   Communist influenced or dominated

MORNING STAR

Launched, August, 1968

Teak plank on apitong frames

Custom builder: Robin Fung, Hong Kong

L.O.A.	46.0'
L.O.D.	42.4'
L.W.L.	33.4'
Beam	13.0'
Draft	5.0'

Naval architect: William Garden

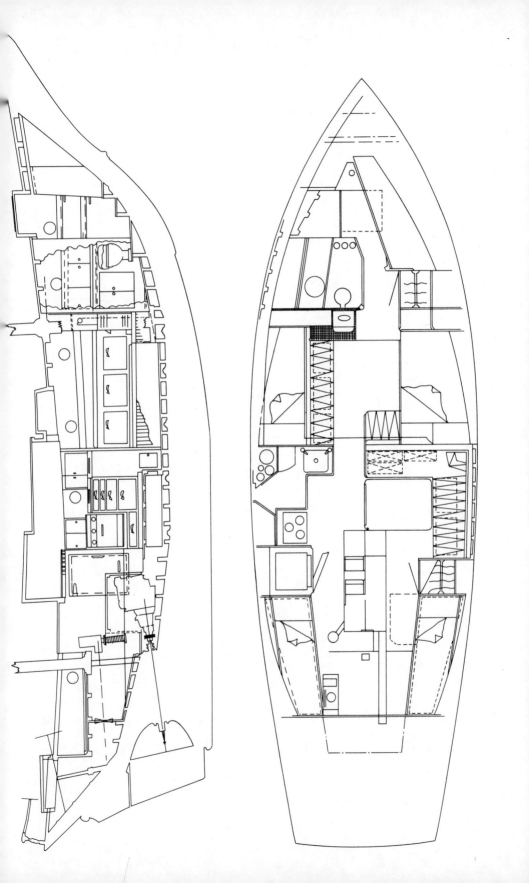

PROLOGUE

It was late May, 1943. The world was convulsed in a global war.

Her holds loaded with seven thousand tons of blockbuster bombs and her decks cluttered with chained-down trucks and tanks, the newly launched Liberty ship U.S.S. *John J. Abel* was staggering around Cape Horn. Lashed by icy, midwinter, sleet-laden, seventy-knot winds and battered by mountainous fifty-foot seas, the *Abel*, powered by her World War I vintage reciprocating steam engine, was barely keeping steerage way. The pitching, rolling motion of the fat-bellied Liberty was grotesque, and no man aboard could retreat into sleep that night.

At 0100 two young officers were huddled in the third mate's cabin, carrying on a whimsically strange conversation. They were the twenty-six-year-old third mate, Lieutenant Junior Grade Bill Musi, and the chief radio officer, twenty-one-year-old Ensign Ray Triplett, fresh out of the Maritime Academy.

This was Bill's third attempt to complete this same mission—to supply the British Eighth Army fighting the Germans in North Africa. On both prior attempts, Musi survived sinking by enemy torpedoes, spending twenty days in command of a lifeboat in the Caribbean, and three days in a lifeboat south of Capetown.

The North Atlantic was virtually under the complete dominion of German U-boats, and the *Luftwaffe* made the Mediterranean from Gibraltar to Suez deadly for Allied merchant
ships. In desperation, the Allies had laid out the only route
available from the eastern seaboard of the United States to the
Middle East for expendable Liberty ammunition ships.

From New York to Florida in a zigzagging convoy, we had
hugged the coast; then, running alone, dragging torpedo
defense nets extended over the side by cargo booms, we proceeded to Panama through the submarine-infested Caribbean.
Then through the canal, down the west coast of South America, around Cape Horn, south of the Falkland Islands on the
border of the Antarctic Ocean, north to South Africa, up the
Indian Ocean to Aden, Arabia, then north to Suez through
the Red Sea. The winter weather is so vile in the deep South
Atlantic that it masked lone merchantmen against attack by
enemy submarines and raiders.

On this storm-lashed night at the bottom of the world, Bill
and I were drinking coffee and confiding in each other our
boyhood dreams. We had shared our dreams many times as
the bond between us deepened. Earlier in the voyage, I had
told Bill that from the time of my early teens I had been sea-
smitten by reading books about high seas voyaging. The most
impressionable books were Jack London's *Cruise of the Snark*
and Joshua Slocum's *Sailing Alone Around the World.* I told
Bill I had determined that someday I would sail a teakwood
ketch around the world alone with my wife. Amazingly, Bill
shared the identical dream.

As a boy growing up on the Mississippi River, Lake Superior,
and the myriad lakes of Minnesota, I had been fascinated with
boats, the water, and the adventure they offered. Inspired by
the writings of Melville, London, Stevenson, and Nordhoff and
Hall, my imagination would become immersed in the adventure of sailing a traditional teakwood ketch to distant islands
far out in the Pacific Ocean; to follow one day in the wake of
the *Snark*, the *Bounty*, and the *Endeavor*. As this embryonic
dream began to infiltrate every cell of my being, I asked
myself, "Is it attainable? Is it possible?"

Within weeks after Pearl Harbor, advertisements began

appearing in Midwest newspapers, "Join the Merchant Marine." "See Action Now." "High Seas Adventure." "Sail to Foreign Countries." "All Can Be Yours within Weeks after Training School." These seductive ads didn't mention that the Germans in 1942 were sinking eight Allied ships a day in the North Atlantic, South Atlantic, Gulf of Mexico, and Caribbean. They affected me like the song of a siren.

So, at age twenty, I was off to the Maritime Academy, graduating six months later as an ensign with a Chief Radio Officer's License. It was during this adventure-packed period of my life that I realized that my boyhood wish—my dream—to sail alone around the world—now expanded to include my wife—became a personal commitment. Once I realized the attainability of this wish—that it was possible, I determined one day *to do it!*

The commitment was irrevocably made! Now there remained how to orient my life to fulfill this commitment.

Bill's and my off-watch hours were filled with shared plans and fantasies. We were inseparable. He taught me celestial navigation and I taught him radio and Morse code.

The boat of our shared dreams, like the *Snark*, was to be carvel-planked teakwood. About fifty feet long overall; ketch rigged; diesel powered. We began drawing sketches and sharing ideas.

Even though the war was not going well for us, we never had a doubt but that we could survive and that we would eventually grind the Axis powers into ultimate defeat. Despite the hardship, danger, enemy attacks, and final torpedoing in the North Atlantic on the last day of the voyage, this dream, this commitment, this common focus kept Bill and me inspired and enthusiastic. We were the victims of the incurable disease called Sea Fever.

After the war, I last saw Bill in the 1950s in Portland. He was then a captain of a merchant ship. He was divorced and his dream had collapsed.

I was busy raising a family and founding my own business in California.

But the nagging dream never left the attic of my mind. To sail a *Snark*-like ketch around the world.

I spent years yacht racing and cruising on various boats that I had acquired, rearing our five kids, instilling into them a love of the sea, sailing with them to Hawaii and back in a thirty-five-foot sloop, cruising the Sea of Cortez, and teaching them the arts of the sailor—but planning—always planning and dreaming about the ultimate voyage—circumnavigation of the world in my own wooden ketch.

Now, thirty years later, the fulfillment of the dream was at hand.

CHAPTER ONE

WHY AND HOW

At age fifty, I felt trapped. My life had become plastic and stale. I felt a sense of urgency—time was running out. At the peak of my career, I was enmeshed in the subtle web of business success. I had long been the stereotyped successful American businessman—highly structured and driven to the top by personal ambition, duty, and sense of achievement.

But I began to reexamine my values and to ask myself, "What real frontiers are there left for personal challenge?" With a sense of desperation, I wanted to emancipate myself from the rigidity of my life-style. I urgently needed to begin to *listen* to my inner self and liberate myself from crowds, traffic jams, jangling telephones, blaring television, money schemes, schedules, deadlines, and itineraries. I wanted to potentiate and reinvigorate my life. I wanted to broaden my horizons and universalize my thinking.

For years I had carried in my pocket this quotation from Robert Louis Stevenson: "Perpetual devotion to what a man calls his business is only to be sustained by perpetual neglect of many other things." We can become so busy *doing* that we give up our chance to just *be*. The good life was beginning to get in the way of the great life. *I simply had to be the master of my life, not its victim.*

1

I sat down one day with my lovely wife, Shirley, to review where we were at midlife. Shirl and I were high school sweethearts, married on Valentine's Day of 1942, a few weeks before I joined the merchant marine. Now, thirty years later, we were blessed with five good children, a beautiful home nestled in the mountains, a successful business career—in short, everything that, according to the American Dream, should make one content.

On the other hand, the kids were finishing college, getting married, going out on their own. The nest was beginning to empty out. The challenges were no longer all that challenging, and we were both experiencing what is currently labeled a "mid-life crisis."

In the back of my mind, the commitment I had made to myself to fulfill another dream was nagging me. The *Snark* wanted to sail out of the pages of Jack London's book and into my life.

One day in 1970, my son Ray and I were sailing San Francisco Bay in my thirty-five-foot sloop *Voyageur*, which we—Shirl and four of the kids—had sailed to Hawaii and back to San Francisco two years earlier. As we returned to our berth, Ray said, "Dad, look at that beautiful ketch!" There, nodding at her moorings, was an exquisite, traditionally designed teakwood ketch—almost the reincarnation of Jack London's *Snark* of my boyhood dreams. She was for sale, and I had to have her. She had been custom-built two years earlier for a rich doctor who specialized in vasectomies. They called him the Sausalito Clipper.

While, over the years of yacht racing and high seas voyaging, I had acquired various brand-new boats, I had now learned to let someone else with a fantasized dream buy the new boat, pour the money in, get the bugs out, and when the mighty sea would more often than not bring his dream crashing about his ears, I would then step in and buy her.

The vessel was almost a replica of the *Snark*—in size, rig, even engine horsepower. I bought her and promptly rechristened her *Morning Star*. This name is mentioned in the Old and New Testaments as well as the Koran—the three great

Pre-purchase sea trial

monotheistic religions of the world. It has deep personal and
spiritual meaning to Shirley and me.

Now came the most agonizing part of all—to actually *do it*,
to break out of the mold of our lives. A large trade-off was
involved. To turn our backs on our life-style, we would essentially forfeit continued accumulation for the "rainy day" that
our Depression upbringing had assured us was inevitably coming—accumulation for our "old age." We both knew deeply
that accumulation of the things of this world was not enough
to satisfy the yearnings of the human spirit. Thoughts and
axioms kept swirling in my brain, "If not now, when?" "Better
now than never, for never is too late." "Grab a chance and you
won't be sorry for a might-have-been." "How rich is rich?"

This question occurred to me, "Really how much difference
is there between *enough* money and all of the money in the
world?" Time, not money, is the real currency of our lives.
Money, when spent, can be replenished. Time, when spent, is
gone forever. Was I prepared to invest the irreplaceable currency of life in order to fulfill a boyhood dream?

Of course, Shirley had to join with me in making the fateful
decision. Should we drastically change our entire life-style?
Should we leave the comfort and the luxury of the life we
knew? Should we trade it for the hardship, discomfort, and
danger of the unknown? Were we able to liberate ourselves
from all that we had, in order to attain a sense of utter freedom
and tranquility?

As Shirl and I began feverishly building up to a peak with all
of the work—planning—preparation—provisioning and coming closer to the day we had set to put it all into action, she,
from time to time, expressed her thoughts: "It's always difficult
to cast off from shore because you are leaving the things you
know and with which you are comfortable. Yet, we also know
the sea and what we may have to endure. We have already
accepted that or we wouldn't be where we are—it is part of
the game." Nevertheless, Shirl and I struggled with doubts
right up to the second we cast off our dock lines to leave
behind the security of our former life-style.

On June 16, 1973, we were under way—out the Golden
Gate—with a maximum ebb tide—heading SSW for Hiva Oa in

Out the Golden Gate

the Marquesas Islands—"The forgotten islands of the South Pacific"—three thousand miles nonstop into the vast Pacific Ocean.

As we glided under the Golden Gate Bridge and began to leave Mile Rock Lighthouse astern, I took my hands off the wheel, flung them to the sky, and shouted at the top of my lungs "FREEDOM." We felt an overwhelming sense of peace.

When the heaving swell of the open sea started to alter our motion and the land began to disappear from view, we had the sense of sailing into our own private world—completely self-sufficient and dependent only upon one another.

At last I was embarked on the fulfillment of my dream.

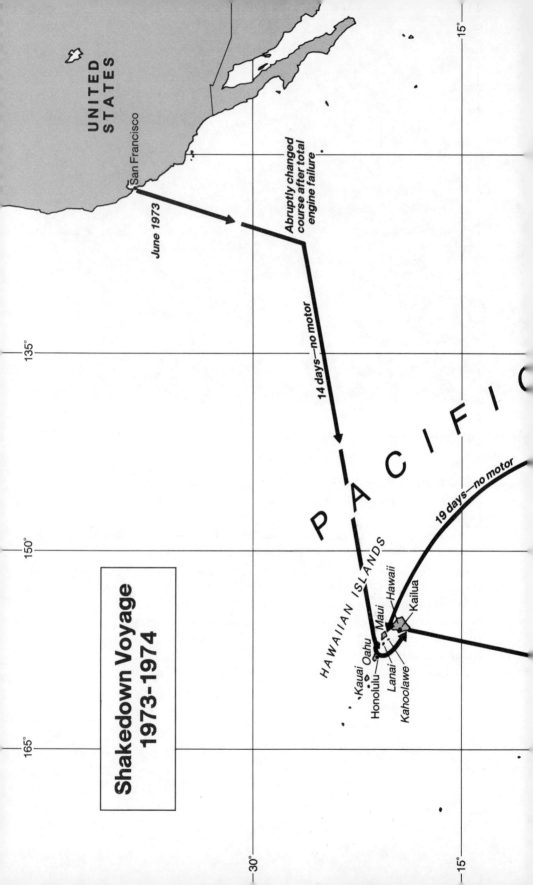

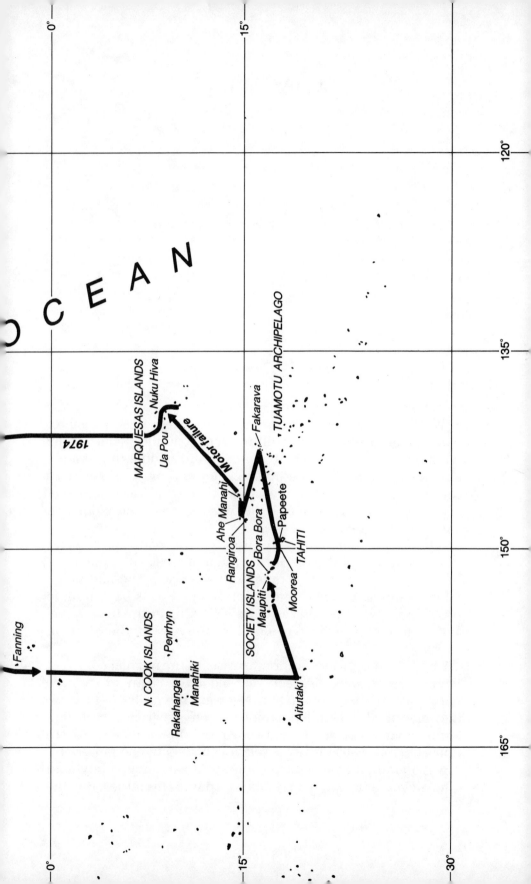

CHAPTER TWO

SHAKEDOWN VOYAGE

⚓ We wanted to give our two youngest kids a year of adventure in the South Pacific, while determining whether we—Shirley and I alone—could handle the twenty-ton *Morning Star*. In addition to Shirley and me, the crew was comprised of our twenty-year-old daughter Teri; eighteen-year-old son Ray, and Peter Fuller, his eighteen-year-old friend and next-door neighbor.

With brisk northwesterly winds, we had sailed eight hundred miles southwest during the first week—the plague of seasickness had run its course with the crew. We had fallen into a seagoing routine. The cobalt blue sea was beginning to warm. Schools of porpoises were frolicking in the bow wave, and all should have been tranquil for the crew of the *Morning Star*.

Unfortunately, this was not the case. In the normal course of family life ashore, eighteen-year-old boys begin to struggle with their natural inclination to assert themselves—to vault into manhood and independence—free of parental restraint. Coping with this adolescent, boy-man phenomenon ashore puts enormous strains upon relationships between father and son. To emerge from this cocoon of dependency, a boy-man often develops a love-hate relationship with his father. But, living ashore during this difficult period, a boy can escape to the reassuring company of his peers, where he can find comfort in pooling problems, insecurities, and ignorance of the ways of the world. Similarly, the father can find surcease from this emotional warfare by seeking privacy alone or with his wife.

When, however, this tense time of life is experienced in the confines of a small craft at sea with five people cooped up in a living space measuring 150 square feet, the situation is combustible. When there is added to this mixture an additional eighteen-year-old boy with whom one has assumed the role of surrogate parent, the relationships become explosive.

On the high seas, there can be only one skipper—literally a master, as a ship's captain is properly named throughout the seagoing lore of centuries. The one captain has the awesome responsibility for the lives and well-being of his crew and his vessel. He alone must constantly make decisions, some of which have sweeping life-death proportions. Unless under military discipline, where orders are obeyed without question, the modern American boy almost never can follow directions issued from a skipper-father without challenge. There is nothing in his experience that would acquaint him with what the military calls the "Theory of Command."

I should have anticipated "crew problems" well in advance of setting out on this voyage. My mind, however, was too engrossed in the end result for which I hoped—a year of unforgettable adventure which I was making possible for these two young men, opportunity that I would have given anything to have had at that age.

As rebellion—usually initiated by Ray and supported by Pete—began to emerge, I tried every approach to thwart it. I was alternately a loving father, a cajoling scoutmaster, a senior counselor, a pal, and finally a Bligh-like tyrant. Nothing worked. Ray had grown up on sailboats and at age thirteen had been a brave and companionable crew member aboard the *Voyageur* on her five-thousand-mile round-trip voyage to Hawaii in 1968. He had been a great crew at age fifteen on the maiden voyage of the *Morning Star* to Mexico and the Sea of Cortez. That trip included a seventy-two-knot hurricane at sea, and Ray's conduct during this ordeal had been outstanding.

But now he was eighteen years old and madly in love with a girl back home. At the same time, here he was trapped with his parents in a floating box twenty-four hours a day, where his only solace from his self-deemed woes was derived from his kindred spirit, Pete, who was equally involved in a youthful love affair.

Pete, however, was more prone to follow orders for a number of reasons. First, the orders didn't emanate from his father, the authority figure of his eighteen years. Secondly, Pete was a bona fide lover of the sea and had the rare capacity to exult in the circumstances of the moment. And, of course, he was a guest and realized as much. Finally, I had obtained senatorial appointment for Pete to enter the California Maritime Academy the following year, and he was extremely interested in celestial navigation, chart reading, and all things pertaining to the sea. He wanted to, and ultimately did make, seagoing his profession. But overriding all of these considerations, he felt an emotional obligation to participate in the daily marginally mutinous conduct of his friend Ray.

I would teach the boys sail handling, watch standing, marlinspike seamanship. They would teach it back to me in a matter of hours, tainted with their own inexperienced embellishment. As alternate orders, requests, and entreaties were issued to them about watch standing, daily duties of seagoing maintenance, and sail handling, they would first hold their plebiscite on the foredeck and invariably come back with assertions of how they thought things should be done—an absolutely outrageous and intolerable situation for any skipper of any ship to put up with for long.

Teri was the mediating peacemaker and brought a ray of sunshine through every dark cloud. She is an outstanding sea cook, whipping up dishes that would seem impossible to concoct in a pitching, rolling galley. Shirley was torn between her motherly instincts and her wifely devotion—an extremely difficult situation for her, as valiant as she tried to be—placing her squarely between the clash of wills of the young bucks and the old buck.

We had observed over the years that the greatest single factor in the ultimate abandonment of high seas voyages was "crew problems." But I had naively felt that this cannot happen with *my* crew. They are "different." I had failed to face directly that the trouble was not so much *who* they were or *who* I am, but rather it lay in the consequences of never-ending close confinement, sometimes monotonous routine, and occasionally perilous conditions.

The best possible crew arrangement, it seems to us, is a man and woman alone, but even with this combination, we have seen many would-be adventurous cruises disintegrate as quarrels clouded the cabins of their little craft. The sea brings out the best and the worst in the characters of human beings. The experience at sea enlightens perceptions of one another, revealing hidden characteristics, both noble and mean, of fellow crew members.

One dark night a tanker came up over the horizon and her red-green lights showed us that she was bearing down on us on a collision course. We were running before the wind with the poled-out twins—similar in effect to the square sails of the old clipper ships—which severely restricted our maneuverability under sail. As the tanker drew ominously closer, I attempted to start the motor. In a cloud of smoke, the starter-motor windings fused and burned out. I hit the bridge of the tanker with a powerful searchlight, and her crew, at last, saw our tiny vessel down in the sea troughs and radically altered course to avoid us.

The next morning, I dismantled the starter motor and determined that it was unrepairable at sea. I did not have a spare. Nor could we hand-crank our seventy-six-horsepower diesel engine. I now was confronted with a capital decision. Whether to turn back and beat 950 miles against the northwesterlies to San Diego; or to continue the voyage through the doldrums to the Marquesas with no engine; or to lay off and run with the trades to Hawaii for repairs. To sail to Hawaii meant that we would lose our precious easting, and would have to alter our one-year game plan substantially. Rather than abort the cruise and turn back, I decided to alter course to Honolulu 1,800 miles

"Dear Diary"

to the west. This decision was met with unanimous and unalloyed joy by the crew. As we came to a course of WSW, they were elated.

With gentle twenty-knot trade winds singing their soft tunes in the rigging, the *Morning Star* hurtled along, leaving a hissing, bubbling phosphorescent wake far astern. Porpoises were all around us. Flying fish began to land on deck at night, and peace descended on our quiet, motorless craft. The morale of the crew soared to the star-filled heavens. Now our bowsprit was pointed toward a relatively near and definite destination—Honolulu—ETA fourteen days. All became right within our small private world, contained only by our horizon on this desert of undulating sea.

Gear failure of one sort or another is almost a daily occurrence. The log is replete with entries:

Generator oil pressure dropping—flushed with kerosene and repaired. Seawater galley pump broken. Dismantled and repaired. Heavy leaking around binnacle base. Salt water

Teri

Sun sight

Ray, Jr.

Running with twins

leaking all over our canned goods stowage. Lying on my back
with salt water dripping in my face. Unscrewed all binnacle
bolts and rebedded holes. No more leaks.

All ships at sea develop problems—especially on a shakedown voyage. The constant—sometimes violent—motion as
well as the saltwater atmosphere causes gear failure that must
be repaired or jury-rigged in some make-do fashion. There are
no mechanics at sea; so you cope with what you have aboard.
Coping successfully with these problems as they continue to
arise gives one a tremendous sense of satisfaction. We called
these failures the "crisis of the day," and began to accept them
as a normal and natural part of high seas voyaging.

During one such "crisis of the day," our log cable broke, and
we streamed astern the whirling rotor of our taffrail log. With
a shriek of despair, Ray, while hanging over the stern, got his
shoulder-length hair caught in the rotating line. Shirl quickly
offered scissors, and with a few snips, several precious locks
were sacrificed. Ray then became the target of merciless teasing from his equally long-haired buddy Pete. Ray got his
revenge, however, when a few days later, Pete got his hair
caught in the same line, and the same solution was employed.

Running before long, foam-streaked seas, the *Morning Star*
rolled and surfed before the trades. Black, ominous line squalls
appeared to windward, and as they inexorably marched like
an army of horsemen in procession down upon us, we prepared for the heavy winds, gusting sometimes to fifty knots, by
shortening sail.

As the rain-filled squalls advanced with the wind toward
our small craft, we were always intrigued by the effect of the
delugelike rains on the breaking combers. The wind-driven
downpour would flatten the seas and rob them of their foaming whitecaps. Then the violent winds would hit us like a giant
sledgehammer. Our technique was to run off dead before these
winds, and in the process the boat would accelerate like a
greyhound.

At first, these squalls were a source of apprehension to Pete,
who had never experienced them. Then I suggested to the
crew, "Why don't you utilize the fresh water to take showers

and wash your hair on the foredeck?" After that, the squalls were welcomed. On several occasions, they would get their hair lathered with soap, only to watch the rains pass over us, leaving them with no rinse, except for the salt water in ample abundance all around us. As they caught on to this, they would prelather their hair with salt water at the first sight of squalls approaching; then rinse it in the fresh water deluge that would inundate us.

When no fresh water was available from the heavens, daily bathing was accomplished by using the saltwater deck flush, which was driven by the diesel generator. Following the salt-water bath, I would ration out of our tanks to each a bowl of fresh water, which, when laced with rubbing alcohol and sponged over the body, would leave one as fresh and clean as though just out of a cold, freshwater shower.

While we had a self-steering Aries wind vane—promptly christened Jonathan Livingston Seagull—which experimentation and practice had taught us to trim in such a manner as to steer the boat, I wanted to teach the kids the fine art of helmsmanship, and they hand-steered throughout their three-hour watches.

There is no situation on earth that I know of which gives to a human being the same opportunity to think, reflect, and meditate, as does sitting alone in the cockpit of a sailboat on the high seas under clear tropical skies filled with glittering stars. As they learned the stars and constellations, the crew began to look forward to the lonely respite of their night watches. They formed fast friendships with Sirius, Spica, Arcturus, Antares, and the wheeling Big Dipper with its pointers directed toward Polaris, low on our starboard beam.

I taught them how to steer by the stars rather than the mesmerizing red-lit compass. As they would come on their watches, I would check them out to see that they were wearing safety harnesses and life jackets complete with whistles, electronic flares, knife, dye marker, and shark-chaser chemicals. They resisted wearing these harnesses, but if they were alone in the cockpit at night, running before strong winds, a rogue sea could wash them overboard while the sleeping crew below would be totally unaware of their plight. We towed astern a 300-foot floating polypropylene line with a loop at its end. If a crew member went overboard, he or she was to make directly for it.

When one is living daily with the sea two or three feet below the rail, a complacency develops and one forgets the lethal nature of the boiling ocean around. The two most dreaded events that can happen to high seas voyagers are falling overboard and being run down by a ship.

We held practice man-overboard drills. "Man overboard! All hands on deck!" We would simulate a man overboard by throwing floating objects over the rail or by retrieving glass fishing balls that had drifted with the currents from Japan. One crew member was designated never to allow the bobbing object to get out of sight. The rest of the crew were to strike sail or jibe the boat around to a reciprocal course.

Running with the poled-out twins made these practice maneuvers extremely time consuming. Increasing awareness of the likelihood that it would be impossible to recover a lone watch stander who went overboard began to make the skipper's rules more acceptable.

One day Teri was emptying a wastebasket over the side when a sea snatched it from her hands. It was high noon—a clear, sun-filled day—and all hands were on deck. By the time we got the twins down and reversed course to retrieve the floating wastebasket in our distant wake, it had disappeared from sight. It was a graphic lesson to the kids that it would only be sheer luck if we were able to save them if they fell overboard.

I know of five people who lost their lives by falling overboard within the last few years—two of them went into the sea in broad daylight. During my yacht-racing years, one of my competitors in a night race lost a man overboard only twenty miles south of San Francisco. It is almost impossible to see a small, bobbing head in trade-wind seas breaking at heights of fifteen to twenty feet.

After the wastebasket incident, there was a noted lack of grumbling—"Do I have to?"—among the crew.

One day we were totally becalmed. There wasn't a breath of breeze. The *Morning Star* lay rolling and slatting her sails on the brassy, billowing sea. The kids wanted to go swimming. I warned them about oceangoing sharks, but yielded to a quick dip by each of them—one at a time—while I maintained a watch at the boarding ladder with a semiautomatic rifle. As the initial interpersonal tensions that had developed during the first week of the voyage relaxed and their sea legs were acquired, the kids began to enjoy this rare adventure thoroughly.

The sea was churning with teeming life all about us. Flying fish, in their desperate efforts to avoid being eaten by the dorado, or mahimahi, would skim the surface of the seas—sometimes for incredible distances. At night they would strike the sails and drop flopping onto the deck—there to die and be served for breakfast to the ravenous crew.

Our beloved porpoises would converge in schools from

Flying fish for breakfast

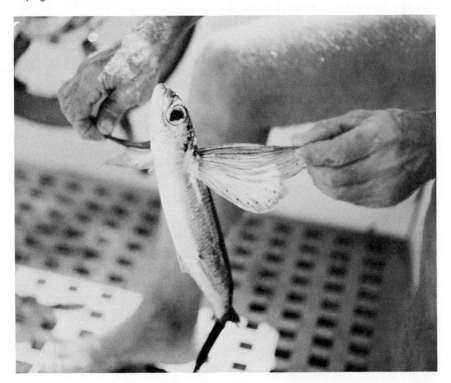

great distances, leaping and playing in our boiling bow wave. Their appearance, no matter how frequent, always evoked shouts of delight from the crew as they dashed to the bowsprit to see and hear the squeaking language of the exuberant creatures performing their happy show exclusively for us.

Shearwaters, puffins, petrels, white bosun birds, and albatross would play around us, dipping and diving, performing their aerial antics in the sky overhead. Our whirling anemometer at the masthead would attract the angered attention of the fork-tailed, alabaster bosun birds. They would dive to the masthead, then pull up at the last minute with an angry shriek.

We adopted two pets. One was a brown albatross that trailed us for days and nights, feeding on garbage in our wake. I told the kids that this bird is a good omen, so it was given the name "Omen." The other was a striped pilot fish that swam unerringly in a designated position just ahead of our bow. This type of pilot fish accompanies sharks and feeds off the remnants of their daily kills. The kids named it "George," and we speculated that George must have thought us to be a huge shark.

As the ascending sun dead astern began to lighten the heavens, I would be in the cockpit shooting dawn star sights. First I had to determine that Omen was still soaring in our wake and that George was in his proper place ahead of our foaming bow wave. Unfailingly, to our delight, they were always there. We wondered when they slept.

We dragged fish lines with a white-feather lure astern and, almost at will, began pulling in the exotically multicolored dorado, or mahimahi. Without engine power, we had no refrigeration and the meat could not be preserved, so Shirl and Teri taxed their ingenuity determining new ways to bake, fry, or broil the delicious fillets.

With daily twenty-four-hour runs averaging 140 miles, the red dots showing our noon position gradually crawled across the chart toward the island of Oahu. Now that a sense of harmony had descended upon the crew, we approached our Hawaiian landfall with mixed emotions. Our self-contained little world was soon going to be intruded upon by the clamor of the "real" world.

One morning revealed that both Omen and George had
abandoned their convoy duties during the night, as though sig-
nifying their dissatisfaction with the approaching land. They
had left us to our own follies ashore. Our momentary sadness
at this event was broken by Shirl's cry "Land Ho!" There, far
off to port, almost indistinguishable from the towering mass of
cumulus clouds, reared the faint, dark outline of the mountains of Maui.

Then as night fell, we saw the loom first, then the twinkling
flash of Makapu light dead ahead of us. Experiencing his first
landfall, Peter, in enthusiastic astonishment, blurted, "It
works. You hit it right on the nose exactly when you said—
fourteen days from when we changed course." I could appreciate his exultation. No matter how many landfalls one makes,
after weeks on the trackless sea, guided only by the heavenly
bodies, it is always an indescribable thrill to see land emerge
exactly where and when you said it would appear.

On a glorious Sunday morning, we had Diamond Head, followed by Waikiki, on our starboard beam, and soon we were
tacking back and forth among the day sailors outside of Ala
Wai Boat Harbor. With the traffic, we hesitated to tack our
engineless heavy ketch into the narrow, coral-reef-bordered
entrance to the harbor. So we gladly accepted an offer
extended by a passing power boat to tow us in.

Although we hadn't set out for Hawaii nineteen days earlier,
this initial phase of the shakedown of crew and ship had been
completed with mixed success.

CHAPTER THREE

DOWN TO THE EQUATOR

It was Lord Nelson who said, "Ships and men rot in port."

In Honolulu, I installed a new starter motor and bought a spare. A laundry list of other jury rigs was repaired over the next month. On a ten-hour-a-day basis, I was totally occupied with these repairs, obtaining charts to cover our revised game plan, along with a host of other demanding preparations for a continuation of the voyage to the South Pacific. The kids were rapidly becoming bored, and tensions among the five of us, living aboard the dock-bound vessel, again mounted. "Port rot" began to contaminate each day.

The role of surrogate parents was becoming an increasingly odious one for Shirl and me. While our own kids would be— although unwillingly—back aboard ship at a certain time of night, parental demands of this nature made of someone else's son produced a different response.

Finally, Shirl rebelled and demanded that I send Pete home to his parents. She said she could no longer live with the responsibility for him. The idea was an enticing one to me because I felt that it would remove the contaminating peer-group influence of the Ray-Pete combination and improve the relationship between Ray and me. For the balance of the one-year voyage to the South Pacific and return, I fantasized that with only our own two kids, we could bring a new and permanent sense of harmony to the crew of the *Morning Star.*

Ray, who grew up as an only son with four older sisters, had become the object of all of the attention a father could lavish on him. I had taught him to hunt and fish, taken him on pack trips into the wilderness, taught him a love of the outdoors, brought him along on yacht races and numerous high seas cruises. He and I were friends.

However, Pete had his heart set on the South Pacific voyage. He had worked diligently with me for months in the preparation for this great adventure. I was attracted to him, when alone with him in this endeavor, because of his outstanding love of the sea, his cheerful willingness to work and learn, and simply because he was an exceptionally fine young man with a superior family background. I loved him as though he was a second son. It was the *combination* of the two boys that was making the confined life aboard the *Morning Star* a nightmare.

Then Pete got a phone call from his parents, telling him that his beloved grandfather had suddenly died. He was heartbroken and sobbed in grief, alone with me. His grandfather had sailed with us on San Francisco Bay, and I was very fond of him. As I comforted Pete, I asked myself, "How can I cap this tragedy in this young man's life with another crushing disappointment by sending him home? But if I don't do it now, we shall be committed to this arrangement until we—if and when—get to Tahiti."

I discussed the whole matter alone with Ray and Teri. They were appalled at the idea of my sending Pete home and pleaded that we try it again with all kinds of reassurances that "this time it will be better." Shirl and I then decided that as we cruised the Hawaiian Islands—Lanai and the "big island" of Hawaii—we would see how it works "just once more."

I told Pete what we were considering and why. He tearfully begged me not to send him home. "Please, Mr. Triplett, let me finish out the year. I guarantee you that Ray and I will shape up together. I am just beginning to learn so much. I really love the life at sea." How could anyone be hard-hearted enough to turn down a sincere plea like this? So we sailed with a renewed spirit of cooperation and adventure, but with some residue of skepticism on the part of Shirl and me.

With stops at Hulopoe Bay on Lanai and Kailua on the "big island" of Hawaii, we cruised south in the Hawaiian Islands chain. On the island of Hawaii, Shirl guarded the boat while I took the kids to the volcano Kilauea and toured the entire island in a rented car. We had a beautiful day, laughing, joking, and I genuinely enjoyed watching the faces of these young people as they beheld the awesome live volcano. I thought, "This is going to work out beautifully. These kids will now shape into not only a good crew but a great crew." Hope springs eternal.

Interspersed with another stop at Kealakakua Bay, where Captain Cook was murdered by the Sandwich Islanders, we headed down the Polynesian Passageway, bound south one thousand miles to Fanning Island. With light winds, we ghosted down to clear the wind shadow of Mauna Kea and Mauna Loa and the South Point of the "big island." We sailed through a pod of whales surfacing, snorting, and blowing right alongside of us. The kids were enthralled at the sight of these mammoth wild creatures, apparently welcoming us as fellow seafarers.

Once clear of the land mass to our port and reaching with shortened sail on a course of due south, we were battered by heavy seas and winds gusting to forty knots. During the month ashore, everyone had softened up and lost his or her sea legs, so the occupational hazard of a small craft at sea—seasickness—began again to afflict those aboard with its devastating effects. No respecter of persons, it can strike at anyone.

Fortunately, I so far have not been afflicted by this debilitating ailment. Those in the crew who were violently retching their guts out over the rail fixed me with baleful glares as I sanctimoniously theorized that it was "mainly a psychosomatic problem." Despite motion-sickness pills, bland diet the day before sailing, no acid intake—there still remains no known guarantee that one will escape this curse, which renders its victims useless.

All notions of high adventure and exhilarating South Sea landfalls fled from the imagination of the crew. They craved just to "get off this thing. Just to be on dry land again!" To get away from their smug, seasick-free skipper. They sprawled all over the cockpit and the cabin with their buckets gripped in white-knuckled fists.

I remain convinced that this condition has a psychogenesis, related to apprehension, and that one can allow it to happen or not allow it to happen by a form of autohypnosis. But these theories fell on deaf and resentful ears for three or four days in the predoldrum heavy seas, as our latitude lowered toward the equator.

A coral atoll is a sunken volcano forming an encircling reef, plunging steeply into the sea on one side, and sloping gently into a relatively shallow lagoon on the other side. Fanning Island is reputed to be the most exquisite coral atoll in the world. The reef itself protrudes only four to ten feet above the seas, but the atoll is thickly covered with coconut palms, the tops of which reach heights of sixty to ninety feet.

Strong currents—the equatorial and counterequatorial— make navigation to Fanning challenging, and many ships and small craft miss it entirely. The only way to find a pinprick of low land, surrounded by currents, is by frequent celestial observations.

At north latitude 7° 44' and west longitude 157° 50', a cross fix of Arcturus, Vega, Deneb, and Spica revealed that we were in the meandering countercurrent pushing us eastward at the rate of one knot, or twenty-four nautical miles, per day. As we continued south, this current accelerated to one and a half knots, or thirty-six miles per day. But I knew that once free of the countercurrent, the west-setting equatorial current would take over, and the precious easting gained would once again yield to the inexorable westerly flow.

Without the use of the heavenly bodies—sun, moon, stars, and planets—there is no way, other than with untrustworthy modern electronic gadgets, which we didn't have, to determine the effect of these currents on your vessel. One can't *see* an ocean current or estimate its effect upon one unless one knows one's precise position. And this can only be determined by frequent observations using, especially, the distant stars.

As we neared the equator, we began to experience frequent squalls and overcast skies rendering celestial sights impossible. Our night watches revealed frequent comets streaking toward their burning deaths in the earth's atmosphere.

At 1100 on the ninth day out from Hawaii, Pete was at my side at the table below assiduously watching me work out a running fix—three morning sun lines advanced and crossed. I said to him, "Pete, climb aloft in the rigging and fix your eyes on the horizon ten degrees to port of our bowsprit. You should see a fuzzy outline just above the horizon. The fuzz you see will be the top of the coconut trees on Fanning, which I figure are exactly twelve miles dead ahead of us." He looked at me with a face full of doubt, but without a word he went topside and climbed up the ratlines while I stayed below.

As his eyes adjusted to the tropical glare, he let out an excited scream, "I see it! I see it! It's right where you said it would be."

Everyone came alive as ripples of excitement washed the spirits of the crew. Pete came clambering down from the ratlines and dropped below to resume his seat alongside me. This young man who, until a few weeks ago, had never been out of sight of land, gazed at me as though I were some sort of magician. He said, "Aren't you going to come up and look?" Masking a thumping heart, I played my detached role well and said, "In a minute, Pete. Just as soon as I put away the dividers, parallel ruler, and sea charts. But I know Fanning is there, and in two hours we shall be abeam of English Harbor."

Pete confessed, "You know, when you hit Diamond Head right on the nose, I have to tell you that I thought it was just luck. Now I know what all of these sights meant, and I want to learn as fast as possible." I was deeply touched by his honesty and enthusiasm and felt a strong bond with this young fellow lover of the sea.

Sailing into the lee of Fanning, we could smell the delicious aroma of land, copra, and cooking fires and see the resplendent white-sand beach with tall, leaning coconut palms waving their gentle welcome. The *Pacific Islands Pilot Book* told us that the pass into the lagoon was about one-quarter of a cable wide (150 feet) with reefs on either side and a depth of 20 feet. The maximum rate of current in the pass was upward of five knots. To gain maximum steerage control, I wanted to wait until the very beginning of an outcoming current, which wasn't due for another two hours.

Also, the *Pilot Book* said that pilotage was mandatory. As we tacked back and forth off English Harbor with our "request-pilot" flag flying, we saw no trace of any other human being. Pete and Ray were told to remain aloft as we entered the pass, while I was at the wheel with the chart. Sitting on the spreaders aloft, they could clearly see the jagged fangs of coral protruding on either side of the pass. As the tide began to turn, there was still no sign of a pilot, but I saw no reason why we couldn't enter the pass on our own.

Just as the tide began to turn, a black squall appeared east over the lagoon to windward and began to bear down on us. The squall would obscure the coral, so I decided to go for it now. Pete chose that critical moment to come scrambling down to the cockpit. I said, "What are you doing here?" He retorted, "I want to see where we are on the harbor chart." I couldn't believe it! Ah, the arrogance of youth! Until a few weeks ago, he had never seen a sea chart, and now he had arrogated unto himself the expertise to interpret and relate the chart to this treacherous pass. I sternly yelled, "Get back in the ratlines and stay there until I tell you to come down. We are going for the lagoon before this squall hits."

With a boiling rush through the turbulent pass, we, within minutes, were safely inside the lagoon and maneuvering to anchor in twenty feet of water off the settlement. Because of strong currents churning within the lagoon, we placed a set of stern anchors, which kept us beam to the beach fifty yards off our port side. Out of the coconut groves appeared a trickle of people curiously staring at the American sailboat that had suddenly appeared out of nowhere.

Then a boat put out with black native officials, whom we greeted aboard. They were somewhat surly and quite unresponsive to our cheerful smiles and extended handshakes. It was Sunday, and they were dressed in their finest. The head man had his son with him, so I produced our Polaroid camera, propped the lad at the wheel, and took his picture. In a minute, when they saw the result develop in color before their curious eyes, their faces broke into wide grins, revealing rows of ivorylike teeth. Nothing would have it then but that I take all of their pictures. From that point on, the island was ours. We served tea and soft drinks, and a bond of friendship was instantly established.

"Did we want to go spearfishing? Would we like a tour of the lagoon? Could we attend a native dance that afternoon?" We were overwhelmed with kindness. When the formalities were completed—endless stamping of passports and papers—they left, only to return in an hour with their rowboat laden with bananas and coconuts.

Fanning's reputation for beauty was well earned. Although at one time a British possession, arbitrarily taken control of on behalf of Great Britain in 1888, it is now included in the Gilbert and Ellice Islands administration and is a part of numerous emerging Third World countries. It is inhabited by five hundred Melanesian people from the Gilbert Islands and two Australian overseers who process copra for Fanning Island Plantation Ltd. of Sydney.

Fanning Island with its neighbors Washington (75 miles to the northwest), Palmyra (still farther to the northwest), and Christmas (153 miles to the southeast) are called the Line Islands because of their proximity to the invisible line forming the equator. Fanning had been the connecting link of the Pacific cable between Canada and Fiji, but the new British Commonwealth cable bypassed the island, and the station was closed in 1963. The sparkling, blue green lagoon encloses an area of about 45 square miles.

We inflated the Avon dinghy and rowed ashore to be greeted by Phil Palmer—the chief administrator of the island—one of the two white men commanding the labors of the restive and sometimes rebellious native population. Phil was a tall, spidery caricature of the movie depiction of white men on lonely South Sea Islands. He ran the island with an iron fist, tempered by persuasion and justice. As with many white men we were later to encounter in the South Seas, Phil was starved for someone to talk with about the matters of the "outside world"— world politics—and we spent endless hours in the cool breezes of his plantation veranda learning from one another. He had been on Fanning for thirty-five years—his wife was in Australia—and he regaled me with story after story of shipwreck, hurricanes, and native uprising while lamenting his plight—"stuck on this lonely speck in the Pacific." But Phil, I knew, could never return to "civilization." We thoroughly enjoyed one another's companionship, and Phil arranged for skin diving, spearfishing, and shelling expeditions for all of us in the vast blue green coral-studded lagoon.

Pete was enthralled with the movielike South Sea Island paradise and drew sketches of native villages and craft. Teri would wander off among the villagers and, with her well-scrubbed, open-faced appearance and glittering smile, was an ambassadress of goodwill. A procession of children and young mothers followed her in her meanderings. She was showered with gifts—precious native shells, flower leis, and coronas.

Ray dove and speared fish, unintentionally revealing to us that he was, indeed, thoroughly enjoying himself. Once committed to the role of reluctant crewman-passenger, he sadly seemed to miss so much in his apparent inability to "smell the roses along the way"—to exhibit youthful exuberance over the almost paradisical setting in which he found himself. Shirl and I would often see our love-sick son disconsolately sitting on the beach, back to a coconut tree, all alone, throwing an occasional pebble into the glittering sun-drenched lagoon. We continued, along with the other kids, to try to draw him out, to "show him a good time," but with little apparent success.

It seems that one of the greatest gifts that one has is the capacity to enjoy the here and now; unbeclouded by events of the past or concern for the future. It is a rare gift, but available to anyone for the asking. We must find it on our own—the daily gift of life.

To me, Fanning Island was our first taste of my version of the "real world." The earthy, guileless, cheerful people who would laugh at or see some good in everything—even the misfortunes that life hands out to others as well as to themselves.

As we squatted in a circle in a large assembly hall built of coconut logs and palm fronds watching the traditional drum-accompanied dances put on for our benefit, we marveled at the continuous, uninhibited, sensuous leaping movements of the almost naked performers. Our applause produced renewed unrestrained effort on the part of the dancers until they finally wilted in exhaustion in the heat of the day.

The two white men on the island were made increasingly uncomfortable by our open fraternization with the "natives," and their attitude, "this sort of thing just isn't done, you know," became increasingly apparent. Evidently their roles as plantation overseers and masters demanded that they maintain an aloofness from their workers. But the creeping death of colonialism was spreading around the world, and we could sense resentment by the "natives" at being treated in the traditional master-semislave fashion.

On several occasions, dugouts would silently slip out from the village at night and come alongside of the *Morning Star*. The uplifted, smiling, childlike faces would ask to come aboard just to sit silently in the cockpit, with wandering fingers shyly fondling the wheel. Always gifts of shells—a fresh fish—a lobster—were proffered with nothing expected in return. But we would give them clothing, canned goods, balloons for the kids, and other trinkets brought from faraway America.

Preliminary to leaving, we reluctantly took on a barrel of diesel fuel used to run the generator on Fanning. It turned out to be polluted with water and was later to cause us enormous engine problems.

When we examined the brackish fresh water in a reservoir on the beach and noted its surface swimming with mosquito larvae, we decided that we would continue to rely on rain entrapped in our awning to replenish our 160-gallon fresh-water supply.

After eight days in Fanning the crew of the *Morning Star* said a poignant good-bye to Phil Palmer and to our newfound friends clustered on the beach to watch our departure. To gain maximum control in the river of current in the pass, we awaited the first beginnings of an incoming tide and with a long blast from our air horn eased out the pass and headed SSE to cross the equator, bound for Aitutaki in the Cook Islands, twelve hundred miles to the south.

CHAPTER FOUR

TO THE SOUTH SEAS

As we neared the equator, we were beset by calms, squalls, and capricious weather. We were now in the throes of the equatorial current, pushing us westward at a one-knot rate in light but frequently tempestuous winds. Crabbing into the current with all light-air sails set, we ghosted along with daily runs as low as twenty-four miles—one mile per hour.

At the equator, we held the traditional first-time crossing ceremony as I initiated the crew into the ancient order of Neptunus Rex. Using aluminum foil, Teri made a kingly crown. A blanket formed King Neptune's robe, and the handle of a gaff hook became his staff.

Finally, free of the equatorial doldrums, our daily runs began to pick up to 130, 140, and 150 miles as we reached ever southward. As sea legs were regained, waves of seasickness passed and our sea routine was again established.

We saw stakes on floats with radar reflectors, denoting Japanese fishing activity in the open ocean. These floats and nets set recklessly anywhere on the high seas constitute a hazard to navigation for a small craft like ours.

Dragging our "meat hook," we daily visited the fresh fish market entirely surrounding us. One day we began reeling in a tuna only to have a shark, in a neat surgical strike, gulp the entire fish abaft the gills, leaving us with only a hooked esophagus.

A fifty-knot squall roared down on us with express-train speed, leaving us with just enough time to strike sail and run off before the twenty-foot seas pushed in its path. But the deluge accompanying the squall filled our freshwater tanks.

Then, at 12° south and 159° west—407 miles north of Aitutaki, we weathered a Force 9 gale. Ray was slammed into the pulpit with such a blow that it bent and was uprooted from the deck. Only his harness, clipped to the headstay, prevented him from being swept over the side into the maelstrom of curling seas breaking over the bow. This event starkly brought home to the crew that the tyrannical skipper's insistence on harness wearing in heavy weather made sense after all.

One night in thirty-five-knot winds, the motion of the boat radically changed, and there was a loud crash on deck. As I charged topside, I found that Pete had become totally disoriented, and the boat had accidentally jibed around despite the restraining jibe-preventing vang. As long as the boom and the mast were undamaged, the only harm done was to Pete's overweening self-confidence. Although we had been at sea only three months, he, in the fashion of the novice, had already begun to show evidence of an almost dangerous overconfidence in his newly learned arts of the sailor.

As I surveyed the situation—the boat wallowing dead in the water—180 degrees off course—with all sails aback, I said, "Let me guess. You got tired of steering a compass course and decided to set the vane." The vane servorudder was in the water, so what had happened was self-evident. Pete sheepishly admitted that this is what he had done, despite explicit orders not to fool with the vane mechanism.

I said, "Okay, now how do you propose we get out of this mess and resume course?" As happens with novice airplane pilots, he was possessed by an almost vertigolike disorientation, and despite glittering stars, along with a full moon, in the heavens above, he simply did not know north from south, east from west, or his relative position between the sea and the sky. He didn't know what to do.

So, I brought the boat off the wind, picked up steerage way, and wore her around with a controlled jibe to the beam reach we had been on. Then I said, "See, Pete, there ahead of us is Acrux—part of the Southern Cross—the compass now reads one hundred sixty-five degrees and you are back on course."

Although the cockpit was illuminated only by the dim red light of the binnacle, I could see tears glistening in the eyes of this sometimes-too-eager boy-man who had momentarily thought that *he*, now, was the master of the unforgiving sea. The next morning, Pete's only entry in the log for his night watch was one word—"Sorry."

A night watch stander has in his hands the lives of his four shipmates deeply slumbering below. If he is not alert and not prone to follow orders, real life-threatening situations can and often do arise. The all-prevailing orders directed to these novice sailors were "When in doubt, call the skipper. Don't guess! Don't experiment. Stay alert."

We continued to have heavy weather, lightning storms, strong squalls—beam seas rolling up, uninterrupted, from the reaches of the great Southern Ocean, for the duration of our passage to Aitutaki in the Cook Islands.

The submerged reef Wairuna was marked on our chart "PD 1915." This meant that its position last charted in 1915 was doubtful, so I directed the *Morning Star* to pass well east of this death trap.

Our course had been laid out to give us a wide berth between the Northern Cook Islands of Rakahanga and Manihiki to the west and Penrhyn to the east. We had wanted to stop at Penrhyn Atoll with its 108-square-mile lagoon, reportedly one of the largest in the Pacific, but the newly independent government with its resident agent was refusing to grant Americans this permission. The native name for Penrhyn is Tongareva ("Tonga in the heavens"). The people of Tongareva have been very friendly toward Americans since World War II, when it was used as an airbase for American forces. Its disputed ownership is claimed by the United States, by New Zealand, and by the newly formed independent Cook Islands government. It is said that the Tongareva Islanders, if given their choice, would vote for annexation by the United States.

It is a reasonable stop for water and provisions, but Americans who had attempted to put in here in the past were summarily ordered out of the lagoon by the resident agent of the Cook Islands government. Rather than get involved with this probability, we reluctantly sailed past Tongareva, heading for what we had heard was one of the friendliest islands in the Pacific, Aitutaki. Twelve days out of Fanning, the dark outline of that island loomed through heavy overcast and squalls. What new adventures awaited us here?

With black squalls obliterating the view, we approached the pass of Arutunga village. The entrance to the pass into the barrier reef surrounding the island is only six feet deep, exactly our heavily laden draft, so we anchored in twelve fathoms (seventy-two feet) outside the reef awaiting a high tide. The lagoon was sprinkled with Maori fishermen in dugouts casting their nets. It was a thoroughly enthralling sight.

As we tidied up our little ship and got into our Sunday-best clothing, a government launch named *Te Avarua* came pitching out of the narrow pass. She was loaded with men all dressed in starchy white uniforms and one sedately dressed, thirtyish woman. They boarded us and almost immediately told us that we were denied permission to enter their precious lagoon.

As they chatted among themselves in the Maori language, I noted that the lone woman, Rima, had a great deal to say—and in a very authoritative way. They offered a variety of excuses. We couldn't enter because we were not fumigated for the rhinoceros beetle—an insect that has ravaged the coconut crop of the western Pacific. We explained to them that we had come from Hawaii and Fanning, where the devastating insect was unknown. It was evident that there was disagreement among them as to whether or not to allow us to enter.

But Rima was adamant. The next excuse was that Aitutaki was not a port of entry for the Cook Islands, and they told us that we would have to sail 140 miles south to Rarotonga to gain formal permission. I told the official party that we and the kids were extremely disappointed—that we had heard that the people of Aitutaki were the friendliest in the South Pacific—but that we would remain anchored out in the open sea near the dangerous reef if we could come ashore with the dinghy. They consented to this with the caution "Just to reprovision, mind you." As the official party left, we did our best to muster wan smiles and a cheerful wave.

That afternoon, fishermen in dugouts would come alongside and ask us, "Why they no let you go into lagoon?" "Too dangerous out here if wind changes." "Papa Jimmy, (the resident agent) he don't like strangers here." "Aitutaki people like Americans, no like Papa Jimmy."

As we invited these lovely, outgoing Polynesian people aboard for tea or a beer, took Polaroid pictures, and showed them around the *Morning Star*, they radiated friendship. Many gave us fish, coconuts, oranges, and bananas as the stream of dugouts continued to pour out of the pass on a family Sunday excursion to see the American yacht. They filled us in on the local politics and explained that Rima was the niece of Sir Albert Henry, the prime minister of the newly independent Cook Islands. Although Aitutaki was Sir Albert Henry's home island, it appeared that there were strong feelings of animosity directed toward him by his own people, and especially toward his resident agent.

These people explained how twenty-five hundred American troops occupied Aitutaki during the war, although a gun was never fired in anger. This contingent of American infantry was lead by a young officer named John Harrington. From that day to the present, Harrington has never returned to America. At the war's end, he was mustered out of the army in the South Pacific as a colonel, and returned to Aitutaki to marry a local Maori girl and set up a trading business. As they chattered, we listened and smiled, but avoided offering our opinions about island politics or getting involved in any controversy.

We pitched and heaved at anchor outside the pass for the next several days, going back and forth to the village in the rubber Avon dinghy—sometimes standing still when the tiny Seagull outboard motor could not overcome the velocity of the outrushing current.

One day, Rima and her husband, Harold Browne, a big, handsome Maori, came out in an outrigger canoe and we cordially invited them aboard. We broke out our guitar, and Rima played it beautifully as she sang Maori songs to us. As we sat in the cockpit, I couldn't help notice the fishermen in their dugouts furtively giving us the universal thumbs-up signal. We had the "right" guests aboard.

Suddenly, Rima blurted, "Ray, we go get *Te Avarua* and Reo, our best pilot, and bring you into the lagoon now. You get up your anchor and wait for us. We shall be back in two hours when the tide changes."

We were jubilant at this sudden outburst of smiling hospitality. The sixty fathoms of chain and the anchor had now become hopelessly entangled in the coral, and there was no way for us to break it free. Pete and Ray, both expert scuba divers, volunteered to dive down. It took them an hour to disentangle the anchor, caught between coral rocks, and to surface slowly to avoid the bends. When they came back aboard, they were wide-eyed as they told us of the monster groupers they had seen in the murky depths on the floor of the ocean. Just before dusk *Te Avarua* swung alongside, and Reo, with his ten-year old son David, boarded us.

With Reo guiding me with hand signals from the foredeck, we scraped over the sandy bottom into the still lagoon, weaved our way among the coral heads, and tied up the *Morning Star* alongside the remains of a coral jetty. Here an immaculately white-uniformed Maori boarded us with a Flit gun and with a few desultory, face-saving squirts pronounced our ship free of the rhinoceros beetle and any and all other plagues and infectious diseases.

For the next month, every kindness was lavished upon us by the friendly Maoris. We attended their nightly wild, sensual native dances. We were invited into their homes on all levels—from squalid, corrugated-iron (left over from the American occupation), dirt-floored shacks, to the relatively palatial clapboard-styled houses of the handful of white men in residence on the island. We learned for the first time from John Harrington, the ex-American officer, of the emerging Watergate scandal, the resignation of Vice-President Spiro Agnew, the Israeli-Arab War, the oil embargo, and all of the news of America gleaned from his shortwave radio.

Here on this isolated Pacific island, caught up in the relatively primitive life-style of these carefree Polynesian people, we could not bring ourselves to become absorbed with the news events of the "civilized" world we had left in our wake. At home, I had been a news junkie—totally addicted to watching two or three network and local televised news programs a night. By design, we did not listen to the shortwave BBC and Voice of America broadcasts while on this voyage. The news of the world and of our "civilization" is almost all worrisome and negative. Absorbed in nature and its native people, we found that our spirits remained more buoyant, tranquil, and positive than if we pondered the geopolitical implications of wars and rumors of wars that nightly filled the airwaves of the world.

Aitutaki with its thirty-five hundred Maori people is a totally self-sufficient off-the-beaten-path island, which epitomizes the South Sea Island paradise as fantasized for centuries by so many white men. The lagoon is alive with edible fish. The land produces oranges, bananas, arrowroot, and wild pigs. It is lush and beautiful. The kids were thoroughly enjoying this adventure and the young Maori people. Ray and Pete camped out on a motu (small island or islet) across the lagoon and came back with wild tales of stabbing to death with a scuba diving knife a three hundred-pound wild pig that they managed to corner.

Apparently, escapism "back to nature" was the prime motivating factor in the lives of the white men on the island. They were an odd mixture of origin and background:

Jack Neale was a Scotsman, who wrote in our guest log, "If tha does ought for naught—do it for thee' sel." Kurt was a Dane and a ham radio operator. Edson Raff was an American ex-paratroop officer who had been in the Normandy invasion and maintained a twin-engine airplane on the airstrip that the Americans had built during the war. Then there was Bill Reeder, a New Zealander, who ran the airport; and the island's doctor, a young New Zealand general practitioner, David Jones, who was, predictably, known locally as Davey Jones.

John Baxter was a British ex-submariner and, along with his lovely Maori wife Mary, the proud owner of Baxter's Store, a tiny general store on the island.

John explained that for one reason or another these men

had become disenchanted with life in their own countries—
with the frantic "hectivity" all around them—and thought that
by marrying an attractive, brown-skinned Polynesian girl,
they could find inner peace, stake out a tiny niche for themselves on this earth, and live a more rewarding life in a place
where the pace was relaxed, and where the people and the
weather were kind.

But John's comments revealed to me that this seemingly
idyllic blueprint for life had not quite worked out as expected
for some of the white men of Aitutaki. Removed from their
own background and system of living, they found accultura-
tion to the civilization of the South Sea Islanders very difficult,
if not impossible. John remarked one day that the only refuge
for such a European (the generic term for all white men) was
to be found in a can or a bottle. And, indeed, the consumption
of alcoholic beverages among the refugees from the main-
stream of their own cultures was prodigious. Crushing boredom seemed to underlie their dilemma. They hadn't found
that for which they had been searching.

John complained that there was no one to talk to intelli-
gently, that you could only discuss fish, coconuts, pigs, and
bananas for so long; that mere subsistence was the central
preoccupation of the local people.

Kurt told me that were it not for his ham radio, he would go
crazy, stuck on this South Sea island paradise.

I had noted the claustrophobic sense of entrapment among
other white men in their self-inflicted South Pacific imprison-
ment. The point seemed to be that without an inner sense of
mission and purpose in life, no solution to discontent can be
found on this earth—no matter where one looks and no matter
how pleasant the ambience into which a man retreats. From
the days of the *Bounty* mutineers to the present, the lore of the
South Seas is replete with the myth of "escape to the South
Pacific—to get away from it all"—that changing one's life by
changing one's habitat would solve one's inner problems and
grant to the white man a solution to his inner torment—the
legendary white man's burden. As a transient adventurer—
here today, gone tomorrow—and as an interested listener, I
found that I provided an apparently much-needed outlet for

the frustrations and disenchantment that seemed to pervade my fellow white men on these islands. Sharing, to a degree, their mythical illusion, I couldn't offer much consolation other than trite observations to the effect "I guess life is what you make it wherever you are."

But in a way I was thankful that I had a mechanism established in the form of a floating home to enable me to keep moving—to continue the search—both interior and exterior. When I became bored with people, places, and things, there always remained, seductively beckoning me, the open sea and what I might find over the next horizon.

It is difficult for a land-bound human being to relate to the almost compulsive lure of the sea. The music of the gurgling bow wave of a silent sailing ship is a tranquilizer not found in any drugstore. Time spent contemplating the pale blue tropical skies, flecked with popcorn puff clouds; or, when night steals the light of day, the tropical heavens aglitter with diamondlike stars—restores a childlike sense of the wonder of it all. I felt that whenever we set out to drop over a distant horizon, there was a faint tinge of envy radiating from the people we left forlornly behind on the docks and beaches of the world.

On Aitutaki, an ancient custom dictated that only Maori women could own land. John Baxter and I became particularly good friends, and he explained to me how and why each *pakaha* (the Maori name for "white man") had ended up in this backwater of the Pacific.

One Maori family, Tiopu and his wife, Nga Tere, literally adopted us and the crew. Almost every night, accompanied by their children, they would visit the *Morning Star*—always bearing gifts—rare conch shells that Tiopu would find at night while fishing on the reef. Nga Tere wove together a border of uniformly sized, exquisite cowry shells for the two-by-six-foot collage of color pictures which adorned the main bulkhead of the *Morning Star*'s salon.

Nga Tere told me that I was unusually fortunate to "get on so well with the Maori people as well as the *pakahas* on the island." With tears welling up in his eyes, Tiopu said to me one night, "I your Maori brother. You come live here. Nga Tere give you land for small plantation." I was overwhelmed and could only say, "Maybe someday, Tiopu, maybe someday."

It would be grossly discourteous to refuse or to offer to pay directly for any of the gifts of carvings, Maori war clubs, seashell headbands, flowers, fruit, fish, and coconuts. But we reciprocated with gifts of clothing, a wristwatch for Tiopu—the first he had ever owned—canned goods, and numerous other items carried with us from America for just this purpose.

In the long evening sessions around the salon table of the *Morning Star*, Tiopu explained to us how Captain Bligh had brought the *Bounty* to Aitutaki in 1789 and how native tradition says that later the *Bounty* mutineers brought the first orange and pumpkin seeds to Rarotonga, where they were established and transferred to Aitutaki.

One day I showed Nga Tere how the rounded binnacle of the *Morning Star* looked like a Maori god's head and the projecting wind direction and wind-speed indicator resembled the arms with upraised fists. I said, "It reminds me of the Maori god of the sea—Tangaroa." I told her that I was thinking of painting eyes, mouth, and nose on it.

To my amazement, the next day Nga Tere appeared on the jetty with her eighty-six-year old father, "Papa Tere," who had walked several kilometers from his village. He had three cans of house paint bought at Baxter's Store—red, green, and black.

Although almost sightless, Papa Tere spent the next six hours painting a terrifying rendition of Tangaroa on my binnacle. The eyes were compelling and radiated blood and fire. The upraised fists were enormous.

As he painted, Papa Tere talked freely to me of his eighty-six years on Aitutaki. He said that from the missionaries of the London Missionary Society, to the Seventh Day Adventists, he reckoned that he had been baptized by no less than twenty-one religions. "Now," he said, "I ready to die and I go straight to God."

With a grunt of satisfaction and a flourish of his crude brush, Papa Tere said, "I super Christian, but Tangaroa still god of the sea. He take you safe where you go."

Disdaining any compensation for his day-long effort, Papa

Tere, supported by his cane and his grandson, began his long, halting walk back to his village.

Tiopu was a fifteen-year old boy when the Americans occupied Aitutaki. He was adopted by the troops and became their official barber. He detested the shoulder-length hair of Ray and Pete. In blunt Polynesian style, he told them, "You men— should not have hair like girl. You want to fish and dive with me. I cut your hair off."

The next day he appeared with his barber tools, plunked each of the boys, in turn, on a jerry can, and ruthlessly slashed off their precious locks. The boys had rueful looks as their tresses began wafting into the sea. But in a sense they seemed relieved. Now they had a new peer group into which to blend. The voluptuous Maori girls began to give them flirtatious glances, and the Maori young men became their fishing and diving buddies.

Devastating hurricanes regularly strike the Cook Islands. The coral jetty that the American forces had built out to the reef had been destroyed in one, and the stump of the jetty to which our small vessel was tied collapsed into the sea one night during a storm while we were in Aitutaki.

In mid-October, with the oncoming hurricane season, it was time for us to begin the 660-mile windward voyage east to Tahiti, where we could feel relatively free from the threat of storms. As the weather abated, I studied the pass through the binoculars and abruptly decided that now was the time to leave.

I walked up to his house and paid my last respects to Papa Jimmy, the initially hostile but now friendly resident agent, and within minutes the "coconut telegraph" had transmitted the message around the island—the *Morning Star* is leaving.

When I got back to the jetty, it was congested with our new-found friends, both Maoris and *pakahas*. Her powerful diesel purring, *Te Avarua*, with both pilots—Reo and Nui—vying to pilot us out the treacherous pass, breasted up alongside.

With lead-filled hearts and tear-filled eyes, we cast off our forward mooring lines as good-byes were shouted and hand-kerchiefs were waved. The broad, powerful figure of Tiopu stood stolidly, our stern line grasped to the last in his massive hands, with unashamed tears streaming down his cheeks. We again scraped bottom in the shallow pass. Within minutes we were in the deep cerulean blue water of the heaving open sea.

Reo and Nui shouted, "God be with you *Morning Star.*" Through the binoculars, we could still see the knots of people on the jetty waving their handkerchiefs in sad farewell. Although the month was brief, we had come to love deeply the generous, free-spirited people of Aitutaki.

As we hoisted sail, I said to myself, "Maybe someday, Tiopu. Maybe someday."

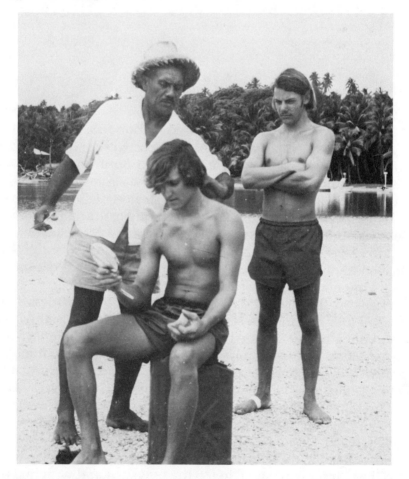

Tiopu, the barber

CHAPTER FIVE

EAST TO FRENCH
POLYNESIA

⚓ Now the loss of easting caused by our aborted voyage to the Marquesas Islands had to be recovered. We strapped down the sails and laid off a course to Bora Bora, lying six hundred miles east-northeast. Hard on the easterly winds with an opposing west-running current, my celestial navigation had to be pinpoint accurate. Just north of our rhumb line to Bora Bora lay the low atolls and reefs of Scilly and Mopelia.

With seas breaking over the bow as the *Morning Star* slogged her way to windward, everything became damp below. The morale of the seasick crew began to sag.

Then, on the second day out of Aitutaki, the stainless steel swaged fitting of the forestay at the masthead fractured with a resounding report. As the headstay let go, we could have been dismasted in an instant, but I spun the wheel to bring the boat before the wind to relieve the pumping action of the mast and calm the severely vibrating rig. With the wind and seas astern, the pressure on the mast was transferred to the backstays. The only momentary problem was that we were heading west back toward Aitutaki. Rather than risk going aloft to the swaying masthead in these heavy seas, I decided to support the mast with the jib halyard shackled to the bowsprit and winched up taut.

Without the jib, the windward ability of our beamy ketch was severely impaired, but I decided that we could tack the remaining four hundred miles to Bora Bora with the forestaysail, reefed main, and full mizzen. We unhanked the jib, coiled the useless wire forestay, and brought our vessel back as close to the wind as I decided that we could safely sail without overstressing the jib halyard, functioning now as a jury-rigged headstay. Then, if we were lucky, the east-southeast trade wind would veer more to south-southeast, giving us a comfortable close reach to Bora Bora. With our speed reduced to an average four knots, we cautiously resumed our windward passage.

We were thankful that we were sailing a ketch with a double head rig—jib and forestaysail—rather than the sloop-rigged boats that I had owned before acquiring the *Morning Star*. Sailors become vehemently opinionated about their notion of what constitutes the ideal boat, the ideal rig, the ideal hull material, the ideal design and construction. Having sailed and raced sloops, cutters, schooners and ketches made from steel, fiberglass, and wood, I had finally come to the long-overdue conclusion that there *is* no ideal. A high seas voyaging yacht is *always* a compromise. One trades off one feature and characteristic to gain another.

My highly personal dream had always been to sail a traditional carvel-planked, wooden ketch around the world. I feel that, properly handled, a traditionally built hull with ketch rig is the best compromise for us—for our ultimate short-handed crew of two. Ketch sailing and the proper use of the mizzen sail takes thousands of sea miles of practice. One can't learn it out of books.

Now, with the full mizzen sail strapped down flat, our bow was held into the wind, where a slightly eased forestaysail, trimmed with the reefed mainsail, gave us sufficient drive to windward to hold a steady course to Bora Bora.

Our crisis of the next day was a first-class galley fire. A sea cook, pitching about the galley of a small craft on the high seas, is a special breed of heroine. Teri is the most heroic sea cook I have ever known. No matter what the weather or the motion of the boat, no matter if she felt slightly seasick herself, Teri would manage to fire up one of man's most obnoxious inventions, our kerosene stove. With its poorly designed, small, shallow priming cups beneath the temperamental Primus burner, the kerosene stove at sea is an abomination.

On one prior boat, we had cooked with alcohol, which is even worse, and on another formerly owned boat, we cooked with butane gas, which, if handled with an abundance of respect for its explosive nature, is our choice of cooking fuels. The specious argument for kerosene for the long-distance voyager is that it is safer and is available anyplace in the world.

While Teri was an outstanding sea cook, she had no patience with either things mechanical or things that required meticulous maintenance. Once our South Pacific shakedown voyage was completed, Shirl and I had fully resolved to replace our kerosene stove with a proper butane installation. But as long as we had the kids aboard, we didn't feel that any of them, especially Teri, would show the liquified petroleum gas the proper respect that it deserves under penalty of death.

There existed between Teri and our Primus stove a smoldering enmity. She would fail to keep the burners and the needle aperture immaculately clean. When her burning alcohol primer would spill from its tiny cup, she would mutter, grumble, and slap "this stupid stove" with a pan or the nearest weapon at hand. The stove would respond with obscene burps and sputters as its embryonic smoking, yellow flame would flare up only to die aborning.

But this day Teri went too far! A pool of unburned alcohol and kerosene had collected underneath the stove. When Teri held a lighted match to the burner, the stove erupted into a ball of flame. As she screamed I came stomping below, to observe sadly the flames blister the varnished interior as the teakwood stove enclosure caught fire.

In one swoop, I had the dry-chemical fire extinguisher squirting its foamy cloud over the fire. As the fire died, Teri sat at the salon table sobbing. Most of her entire meal had been ruined by the smoky fire and what was spared had been rendered inedible by the chemical fire extinguisher. It was late, and she had to begin the whole miserable process anew.

I said, "Come on, honey, make your peace with that stove.

Do it the stove's way, not your way! I'll tell you what. When you learn how to take care of that stove, I'll give it to you as a wedding present." She merely fixed me with a malignant glare and reluctantly began to swab up the incredible mess. Another "crisis of the day" met head on and resolved in the tiny, isolated community on the *Morning Star.*

At 0500 on the beginning of the fifth day out of Aitutaki, Ray shouted at the top of his lungs, "Land Ho!" Rubbing the sleep out of their eyes, the crew climbed out of their warm berths and assembled on deck. There! Etched on the eastern horizon by the predawn rising sun were the spectacular 2,100-foot-high twin peaks of Mount Pahia on the island of Bora Bora. Off our port beam, low on the horizon, was the 1,200-foot-high island of Maupiti. We had made it with our mast intact! Six hundred miles to windward in slightly less than five days. Not bad, considering our crippled condition.

In a few hours, with the sun high in the sky, we proudly sailed through Te Avanui Pass into the glittering azure green lagoon formed by the barrier reef surrounding Bora Bora. As I listened to the excited plans for diving, hiking, spearfishing come pouring from the mouths of the kids, I thought to myself, "What a truly fascinating adventure for them." It is just as well then that I didn't know what awaited us in Tahiti.

James Michener reputedly has referred to Bora Bora as the most beautiful island in the world. Its scintillating blue green lagoon, peppered with small motus with leaning coconut palms—all formed a stage setting for the verdant cone-shaped peaks clutching for the pale blue heavens above.

Bora Bora, Huahine, Raïatéa, and Tahaa are among the Leeward Islands—Îles sous le Vent, or "islands under the wind"—of the Society Island Archipelago. Captain Cook of HMS *Endeavor* named them the Society Islands because "they lay contiguous to one another."

We spent days swimming, diving, and spearfishing in the lagoon and on the reefs of Bora Bora, Huahine, Tahaa, and Raïatéa. Raïatéa is the ancient Havaiki of Polynesian lore—the legendary home of the gods. It was from here that the Polynesians set out to populate the islands in the Polynesian triangle—Hawaii to the north, Easter Island to the east, and New

Zealand to the south. We were fascinated by the former places of Polynesian religious significance and human sacrifice that our newly made Polynesian friends on Raïatéa showed to us.

In Huahine, we rigged anchors to the masthead and "careened ship" first on one side, then on another as we scraped the gooseneck-barnacle-encrusted bottom and caulked and painted it with antifouling paint. The gooseneck barnacle will fasten onto a swiftly moving hull, beating hard to windward, and short of a putty knife, there is no way to break its tenacious grip. Scientists are analyzing the gluelike substance that it exudes, permitting it instantly to adhere under water to a moving vessel.

Sailing eastward toward Tahiti, we came to what *we* consider—far and away—the most beautiful island in the world—Mooréa. We entered Opunohu Bay and anchored in Robinson's Cove, with our stern tied to a coconut tree. The tourists call Mount Muaputo, a toothlike peak overshadowing Opunohu Bay, Tiger Tooth or Bali Hai Mountain.

During our days cruising and diving in Mooréa, we were befriended by two most gracious and friendly Americans, Med and Glad Kellum. The Kellums sailed into Mooréa in Med's father's yacht over forty years ago, fell in love with the island and its people, bought property, and made their permanent home in French Polynesia.

They showered on Shirl, the kids, and me such copious hospitality that there is no way that we can ever reciprocate. Both Med and Glad speak French and Tahitian fluently, and we never tired of hearing the stories of their experiences and the lore of the South Pacific.

We had the entire bay to ourselves and found ourselves to be a tourist attraction. Two or three times a day tour buses would stop on the road bordering picturesque Robinson's Cove and eject herds of camera-necklaced tourists, who would point their lenses at the palm-framed *Morning Star* and shoot pictures with the spectacular spires of Bali Hai Mountain forming the background.

Then, twice a day, we would have a tourist-laden outrigger canoe come sweeping around by sea from Paopao (or Cook's) Bay, where hotels are located. Similarly, tourists would be

Mal de mer

Peter Fuller, crew of shakedown voyage, with Maori girls

Majestic Moorea

Sunset over Moorea

brought around from the Club Mediterranean on the west side of the island. Many of them were Americans visiting Tahiti, lying only twelve miles to the east.

As the cameras clicked, the questions flew. We were to learn to encounter these same questions, almost verbatim, in every port of the world during the next eight years.

Question: "Did you sail that boat all the way from San Francisco?"

Answer: "Yes."

Question: "Did you get into any storms?"

Answer: "Not too many."

Question: "What did you do at night—anchor?"

Answer: "The ocean is too deep to anchor. In some places, over three miles deep. So we sail night and day."

One paunchy man bluntly volunteered, "I think you are nuts to expose your wife and kids to such danger." I simply stated, "Do you feel that way when you pack your car with your wife and kids and drive down the freeway?"

In my mind, the hazard could be greater on the freeway, but the point is, it is a hazard to which my impertinent questioner had grown so accustomed that he no longer thought of driving the freeway as dangerous. It was his element. The open sea presented a totally hostile environment to him. He simply did not have the ability to relate to life in a small sailing craft.

One day while anchored in Robinson's Cove, Ray said, "Just think of the thousands of slides and movies of the *Morning Star* anchored in Mooréa that will be shown on these tourists' screens all over America and Japan. I wonder what kooky things they will say about us?"

On December 3, 1973, almost six months out of San Francisco, we sailed into Papeete Harbor on the fabled isle of Tahiti.

CHAPTER SIX

HEARTBREAK HARBOR

Tahiti—the very name has an allure. Ever since the early European navigators—Wallis, de Bougainville, Cook, and Bligh—beginning in 1767, "discovered" Tahiti, it, more than any island of the South Pacific, to this day conjures up images of the South Pacific island paradise in the minds of the white man. Artists such as Gauguin, poets such as Robert Louis Stevenson, authors such as Nordhoff and Hall, actors such as Gable and Brando—all have contributed to the magic that Tahiti symbolizes to millions of people around the world.

The island of Tahiti with its lush, verdant, strikingly beautiful mountains, flowers, waterfalls, and forested pools must certainly be as close as one can get to a geographical paradise on this earth. The tourists in Papeete have spoiled some of the Tahitians, but the vast majority are still an inherently kind, fun-loving, and lovable people. I often thought that had I been on the *Bounty*, anchored for months in Matavai Bay while my harsh captain awaited the breadfruit seedlings to mature, I too would have mutinied—would have done anything rather than return to dreary old England.

We anchored the *Morning Star* with stern lines extending to the shore in front of the de Gaulle monument; checked in with the immigration, customs, and police officials; and settled down to enjoy the wonders of Tahiti.

It was the middle of the rainy season. Almost daily, the dark clouds rolling over the mountains of the island would discharge torrents of cold rain on the decks of the *Morning Star*, creating the musty atmosphere of a wooden vessel below decks. The incessant rain had a depressing effect on the five boat-bound crew members.

One day the French navy towed a derelict sailing vessel *Greenpeace* into Papeete and anchored her alongside the *Morning Star*. She had been involved with the vessels *Fri* and *Spirit of Peace* in the protest sail to Mururoa Atoll in the southern Tuamotus, where the French government—nonparticipants in the atmospheric-test-ban treaty—were exploding nuclear devices suspended below barrage balloons above the atoll. The crew of *Greenpeace* had been violently arrested by French commandos and deported from French Polynesia. But their bedraggled vessel was towed to Tahiti and anchored unattended right alongside of us. Despite my vehement protests, the French sailors tied her stern to a bollard ashore, threw the *Greenpeace* hook over the side, and in their navy launch swept across rainy Papeete Harbor.

The constant rains in the mountains to windward were causing a debris-laden, brown muddy torrent to flood out into the harbor just astern of *Greenpeace*. Predictably, she began to drag her bow anchor and swing ominously down toward the *Morning Star*.

Ray and I, with the help of a German yachtsman, Uwe, anchored nearby and equally threatened by the dragging vessel, took one of my several spare anchors out into the harbor at an angle. Then we boarded *Greenpeace* and secured my anchor to keep her swinging bow away from us. With this temporary solution, Uwe and I hitchhiked a ride around the harbor to Fare Ute to see the French harbormaster.

The issue of French atomic testing in Polynesia was so politically combustible with the Tahitian independence movement (*Autonomistas*), the Tahitian and Paumotuan people, that we had to be extremely diplomatic in asking the *capitaine du port* to remove *Greenpeace* from her threatening position next to us. Initially, he said, "If you don't like *Greenpeace* near you, then *you* move." No one likes to be told how to run his business.

Uwe got a little hot under the collar and started to talk about the French and German common partnership in the European Economic Community. Paradoxically enough, these historic enemies—the Germans and the French—now have a "special symbiotic relationship," and Germans abroad get preferred treatment from the French in visa requirements, customs, and many other areas.

Listening to Uwe's desk-pounding tirade, I knew that we weren't going to accomplish our mission in this manner. As far as the Frenchman was concerned, the interview was over. It was nearing noon, and everything closes in Tahiti for two or more hours in the afternoon.

When Uwe and I got outside the office, I looked him in the eye and said, "Cool it, will you? Stay here and relax for a minute. I'm going back to see the *capitaine*."

I walked back into the office and asked for one more minute with the fiery official. Stumbling with my pathetic fractured French, I told him that I thought he was right. "We both should move our yachts. But it occurred to me, as I was leaving, that when we do, someone else will come in and anchor where we were. After I take my anchor back, you may have *beaucoup* trouble *redoublé*." Also, I said, "If the Canadian vessel, *Greenpeace*, drags onto the *roches* ("rocks") or *le plage* ("beach"), you may have a *naufrage* ("shipwreck") in your harbor—then, *beaucoup de problèmes pour vous avec* the Canadian government. This *condamné bateau* has already caused your government so much trouble that you may want to reconsider our *petit problème*."

The *capitaine* pulled a little grin, stuck out his hand, and said, "I'll think about it, *mon ami*." (On subsequent calls in Tahiti, the *capitaine du port* and I were destined to become good friends.)

With that, I waved *"à bientôt"* ("see you soon"), collected Uwe, still fuming outside the door, and started to leave the building. As we walked out into the drenching rain, the *capitaine* came after us and said, "Your yachts are *très loin* ("very far") for you to walk in this rain. Come, I will give you a ride back."

Within an hour after Uwe and I returned, a group of sailors with an officer in charge came alongside the *Morning Star* in a gray launch. They politely explained that they were going to tow *Greenpeace* to the other side of the harbor, and they wanted to return my anchor to me. Within the next few days, we learned that *Greenpeace* was loaded onto the deck of a freighter bound for Vancouver.

This episode again taught us that human beings are essentially the same all over the world. In dealing with officialdom, as guests in their country, we found that we received just about the same treatment and attitudes that we projected. If we projected cooperative friendliness, we received, more often than not, abundant friendliness and kindness in return.

Port rot again started to gnaw at the vitals of the crew of the *Morning Star*. The Arab oil embargo was beginning to affect Tahiti. Petroleum products of all kinds were coming into short supply. The French were allocating a liter a week of diesel fuel to yachts. Long lines were forming at the gasoline stations on the island. Flights out of the island were being canceled and severely curtailed. No one had any idea when, if ever, the embargo would be lifted. Panic buying of kerosene, butane, and all petroleum supplies including accessories—lamps, cooking stoves, jerry jugs—quickly emptied the Chinese stores of Papeete.

We were stuck in Tahiti for at least three months awaiting the passing of the hurricane season in the Tuamotus. The Christmas season was approaching, and the kids were becoming bored and homesick.

The uncertainty of the duration of our stay in Tahiti compelled Shirl and me to bite on the bullet and send Pete home. On December 11, we sadly put him on a California-bound plane in the hope that with just our own two kids aboard, during our enforced port-bound period in Tahiti, harmony would be attained. It was an exorbitant expectation. Teenage American kids cannot be confined with their parents twenty-four hours a day, no matter how exotic the surroundings.

Howard Hughes's ocean-floor research vessel, *Glomar Chal-*

lenger, docked in Tahiti one day. I became acquainted with the captain and the radio officers.

There is a fascination among professional seagoing men of all nationalities with high-seas-voyaging sailing vessels. The officers of the *Challenger* visited us on board, and I arranged to buy diesel fuel from them. So, Ray and I ferried jerry jugs of fuel from the engine room of the ship to our little craft, and in a day our tanks were topped off and our fuel problem for the return trip to Hawaii via the Tuamotus and Marquesas was solved.

We then had a family conference. I proposed, "I'll buy one-way plane tickets for you both to go home before this fuel shortage terminates all flights out of here. You go back to college for a quarter. If you want to rejoin us in Tahiti to sail through the Tuamotus to the Marquesas and back to Hawaii, you will be welcome. If not, mom and I shall sail on alone."

They jumped at the chance to go back to their friends and sweethearts. On December 23, they were winging their way back to California.

As Shirl and I returned to the boat, we had mixed emotions. We were depressed by the sense of emptiness created by the sudden departure of the kids, while at the same time we experienced a sense of peace and relaxation that we now no longer had the responsibility to "show anyone a good time."

Before Ray and Teri left, we had sailed the boat inside the barrier reef around to Punaauia on the west coast of Tahiti to get away from the bustle of Papeete Harbor. Now we were in a lovely, reef-bound anchorage. Our dawns were heralded by the sun shooting its golden lancelike rays up and over the green peaks of Tahiti towering above us. The land breeze wafted with it the smell of cooking fires, permeated by the delicious perfume of the flora of Tahiti. The lagoon was dotted with wading Tahitian women fishing patiently, pulling in fish for breakfast. Out near the reef, Tahitian men were paddling their outrigger pirogues in the calm lagoon.

In the evenings, our eyes feasted on the multihued, cloud-filled sky as the sun dropped behind the majestic mountains of Mooréa. The calm beauty and tranquility of our setting was as a much-needed balm to our on-edge nervous systems.

Once or twice a week, we would go to the market in Papeete via "le Truck"—the mode of public transport of Tahiti. Each trip on "le Truck" was an adventure, as we watched the laughing, jovial Tahitians board this open buslike vehicle with everything from automobile tires to fish and squealing piglets. Articles that couldn't be accommodated inside on the bumpy benches were heaped on the roof by the driver and helpful fellow passengers. When "le Truck" became overloaded, the Tahitians would simply sit on each other's laps. No matter that the lap belonged to a total stranger.

Other days would find us swimming and diving on the reef, exploring in our dinghy, or hiking in the lush Tahitian mountains.

Shirl and I made many friends during our stay in Tahiti. We were invited into the homes of Tahitian, Chinese, and French friends and would entertain them aboard the *Morning Star.*

Boat repairs and maintenance were an ongoing, never-ending discipline. I would make up lengthy project lists, and as I would strike one completed project from the list, I would find myself adding two more.

We cruised inside and outside the reef down the coast of Tahiti to Port Phaeton, the best natural harbor in Polynesia. Then, back to our anchorage near Paul Gauguin's former house at Punaauia.

We dry-docked the *Morning Star* in Papeete, antifouled and caulked her bottom while living aboard, high on the marine railway of Warren Ellicott's efficient boatyard.

Despite the idyllic setting of Tahiti, it can be, indeed, "heartbreak harbor." During our months there, we sadly observed the collapse of many dreams and commitments. Families would break up—couples would separate—crews would go their separate ways. Boats would be put up for sale, or professional yacht deliverers would be hired to sail them sometimes back to Hawaii or mainland America, and sometimes to New Zealand or Australia. Disenchanted, frightened people would run out of motivation or determination and scurry back via airplane to the security and safety of their former lives. The wakes of many a husband-wife sailing team are littered with crumpled divorce papers.

Life together on a small craft at sea is a lot of "togetherness." You can't get out and walk or find a distant corner in which to pout. It is no place for a fragile marriage. Disillusionment, it seems, can set in because we may have been the victims of an illusion in the first place. "If only we could get away from it all. Get out of the rat race or rut of our lives. Sail away from it all to find paradise on earth in the South Sea Islands."

We fail to realize that wherever we go—wherever we seek—we bring ourselves with us. When we get "there," we find that there is no "there" *there.*

High seas voyaging can be an exciting, challenging, supremely healthy, ever-changing, extremely interesting lifestyle. But, as with everything else in life, if high expectations, nurtured by vivid imagination, don't measure up to reality, then the tendency can be to toss in the towel, give up, and proceed on a new search elsewhere. Shirl and I are no different in this respect from other human beings. We talked about quitting this seeming folly, sailing back to California, "settling down" at least once a week.

One day, a young couple rowing out to their yacht stopped by the *Morning Star.* They were depressed and dejected. As we sat down in our cockpit, the man—a trial lawyer—opened the conversation with, "Well, another crappy day in paradise." We then listened to a whole litany of complaints—hardnosed pompous officialdom, flies, heat, mosquitoes.

"We just wanted to say good-bye. We are having the boat delivered back to L.A. and are flying out of here tomorrow." They had had a rough passage down to Tahiti, and the young wife said, "I never want to set foot on another sailboat as long as I live. What's to like about being cold, wet, and scared half the time?"

As they showed us their airline tickets, I said, "We feel this way often. We frequently ask ourselves, 'What are we doing out here?' As an antidote to this line of negative thinking, I say to myself, 'Okay, if we were home right at this moment, I would be locked into the freeway rush hour, breathing polluted air, while glancing at the monster on my left wrist, which tells me that I *must* do this and I *must* do that when *his* dial so indicates. We would be living a vicarious life. Vicariously adventuring via movies, television, and spectator sports.'

"When I conjure up the reality of that world against the healthy life of freedom that we are now living, it tends to make this life-style vastly preferable, with all its flaws and frustrations, *for us* at this period in our lives.

"I just hope that when you get home, you will not look back and regret having abandoned your cruise."

With mixed, puzzled emotions flashing across their faces, they climbed into their dinghy and waved good-bye to us. They flew out of Tahiti the next day.

In the marinas of the world, so many people have shared with Shirl and me their fantasized dreams of "doing what we are doing someday." It is extremely difficult for us to inflate, remain neutral to, or deflate their dreams. To portray reality—both the good and the bad—to others is often a losing situation for everyone involved.

But *for ourselves*, we know that voyaging under sail on the high seas is a terminal proposition in and by itself. The health and energy reserves that God has gifted us with today must melt away very, very soon. We feel at this brief moment in our lives that what we are doing will prolong good health—physical, mental, and emotional. While it may not be for everyone, we are doing what we want to do with an ongoing sense of achievement, interest, and exhilaration.

CHAPTER SEVEN

THE SHAKEDOWN ENDS

The hurricane season was nearing its end. It was time to leave Tahiti.

Toward the end of March, we received a letter from Teri and Ray. They had completed a quarter of college and were looking forward to finishing the South Seas shakedown voyage of the *Morning Star*.

As they deplaned in Tahiti, they exuded a new enthusiasm for more adventure. A few months ashore will almost always produce within the heart of a sailor a nostalgic longing for the freedom and adventure that voyaging under sail can offer. This gift was theirs for the taking, and "this time it would be different."

Robert Louis Stevenson referred to the Tuamotu Archipelago as a graveyard of ships. On some charts, it is alternatively called the Paumotu, Low, or Dangerous Archipelago. The inhabitants refer to themselves as Paumotuans and their language as Paumotuan. The archipelago of seventy-eight atolls extends for about 950 miles in a general southeasterly direction, from a position about 180 miles north-northeast of Tahiti. Thirty of these atolls are uninhabited. Wrecks of ships, yachts, and copra schooners are everywhere. Hurricanes that sometimes develop in the Tuamotus between December and April devastate these specks of decomposed coral rising just a few feet above the pounding sea.

The west-setting current strikes the atolls, deflects, reverses into back eddies, and ricochets from atoll to atoll like a billiard ball. The unpredictable direction and velocity of these currents, along with numerous submerged reefs and low flecks of coconut-palm-topped motus, create severe hazards to navigation. Sailing at night is extremely dangerous in any kind of weather.

No other group of islands is so remote from any continent. Most of the six thousand inhabitants never see tourists or visitors other than the occasional copra schooner from Tahiti. Lacking a topsoil surface, the coral will not support normal vegetation, and only the coconut palm, pandanus, and breadfruit trees prosper. The Paumotuans living on these lonely wind- and sea-swept atolls are a fiercely independent and self-sufficient type of Polynesian. The sea, with its fickle ever-changing moods, is constantly at their very doorsteps; so over the centuries, they, perhaps more than any other island dweller, are truly the children of the sea.

To avoid the hazards of the Tuamotus, most yachts plying between the Marquesas and Tahiti skirt the northern edge of the archipelago, leaving themselves open sea to their starboard. If they stop in the Tuamotus at all, they usually call at Takaroa, Manihi, Ahe, or Rangiroa, fringing the northern tip of the archipelago. Even with these precautions, numerous craft have been wrecked on the remorseless reefs. Among the wrecks rotting on the reef at Rangiroa is Sterling Hayden's former magnificent schooner *Wanderer*.

Pinpoint celestial navigation is the name of the game if one wants to risk weaving through the treacherous central Tuamotus. We felt that the rewards of departing from the beaten path offset this risk, so I laid an ENE course bound for Fakarava.

We were beating against easterly winds and a west-setting one-knot current. In March, the weather was still unsettled, and we were encountering numerous black squalls, slamming into us from the east. On the second night out, a moon sight crossed with the stars put us seventy-six miles from the northwest edge of Fakarava Reef.

At 0700 of the third day, with the rising sun twenty degrees above the horizon, we spotted land birds, and far off our bowsprit a faint greenish hue to the pale, blue sky—the reflection of the lagoon of an atoll. Six hours later, we sighted the fuzzy fringe of Fakarava dead off our bowsprit, with Niau abaft our port beam.

Fakarava is the second largest atoll in the group, and its Passe Garuae is wide with ample depth. We had timed our entrance for slack water at the pass—two hours before the moon's meridian passage.

Tide and current tables for these remote atolls are difficult to get and lack total reliability, so we would preestimate the current at the pass with the following system:

2 hours before moonrise: Outgoing stream begins

1 hour after moonrise: Outgoing stream at its maximum

2 hours before the moon's meridian passage: Slack water of about 30 minutes duration

1½ hours after the moon's meridian passage: Ingoing stream at its maximum.

In bad weather, the rate of the tidal streams may increase by about two knots; their periods are also altered by the wind. With a strong southeast trade wind, the heavy seas, battering up and over the windward reef, fill the lagoon like a giant bathtub, and the strength and the duration of the ingoing stream decreases while the outgoing stream attains a venturi-like velocity, against which we wouldn't be able to make headway. So it is vital that these passes be entered and exited in ideal conditions, and that maximum control of the vessel be maintained.

As we lined up to enter the pass, we struck all sail and started the engine. With full throttle in the middle of the pass, the water-pump belt broke. The engine instantly overheated and had to be shut off.

Ray immediately hoisted the jib while I raised the mizzen as I tried to keep our heading in the turbulent pass. Suddenly we were in the enormous lagoon infested with coral heads. We proceeded to tack around the patches of coral, heading for the belfries of two churches standing proudly in the village of Rotoava.

Tacking an engineless heavy ketch among the coral heads and reefs is white-knuckled sailing at its most demanding, for which there is no better training than years of San Francisco Bay yacht racing.

At 1600 we rounded up into the wind in front of the village, and with sails luffing as the *Morning Star* slowed, we probed for a clear sand patch into which to drop our anchor. A great sense of relief and peace descended over the crew as the anchor dug firmly into the hard sand twenty feet beneath our keel.

A welcoming fleet of outriggers paddled from the village, and smiling, handsome, brown-skinned Paumotuans greeted us with clusters of drinking nuts (green coconuts). I invited them aboard. They ceremoniously draped heis ("shell neck-laces") around each of our necks as they wished us *Iaorana* (the Paumotuan aloha, "welcome").

With a few surgically deft swings of their machetes, they lopped off the ends of the coconuts and we were draining the nectarlike, always refreshingly cool coconut water down our parched throats.

Among our visitors was the chief Taire, whose "Christian name" was Daniel Snow. He spoke not only French, but also English, much to our delight. Taire was the chief of a group of four islands with Fakarava as its headquarters. He invited us to his house for lunch the following day and said in parting, "I see if I can find right-size belt for your motor—Chinaman store here might have." Although Chinese stores dominate the com-merce of Tahiti and the Îles sous le Vent, I couldn't believe that somehow a Chinese merchant could prosper in the remote atolls.

When the last smiling *Iaorana* was said, we had a quiet din-ner in the cockpit and watched the sun drop over the western fringe of the atoll as we listened to the deep, drumlike sound of the surf pounding on the reef. At that moment, we felt that we were in the most peaceful place on the planet.

The sound of barking dogs and the smell of cooking fires announced a new day. As we prepared the dinghy to go ashore, I thought, "How absolutely identical one day must be to the next. Time loses all meaning in this desolate corner of the earth."

Taire greeted us at the beach with "Chinaman has some belts. We go look." The sole Chinese on the atoll opened his store, piled to the ceiling with all manner of goods. He had a few worn, used belts, but none the exact size. He said, "You take—see if fit—then pay."

There are no automobiles on Fakarava, so Taire took us for a walking tour of "his" atoll. We ended up at his neat, clapboard, house (built on stilts) for lunch, which was immaculately set out for us by the women of his village. The menu included a refreshing repast of rice, *poisson cru*, breadfruit baked in the coals of the coconut-husk cooking fire, lagoon fish dipped in coconut milk, and grated coconut for dessert.

Taire had a poignant story to tell. He was thirty-seven years old. His wife had left him with an eight-year-old son. She had been attracted to the bright lights and excitement of Papeete. This was not an uncommon situation in the Tuamotus. Polynesian women will have a baby, leave it with the father or her parents, and look for a life-style with more excitement and less hard work than that offered by the harsh life on the lonely atolls.

Children are always welcome in Polynesia. The more the better. There are always relatives eager to take a new baby. There is no such thing as an orphanage or child-care center. The very concept of institutionalizing children or the elderly is totally abhorrent to the Polynesian culture.

Taire also expressed great bitterness toward the French— "Franay"—for exploding atomic devices in the atmosphere above the Tuamotus. He said that his atoll had been exposed to radioactive fallout, that he had suffered contamination, and that the French flew him to Paris each year to undergo physical tests and observation. As an American, whose country had engaged in atmospheric testing on another Pacific atoll— Bikini—I didn't have much to say.

We adapted one of the belts to our motor by revising the alternator bracketing. Two Paumotuan boys about Ray's age watched his mechanical skills in the cockpit with great awe.

But finally, as Ray worked on the alternator, the Paumotuans curled up on the cockpit seats fast asleep. They weren't afraid of hard work. They could lie down and go to sleep right alongside it.

The next day Taire and his assistant, Tekurio, came by in a large outrigger and invited Ray and me to go on a spearfishing-diving expedition in the pass. The Tuamotus at one time were renowned for their pearl diving, so the Paumotuans are expert divers who can free dive to incredible depths. To dive with these men was a rare opportunity, so we lost no time in getting our masks and flippers. When Taire saw our fancy spear guns, he told us to leave them behind. He had spare, crude Polynesian spear guns that were very long and, we were to learn, infinitely more effective in shooting fish.

As we paddled the outrigger across the mirrorlike lagoon, Ray's excitement mounted. He had been fishing and hunting with me ever since he was a small boy, and he is an expert diver. At the pass, Tekurio threw over the side a boulder wrapped in a rope, and we were anchored in forty feet of water.

As Taire slipped over the side, he commanded "Follow me." Down, down he spiraled in the gin-clear water. As we watched, the long spear was brought up next to a large grouper cruising on the bottom and—"click"—the trigger was pulled. Taire began to rise to the dugout floating above us with the impaled fish squirming on the crude spear tip dragging behind him.

After this demonstration, Ray and I dived repeatedly and each dive resulted in a fish because of the deadly efficiency of the Polynesian spear gun. They are so long that the tip can be brought up right next to the fish without the body of the diver spooking him.

We were diving in a beautiful marine zoo—an exquisite coral garden—populated by multiple species of fish. Angel, parrot fish, cod, and groupers darted among the waving fan coral. But our reverie was broken abruptly by the sudden appearance of sharks—treacherous, unpredictable Pacific grays!

Attracted by our spearfishing, groups of two—three—five—

began to buzz us; curving away from their approach about ten feet from us. Then as we continued to dive, squadrons of sharks would come out of the blue pass, becoming ever bolder. They could go into a feeding frenzy at any time, and the situation was becoming dangerous.

On our last dive together, just as I pulled the trigger of my gun, a cruising shark broke away from the pack and headed right for me. I signaled Ray to get to the top—fast! Then, as I turned to keep facing the shark with my long spear gun extended, he rolled over, showing his ugly, slitlike, fang-studded mouth, and tore the fish from my trailing spear arrow as he peeled off from his approach about four feet from me. With a surge of adrenaline, I hastily followed Ray's flippers over the gunwale of the outrigger and said, "No matter what Taire says, there will be no more diving."

Taire hung over the dugout gunwale and laughed at us as he taunted, "Aha, Raymond, you are afraid of the mako." I said, "That is right, Taire. The mako is coming too close for comfort. Next time he attacks." Then Tekurio flipped another fish into the now-writhing bottom of the dugout, and with an apprehensive look over his shoulder, he climbed into the pirogue.

But, Taire, as chief, was trying to prove his fearlessness. We watched him plunge once more. With our masked faces in the water, we saw him spin down among the cruising sharks. He shot a red fish and began his ascent. We were horrified to see two sharks peel off the pack and head for him. With a lightninglike maneuver, one shark brushed his coarse body against Taire's struggling form. The other rolled over, opened his gaping mouth, and grabbed the impaled fish from the spear. With our outstretched hands helping him, a laughing Taire flopped into the fish-laden canoe.

As Tekurio pulled up the rock anchor, Taire reached into a plastic bag he had brought and took out a sack of tobacco. Seated in the bottom of the canoe, Taire laughed, but he could not disguise his inner fear, revealed by the trembling, shaking fingers futilely trying to roll a cigarette.

As we paddled back to the village, Taire showed us his abraded skin where the shark's sandpaperlike body had scraped against him. He explained that the sharks often brush against their victim just before a biting attack. He said that they were cowards and wanted first to learn what kind of animal they were going to attack.

We had noticed a large, ugly scar on one of Taire's upper thighs. He pointed to it and said that when he was a teenage boy diving in the lagoon, a large barracuda that he had speared had attacked him and torn away part of his leg. He remarked that "Lucky, Franay come with seaplane and get me to Tahiti, or I would have bled to death."

Then he showed his flashing white teeth in an ear-splitting grin and said, "Fish *manger* ("eat") me; but village *manger* fish."

How I admired the good humor and tough resilience of these children of the sea.

During our stay in Fakarava, Taire showed us a game with spears. He had a group of young men impale coconuts on the top of a long pole standing about thirty feet above the ground. Then they would hurl their javelinlike spears skyward in an arching curve, and more often than not the spear would pierce the waving coconut. Ray and I tried again and again, but couldn't begin to get the spears anywhere near the target.

Ray and Teri played volleyball with the young Paumotuans, as Taire did everything he could to entertain his unexpected visitors from the "Yate Fetu Poipoi" (Paumotuan for *Morning Star*). But as with all things in life, each season has its time. Thére is a time to arrive and now there was a time to leave.

Taire had a village banquet for us, and at 0530 the next morning, we were heading out the pass between white seas breaking heavily on the reefs on either side of us. Our motor was surging and quitting, so we cleared the pass with all sails set. With a fifteen-knot sailing breeze on our starboard beam, we reached past Toau and Kaukura, and our local noon found us between the atolls of Apataki and Aratika.

Ringed by atolls and submerged reefs, I wanted to get into an area east-southeast of Rangiroa where I could have searoom to work on the engine before night fell. Even though we had timed this leg of our passage through the Tuamotus with the presence of a full moon, I did not relish sailing without auxiliary power among the dangerous atolls at night.

I cleared the air locks in the injectors and got the engine running again, but the worn belt we picked up in Fakarava broke with a resounding snap. In our spare-parts locker, we had an adjustable belt that is sold to unsuspecting yachtsmen as a solution to the problem we were having. The belt was held together by metal clips and would continually part at the clip, so we couldn't rely on the engine for any sustained time.

I decided to shorten sail to jib and mizzen and ghost through the night with Takapoto, Manihi, and Ahe forward of our starboard beam, and Arutua and Rangiroa forward of our port beam. I shot a round of stars at dusk and got a perfect fix on our position. These sights revealed that we were in a 1.25-knot southwest current setting us down toward the reefs on our port side. My moonrise calculations showed I should have slack water at the narrow pass into Ahe at 1600 the next afternoon.

Now it was simply a question of establishing a course that would crab us into the invisible ocean current, and sweating out the next twelve hours of darkness. If only the wind would hold!

With submerged reefs in our lee, we sailed our engineless craft all night through the "graveyard of ships." My dawn star sights showed that despite the calculations the night before, the current had subtly shifted during the night to set us farther south. It had silently swept us twenty-three miles during the last seventeen hours.

Another course alteration and from high in the spreaders, Ray called, "Land Ho." There—like a fuzzy duck blind six miles off our bow—was the island of Ahe. At the last minute, we started the motor and slipped into Passe Tiarerroa, turned into the coral-patch-fouled fairway, and sailed across the lagoon to Tekukupara village. As we approached a small motu with a grass shack, white beach, and leaning coconut palms standing off the village, Teri commented, "That island is right out of the movies."

Ray was on the bowsprit looking for a sand patch into which to drop the ninety-pound Danforth anchor. As we neared the reef in front of the motu, he shouted "Reverse!" I threw the Morse combination throttle and gearbox control into reverse—but the boat shot forward toward the reef. The gearbox linkage had broken, and it was stuck in forward! I shouted to Ray, "Let go the anchor!" Out rumbled the anchor and 200 feet of chain. As the anchor dug in, the bow dropped, and we spun around just short of the reef!

The villagers on the beach were standing agape at what they must have thought was the crazy *popaa's* (white man's) way of anchoring his "yate." We had arrived in Ahe and survived another "crisis of the day."

Two Paumotuans came out in a pirogue, and again we were met with smiling hospitality and a cluster of drinking nuts. Our welcomers were the chief, Papa Toa, and his assistant, Piu Père. Ahe was becoming an "in" place for yachts to stop, so the greeting system had become a little more formal, and Piu Père asked to see our passports.

During our days in Ahe, we were fortunate to be the only yacht there, and Mama Fana, the Chief's wife, had an elaborate banquet for us. Surely these Paumotuans had to be the friendliest people in the world.

During our stay in Ahe, we learned an important lesson in human behavior. We discovered that all was not right there. Two feuding factions existed. Where once, in the tradition of Polynesian communal life, the people shared everything—fish, coconuts, breadfruit—rivalries, turning on greed and acquisitiveness, did not exist until one sad day the "treasure of Ahe" arrived.

The "treasure of Ahe" was the Canadian yacht *Que Vive*, which had been wrecked on the reef on the north coast of Ahe several months before we arrived. Apparently *Que Vive* was coming from the Marquesas and spotted the motus of Manihi. Lying just to the east of Ahe, Manihi has an eighteen-mile-long northern submerged reef, interspersed with small islets with coconut palms growing thickly upon them. But these motus have wide, barren gaps between them. When you are abeam of one motu, the next can be below the horizon and you think that you have cleared the west end of the atoll. Your eyes will deceive you into believing that you are looking out over unbro-

ken sea unless you have established exact celestial positions or
have counted the motus, as is the practice of the skippers of
the copra schooners.

The villagers of Ahe told me that as night began to fall, the
skipper of *Que Vive* thought he had cleared Ahe. What he had
actually cleared was the last distant motu of Manihi. He
changed course to run down the wide passageway between
what he *thought* was Ahe and Rangiroa. In the middle of the
night, *Que Vive* found herself in the breakers on the unforgiving reef of Ahe—a total loss.

Although suffering coral cuts as they clambered off the
wreck through the breakers, the crew survived. The local people helped them in stripping the yacht of everything remova-
ble, which was later sold off piecemeal to visiting yachts.

After the skipper and crew had left Ahe in despair, the local
people, with what must have been Herculean efforts, removed
the diesel motor and rolled it on coconut logs over the reef to
the village. In my search for the belt that we needed to make
our motor operate, to get us out of the turbulent pass, I was
shown this motor, carefully covered with a canvas tarpaulin—
"the treasure of Ahe." I bought from Piu Père a belt from the
salvaged motor. An hour later I was visited by a representative
of the feuding faction. He was bristling with anger.

He said "Piu Père has no right to sell you belt. It belong to
us." Rather than get in the middle of this pathetic strife, I said,
"Okay. Suppose I pay you for belt—same as Piu Père?" This
seemed to satisfy him and his group, and I was able to keep
the belt.

The motor was still functional, and I was asked what it was
worth. I said, "Here in Ahe it is worthless—just an inanimate
chunk of iron. If it was in Tahiti, it could probably be sold for
two thousand dollars. The whole problem, it seems to me, is
that it is *not* in Tahiti. I don't know what it would cost you to
get it there, and even if you could transport it, who would
arrange for its sale?"

The schismatic effect of this rusty motor—in their eyes a
prized possession worth cash money—was brought about by
the question of its ownership. Quarrels and bickering had split
the community asunder. Who had contributed the most labor

in its salvage? Did Papa Toa, as the chief, own it, or did a rival chief and his constituency own it? As suspicion and disharmony without a mediator descended on the village, insults were exchanged, fights broke out, heretofore unlocked doors were now padlocked every time their owners left their homes. Deep-seated hatreds developed as the feuding continued. The communal spirit of Ahe was forever shattered.

As each side sought arbitration from us, we were drawn into a small-scale political dispute that seemed to have no solution. Greed and avarice, which so contaminate the "civilized" world, had now found evil expression in paradisical Ahe. Even if they could convert the "treasure" to cash, that cash would be spent only on wants—not on needs—wants such as transistor radios, motor bikes, whiskey, and tobacco. The obvious Solomon-like solution of splitting any profit down the middle was unpalatable to each side, which had established its prideful position.

As we sailed away, we discussed how this microcosmic quarrel had all of the basic ingredients of the eruption of devastating wars in the world we knew, sparked by territorial or material claims on the fruits of the earth, which its Creator had intended for all of his creatures to share in peace and harmony. They didn't seem to realize that a restoration of peace—forgive and forget—was far more priceless than was the hoped-for transient, divisive victory that either faction could possibly hope to attain.

As we cleared the pass and set a NNE course for Nuku Hiva, our engine failed permanently. The fuel-injection pump had collapsed—probably as a result of water in the fuel obtained months earlier on Fanning Island. It was irreparable. We could have given up right then and headed NNW for Hawaii—an easy reach—twenty-one hundred miles from our position. But I was obsessively determined to get to the Marquesas, which had been our goal when we set out from San Francisco ten months earlier. So for the next four days, we beat our engineless craft against the current to our landfall—a rock called Motu Iti standing just northwest of Nuku Hiva.

We then tacked for two more days between the dark, ominous-looking, high island of Nuku Hiva and the uninhabited island of Eiao until we could turn southward along the windward east coast of Nuku Hiva and slowly tack into fabled Taiohae Bay.

A French warship, the *Oueregon*, came into Taiohae with expert mechanics and a machine shop aboard. At first her engineers assured us that they would fix the injector pump and have our engine operative before nightfall—"no *problème.*" Subsequently, despite all of their ministrations and expertise, their launch brought a crestfallen group of engineers over to the *Morning Star* to report that the pump was unfixable.

One day our eyes feasted on the spectacular sight of Gordon and Nina Stuermer's beautiful square-rigged ketch *Starbound* sailing into Taiohae with their son, Ernie, and a crew aboard. As Gordon and I became instant friends, we commiserated about the problems we were both enduring between fathers and sons.

Starbound was heading westward to Tahiti, and Gordon couldn't figure out why I wouldn't try to radio for a new pump to get the motor going again. But I felt that we could sail through the Marquesas without a motor, just as did the many whalers of decades past. The shakedown voyage of the *Morning Star* was just about completed. Despite numerous setbacks, we had determinedly reached our original destination—the brooding Marquesas Islands.

Just at dawn, one breezeless morning *Starbound* swung by us to receive a tow line, and Gordon towed us out of Taiohae Bay. As we began to catch the first whisperings of the trade winds, *Starbound*, with a puzzled "bon voyage" from our friends Gordon and Nina, cast us off. As silence descended upon us, we were utterly free—free of dependency on a cantankerous, clattering motor; free of fumes; free of anything mechanical or electrical—dependent only on God's winds, however and whenever he decided to send them to us. This surrender to our condition brought a peace that far outweighed any anxieties about being becalmed for days in the doldrums on our sail back to Hawaii.

We had an exhilarating sail south. As we neared the cathedrallike spires of Ua Pou, we had to find a sheltered bay not only into which we could safely sail, but one that offered us wind and land configuration that would allow our engineless craft safe emergency exit as well.

We attempted to enter Hakatou Bay on the western side of Ua Pou, but as the reefs drew near, we saw how dangerous this rolling anchorage could become. So we jibed the ship in a tight 180-degree turn, and I announced to the crew that we were heading for Honolulu, twenty-two hundred miles NNW.

Now the end of the shakedown voyage was the next goal. Despite my warnings that we could be becalmed for days in the doldrums near the equator, it was no matter. We were going home. That wouldn't happen to us.

Ray and Teri's response was ecstatic. "We proved before on *Morning Star* and other boats that we could sail thousands of miles with no noisy, stinking motor. What fun this will be. Just like the sailing vessels of history." A school of porpoises appeared around our bow and confirmed that this was a good decision. But I said to Shirl privately, "We shall return to the Marquesas alone and linger for months, just you wait and see."

The next nineteen days were to prove to be the most prolonged tranquil sailing voyage of our lives. With no power, no electric lights, no radio, no refrigerator—nothing mechanical or electrical to worry about—we were entirely back to nature—at the mercy of her uncaring ways.

A glorious, unexpected peace enveloped us as we, voluntarily or not, forfeited dependency on the things that we wanted but didn't really need. With this surrender and acceptance, our nerves were calmed. We were in harmony with ourselves, with one another, and with the universe.

Selected log entries by the watch standers—Shirl, Teri, Ray, or me—best describe this silent passage:

> April 27: Big dipper off bow. Southern Cross astern. Ghosting at 3 knots with Genoa. 401 miles South of Equator. Current and leeway pushing us west. Must retain easting. Easting like money in the bank—you can always take it out—but can't always put it back. Silently hissing through the

water at 5 knots. Diamondlike phosphorescent wake.

Shirley's entry: This is heaven. Wish it would never end. Steering by stars.

Teri's entry: Dad teaching Ray celestial navigation. They are friends again.

April 29: Happy 19th birthday, Ray. Teri baked big cake.

6th day out: Crossed Equator. Winds dropping to 5 knots. Barely able to maintain steerage way. Sails slatting but slight ripple astern. Shows that we are moving. ⅞oths mile in 4 hours. 27 miles in last 24 hours. Where is the wind? Calms worse than squalls. Killer whales around us. Hope they are benign like in Marine World aquarium at home. Bathing out of buckets. NE swell promises wind. Squalls, calms, variables. Fickle equatorial weather. It's hot. Another Japanese fishing ball.

10th day out: Shaking free of doldrums. Winds NNE 25 knots. Beautiful fast sail in calm seas. 1,110 miles to Honolulu. Heavy beam seas. Rogue sea flooded cockpit. Broke over boat at level of first reef points of main. Lucky we were battened down.

Ray's entry: 158 mile run—Wow! Best day's run yet. Strike main—run off before 50-knot squall. Turbulent heavy seas. Green water breaking over boat. 11° North. Buffeted by enormous beam seas.

14th day out: Sea moderate. Reefed main.

May 10: Sun on its northward passage directly overhead—meridian passage sight useless.

15th day out: Teri's entry: Loom of light below horizon off port beam. Hilo broadcast station playing Hawaiian music. Fantastic!

16th day out: Land off Mauna Loa. Loom of Kumakahi light bearing 45° off port bow.

18th day out: See lights on shore—estimate eleven miles off Big Island. Running along Molokai coast with twins.

19th day out: Coast Guard on VHF instructs 'do not tack into Ala Wai. We will pick you up at Alpha Buoy.' O.K. Coast Guard Service boat lashed alongside to breast us into fuel dock. Swarms of Immigration, Customs and Agricultural officials all over boat.

Eleven months after sailing out the Golden Gate, the shake-down voyage of the *Morning Star* had terminated. Although it had almost ended on the reefs of despair, we had survived our own personal heartbreak harbor.

Shirl and I now knew that we had shaken down and settled not only the vessel but our own human problems. We had gained the deep inner confidence that we were ready—ready emotionally, spiritually, physically, and mentally—to set out alone to circumnavigate the globe. To sail with the wind and the seasons without itineraries, schedules, or deadlines. To find and enjoy ourselves and each other without the discordant presence of anyone—no matter how much we loved them. In our minds, the challenge of the logistics and sheer magnitude of the undertaking gave us new goals and purpose.

CHAPTER EIGHT

WE GO IT ALONE

⚓ Now began a seven-day-a-week feverish round of activities centered on preparing ourselves and the *Morning Star* for open-ocean voyaging without a crew.

During our enforced stay in Tahiti, I had earned a French-issued scuba diving certificate. The American National Underwater Instructor Qualified Scuba Diver's Certificate was much more difficult; so to become as proficient scuba divers as possible, we both enrolled in an eight-week course in scuba diving, and I got my American certificate.

We took lessons in French, and had French language tapes playing over our stereo system as we worked on the boat.

While I had, over the years, taught the fascinating art of celestial navigation to Shirl, we found that her skills in this discipline were sharply improved by her completing a course in the planetarium at the Bishop Museum in Hawaii.

Ham radio is the most valuable communications tool for a circumnavigating yacht. Much more so than commercial single sideband radio. At the flip of a switch, we could always find an eager ham operator anyplace in the world who could keep us in contact with our family, help us in procuring much-needed parts and charts, put us in contact with medical advice for ourselves or others, and, via phone patches to our navy's Fleet Weather Service or the National Weather Service, give us up-to-the-minute weather reporting gleaned from the American satellites whirling around in outer space. But a ham radio license, like everything else worthwhile, must be earned. To pass the American examination requires a steadfast self-discipline.

Intermixed with this education was the reorganization of the vessel. We enthusiastically tore out the kerosene cooking system, and I engineered a butane-gas installation which would enable us to cook safely with a clean flame and a minimum of travail. With all of this outpouring of planning, preparing, and provisioning,—the months in Honolulu evaporated.

Preparation is vital—one tries to anticipate every contingency. But it is not possible to cover everything. We had often observed that the "preparation syndrome" assumes a life of its own in the "getting-ready-to-get-ready" activities of many would-be blue-water sailors. They prepare and prepare, but they are never quite ready to cast off and drop over the distant horizon into the unknown.

There is always one more thing to do—one more gadget to install. As the moment to head out into the open sea approaches, they are psychologically restrained by the self-rationalization process, which tells them that they are not quite "ready." The "preparation syndrome" is therapeutic in and by itself. But if it isn't accompanied by the dream—the end result—it will lose its life spark and become an exercise in futility. There are yacht builders, yacht varnishers, yacht fixers, whose numbers far outweigh the relative handful of yacht sailors who *do it*—sever the umbilical cord tying them to the known and the secure.

Then, there is the phenomenon I call the "harbor stallion." A common characteristic of the "harbor stallion" is that despite the fact that he has not yet "been there," he lavishly exudes unsolicited advice. "If I were you, I would do it this way. That system will never work. You are carrying too much chain—it's too heavy in the bow section. She will run bow

down. Use rope and chain." You have to be very patient with
these dockside, harbor-manacled experts because they out-
number you overwhelmingly.

Most of them are of good will with their proffered advice,
but it is sometimes tinged with deeply subconscious guilt and
envy. "Damn it, I know I'm copping out. Why don't I force
myself to get out of here? If this guy can get a ham license, I
can do it—why don't I? Ah, well, maybe I'll start tomorrow."

Every human being has his world to circumnavigate—his
mountain to climb—his private dreams. And we all have
within ourselves an enormous, God-given power—too often
undiscovered—to realize them. But, in my observation, many
men and women confuse attainable dreams with mere vacillating wishes. What is sad is that the vast majority of people
are unaware that within themselves—so near, so close at
hand—they possess a power, a gift of God as part of their
humanity, that, once recognized, can be, with effort, brought
into functional operation. The use or nonuse of this power is
at the heart of the cause of success or failure, regardless of the
enterprise undertaken—circumnavigation of the world in a
small boat or whatever other dream we may entertain.

The preparation and maintenance of a boat must have as its
end purpose a voyage—a secret dream. Boats exist to be
sailed—to be a magic carpet to transport their owners into
high adventure.

Dozens, if not hundreds of times, Shirley and I have had people with vague, undefined dreams say to us, "One of these
days, I am going to do what you are doing. I am going to 'get
away from it all,' 'get out of the rat race,'" and sail into the
adventure, the escape, the excitement, the South Seas, or whatever they fantasize is "out there" over that unknown horizon.
The "getting away from it all," when translated, sometimes
means running from the crushing boredom of their lives.
Escape from themselves or their circumstances.

Our hearts go out to these people, but it is difficult for us to
encourage them—if they will not form the firm spirit of commitment; or won't pay the price of learning what they must
know.

It is equally awkward for us to discourage them. We may risk puncturing the balloon of their dream, which is possibly the only thing that they have to cling to desperately as an escape from their stultifying lives.

But I often ask, "When are you going to do this?" Answer always: "One of these days, when I have time."

When told this, I usually say, "Look, you have the same amount of time as I have—twenty four hours. That is all that there is! The question is: What do you freely choose to do with this time? Isn't it?"

Time, not money, is the real currency of our lives. Did you ever stop and think that as you spend money, you can usually replenish the supply one way or another? But when time is expended, it can never be replenished."

The *Morning Star* was as ready as we could make her, and now the time was at hand to cast off our lines and leave the cocoon of security of Ala Wai Boat Harbor. A source of wonder to us has always been reading news accounts headlined "Couple Sets Out to Sail Around the World." Newspaper people gather, pictures are taken, farewell parties are given, and off into the wild blue yonder sail the intrepid mariners. We know of countless scenarios exactly like this: When heavy weather strikes, gear failure begins, seasickness sets in, the would-be adventurers turn back, sometimes slink into another port, put the boat up for sale, and say, "We have *had* it! Never again."

Realizing that we are just as fragile in our resolve as is every other human being, we entrusted only one close friend with the magnitude of our plans and the time of our departure.

On July 8, 1975, this trusted veteran high-seas sailor, Louis Valier, was on the dock with aloha leis and gifts of macadamia nuts. As Louis cast off our dock lines with quietly spoken alohas, Godspeeds, and bon voyages, all others bustling around the harbor thought that we were just going out for an inter-island cruise for a few days. No fanfare, no grandiose announcements, no publicity. At 0900, with strong channel trade winds blowing, we were again heading down the Polynesian Passageway, obsessively bound for the Marquesas Islands.

The first night out, about thirty-five miles west of Lanai, the seas and winds were so rough and so many things went wrong with the boat that we spent the night hove to in forty-knot winds and steep channel seas. The months in port had softened us and opened up the seams of our ship. "We could head back right now. Only Louis would know. He would understand. No, let's anchor at Lanai and get some rest." Many a cruise has been aborted in the rough channels in the Hawaiian Islands.

A few days in Lanai, and we decided that there is "no way we are going to give up." With winds howling at thirty-five knots, we spent another wild night anchored among the reefs of Smugglers' Cove, Kahoolawe Island. Then across one of the roughest bodies of water in the world, Alenuihaha Channel to Kailua Kona on the "Big Island," Hawaii. Crossing this turbulent channel between Maui and Hawaii, we broke our staysail boom and suffered other damage, making it necessary to anchor in the rolling open bay at Kailua.

We stayed in Kailua one month, rolling at times from gunwale to gunwale. As I proceeded to repair the damage handed out to us by the channel seas, I had a daily ham radio schedule with Louis and another friend, Earl Schenck. Louis asked, "Why don't you come back to Honolulu where these repairs could be done much more efficiently at the dock?"

I told Louis, "To turn back, even a few miles, was too risky. The risk was that it is too easy to get trapped again into the 'preparation syndrome' in Honolulu. This lousy, rolling anchorage will toughen us up for the hard beat to the Marquesas. No way are we sailing back to refasten the umbilical cord."

Earl's only comment was "I think you're nuts."

After one month of repairs and additional preparation, we were so anxious to get out of Kailua that we would have taken on anything that the open sea had to throw at us. Our little ship was repaired. The emotional, psychological, and physical strain was erased. Our motivation was renewed. Without the never-ending responsibility of "showing someone else a good time," we had a whole new sense of freedom and independence. A new beginning awaited us.

On August 8, we rounded Hawaii's south tip, sheeted down the sails, and began the long ESE windward passage to Nuku Hiva, where our Marquesas cruise had been aborted in 1974. What new adventures awaited us as we finally began the fulfillment of the dream and commitment born in boyhood and finalized so many years ago on a midwinter night off Cape Horn? To sail alone around the world—just the two of us—in our traditional teakwood ketch—to follow in the wake of Jack London's *Snark*. We had taken the first step on the long journey into our souls.

CHAPTER NINE

THE IMPOSSIBLE TRAVERSE

In Jack London's book *The Cruise of the Snark*, published in 1908, he quotes the *Sailing Directions* regarding the passage between Hawaii and the Marquesas Islands and says that "no voyager should make himself weary attempting so impossible a traverse. But the impossible did not deter the *Snark*—principally because of the fact that we did not read the Sailing Directions until after we had started."

Jack London, with his wife, Charmian, and a full crew—captain, cook, navigator—had taken sixty days, beating against the easterly winds and the west-running equatorial current, to make the impossible traverse in his fifty-four-foot ketch.

Shirl and I knew that to follow in the wake of the *Snark* would be a grueling, exhausting experience. But we knew that the achievement of any difficult feat—overcoming the harsh conditions of what could be at best a month-long windward passage—would give us a special sense of achievement. We also knew that if we could endure this long beat to windward, the rest of the circumnavigation—largely before the wind— would seem far less difficult.

Our thoughts could best be paraphrased: "If we beat our heads against a stone wall now, think of how good it will feel when we stop." Our nineteen-day engineless passage NNW from Nuku Hiva to Hawaii was an exhilarating, relatively easy experience. Everything—wind and current—had been in our favor. But now, heading ESE to return to Nuku Hiva, these same elements were opposing us.

Our log entries can best describe the raildown passage:

> Short steep seas with easterly 30-knot winds—land effect of South Point.
> Reefed main bashing into heavy head seas.
> Heavy squalls at night.
> Shirl sick in bunk. I have to cook.
> Both bunks leaking right over our heads.
> Slow, wet miserable beat.
> Tropical storm east of us producing confused seas.
> Hard to get reliable sights in rough seas.
> Magic 5th day out. Shirl coming alive.
> Making easting with 130° course. 131 mile run. Best yet.
> Generator exhaust pipe broke. No more refrigeration. Who cares? We can live without refrigeration. Will not turn back. Jury repaired exhaust pipe with 7-UP cans and chemical bandage. Back in refrigeration business.

As the seas would smash into the boat, the crashing, creaking, and groaning of her shuddering timbers put us in awe of how a wooden boat screwed, bolted, and riveted together by the hands of men could take the constant pounding. There were many times when a heavy sea would break over the bow with such an explosive crash that we were sure that the mast, bowsprit, or the planking would disintegrate into matchwood. But as the valiant *Morning Star* continued to endure the beating, we knew that she was stronger and could take more punishment than could her crew of two. Fatigue can be lethal. It warps judgment and clouds the clarity of thinking. To enable us to continue this punishment for weeks, we had to have more rest.

In this remote part of the ocean, we decided to trade off the uncertain risk of being run down by a ship at night for the certain risk of excessive fatigue. So, we stopped our initial night-watch-standing routine of four-hours-on and four-hours-off and went to bed after dinner and my round of star sights every dusk. But I would awaken every two hours or so, peer over the maelstrom around us, and, seeing nothing, crawl into the soothing embrace of my damp but warm bunk.

When electronic strobe lights were first invented, I installed them on each of the four different airplanes that I had owned after the war. Although at that time technically illegal, I installed aircraft strobe lights on the masthead of each boat I had owned. Immersed low in the giant troughs, a small vessel at sea is very difficult for a lax watch stander of a freighter or tanker to see. Conventional yacht lighting is usually a joke, especially running lights inset two or three feet above the sea into the wave-washed bow.

All naval architects should be forced to go to sea in the creatures of their design. While our running lights were set well up into our rigging, I still knew that they were too dim to be seen clearly from the two- or three-story-high bridge of a supertanker. Every night, the *Morning Star* charged and crashed through the seas with her lee rail awash, her strobe light flashing brightly from her masthead, guided by our faithful helmsman—the Aries self-steering vane, Jonathan Livingston Seagull—while her crew of two slumbered below.

A sailor at sea develops an uncanny sixth sense. I would be awakened out of a sound sleep by an increasing or decreasing of wind velocity, by a shift in wind direction—or by any other out-of-the-ordinary noise discerned through the cacophonous din below decks.

Shirl's bunk is on the port side—on the windward or high side of the heeling craft. The foaming seas would break with a crashing explosion one and a quarter inches—the thickness of the ship's planking—from her ear. My bunk on the leeward, or low, side would reverberate with the slamming detonation brought about when we would fall off a wave into a trough. It was like sleeping inside a massive, violently tossed-about bass drum.

The timbers had dried out and separated during our months under the hot sun of Hawaii, so both bunks had maddening leaks that dripped on our faces and soaked the berths. We couldn't stop the leaks, so we rerouted them with channels made of Vaseline and silicone smeared onto the overhead to form canals to guide the drips away from our faces. We were secured into our bunks by strongly lashed high canvas lee "boards," making it almost impossible for us to be thrown out.

Jonathan would track the wind. He wasn't interested in the course. I would trim the sails and the vane, and as the wind shifted, Jonathan would faithfully vary the direction of the yacht into the same relationship to the wind as I had originally set. The *Morning Star* is so well balanced that she can steer herself to windward with no assistance, but Jonathan made this fascinating process more exact. The next day my observations of the heavenly bodies would pinpoint our position and show us where Jonathan had guided us through the long tropical night. What a godsend was Jonathan! Here was a crew mate who didn't complain, didn't eat or sleep, was on duty twenty-four hours a day, and who didn't mutiny, talk back, or fix me with baleful glares.

I steered the boat only in severe squalls, and Shirl steered while I was sail handling on the foredeck. Despite the hardship and discomfort, at the end of the first week out, Shirl came alive, began to cook, and we both felt marvelous.

Then on the eighth day out, the wind began to drop, finally fell to zero, and we lay becalmed. Not a ripple of breeze to disturb the mirror-smooth surface of the oscillating deep blue sea. We were in the doldrums, the space on the earth between two wind systems: the northeast trades and the southeast trades.

In the damp, clammy, hothouse atmosphere of the doldrums, we started the engine and slowly ticked along at 1,000 rpm doing four knots due east. At this speed, we burn only two-thirds of a gallon of diesel per hour. Twenty-four hours will give us ninety-six miles through the water, diminished by the one-knot equatorial current to seventy-two miles over the bottom. But every mile to the east counted heavily.

As we ghosted out of the doldrums, we encountered characteristic tempestuous weather as the two systems converged: frequent squalls, heavy rains, and lightning storms. A breath of breeze started to ripple the surface—"up sails"—"wind quit"—"down sails." Frustrating on-again, off-again wind behavior.

In order to make it to the Marquesas, we had to cross the

equator east of the 140-degree meridian. No cruising ketch can sail close to the wind. No matter what lies I have listened to, I don't believe that any beamy, heavy-cruising ketch can get any closer than 55 degrees off the wind. As a comparison, I used to beat my racing sloop 25 degrees to windward. The *Morning Star's* optimum windward performance to keep her footing was about 55 degrees, depending upon sea conditions.

On the fourteenth day out, we were at 140° west longitude, and it became apparent that we could not make it to the Marquesas fighting the three musketeers opposing us—wind, current, and leeway. We had not been given the break I had hoped for—winds backing into the northeast. Rather the winds had, perversely, been east or east-southeast.

We had been in daily radio contact with the yacht *Fantasia*, which had left Hawaii when we did. She was skippered by Win, a young ex-navy pilot. He hadn't been able to make the necessary easting either, and on our last radio contact, Win said he was giving up on the Marquesas, falling off and heading for Tahiti.

Another participant on our daily ham net was Bill Whipple. He and his wife, Betty, had it made—coming from mainland U.S.A. on their fifty-three-foot ketch *Tyee*, they had easting to spare.

My only hope was to find the narrow, meandering equatorial east-running countercurrent; then, once having found it, to stay in it. We could quite conceivably sail through it in one twelve-hour night and not know the difference. The only way to know whether or not you are being affected by an invisible ocean current is by frequent and accurate celestial observations.

At 7° north of the equator, my running sun lines worked in with dawn and dusk star and planet sights showed that, first, we were getting an accelerated push to the west. This could be the west-running equatorial current's preamble to its east-running countercurrent opposition.

Sure enough, at 6° 36' north, I began to make easting coinciding with my course—then east of my course. I had found it! The equatorial countercurrent would do the job if we could only stay in it—if we didn't inadvertently sail out of this sub-surface stream.

As we tacked on an ENE heading for the first time in twelve days, everything on the *Morning Star* was reversed. High sides had become low sides. Our teetering passage back and forth below decks demanded that we lean and grab support in the opposite direction. It was a weird feeling. We continued to tack ENE back to ESE for the next four days. The teasing from the armchair admirals and the harbor stallions on the ham net back in Hawaii was relentless. "You are heading the wrong way! The Marquesas are southeast of you," and on it went.

Swept by the two-knot countercurrent, we had one run of 180 miles over the bottom almost due east—incredible for us. The strategy had paid off in big dividends. Finally, at 6° north, I tacked back and resumed an on-the-wind course of SSE to Nuku Hiva.

On our fifteenth day out, a large ship came up over the horizon—the *Cape York* out of Glasgow. She was a supertanker, probably heading from Tahiti to San Francisco via the great circle. She came alongside. We waved all is well. With that, she gave a loud blast of her horn and disappeared over the northern horizon. The first sign of humanity for over two weeks.

As we headed SSE, we quickly sailed out of the approximate sixty-mile-wide countercurrent and were pushed westward inexorably by the resumed equatorial current. But we were now going to make the Marquesas.

We crossed the equator at 138° north longitude, and had to avoid the vigias shown on the chart. One said, "Discolored water reported 1956"; another, "Breakers reported 1964"; and still another, "Breakers reported 1953". While these vigias may not, in fact, be navigational hazards—no prudent navigator is going to risk finding out. All around us were depths of 2,300 fathoms (13,800 feet)—over two miles of ocean, so we had no inclination to test the reliability of the charts.

We had now been at sea for three weeks. Our landfall was estimated to be only five more days ahead of us. Despite the beating we had taken, we now really didn't want it to end. We were in a glorious routine. We luxuriated in daily showers under the deck-flush hose on the foredeck. We felt very much alive. Danger seems to enhance this sense of aliveness. We exulted in the abounding sea life around us.

Many times in the early discouraging days of the passage, we would say to each other, "What are we doing out here? We must be crazy." Yet, with all of the gear failures, we found deep satisfaction in the very self-sufficiency required to cope with every situation without yelling for help.

Many of our friends and relatives have great difficulty in understanding what or why we are doing what we are doing. Their inability to understand is not their fault. They simply have no frame of reference to enable them to relate to this activity.

At home, "self-awareness" and "self-improvement" courses are very "in." On the *Morning Star*, I enrolled in my own personal "self-awareness" course in my personal night school. I step out into the cockpit. Shirley may be below cleaning up the galley, reading or sleeping. Jonathan is steering. The *Morning Star* is silently gliding through the seas, trailing a bubbling wake of diamonds. She is powered by God's balmy trade winds, crooning in our rigging and sails. No noise, no clamor, no fumes. Alone on a vast desert of water.

I have a sextant in my hands. By observing my relationship to the planet Venus, the moon, and the stars Sirius, Capella, Canopus, Arcturus, Antares, or any three heavenly bodies of choice, I can pinpoint my position on this spinning planet called Earth. There! Off our starboard bow is the Southern Cross—Acrux, Gacrux—curious names! We are reliving the experiences of Captains Cook, Magellan, de Bougainville, Tasman, and the other great navigators of the past. Hurtling through the tropical star-filled night on a wooden, wind-driven vessel. Sheer exultation!

And I think about how far away these stars are from me. Mind-boggling thoughts! The twinkling light now being observed through my sextant emanated from this star five thousand years before Christ. At the rate of 186,000 miles *per second*, that light is just reaching my eye now. At the time the light left my next star, Hannibal, Alexander, Plato, and Socrates walked on the soil of the earth. How puny am I! How insignificant is the Earth and the solar system compared to other "solar systems." For example, the sun in size, in relationship to the Earth, bears the same relationship as does the Earth to an orange. But the sun in size is as an orange to my navigational friend Arcturus. The symmetry, the precise order of things, the guiding intellect that arranged all of this—I am overwhelmed! By spherical trigonometry, invented centuries ago, I can, with exact precision, use these "beacons in the heavens" to determine where these two frail souls in this frail craft are at this instant.

That is my lesson in self-awareness for that night. These thoughts will now nourish me during the next four hours of my watch. A mantle of deep inner peace envelopes me during these interludes, and the continuous effort to go on seems very rewarding. I am never less alone than when alone.

As the sun rose on the twenty-sixth day out, it outlined the rock of Motu Iti—exactly my landfall—jutting out of the sea north of Nuku Hiva. Frigate birds prowling their soaring beats overhead, fork-tail white bosun birds darting at our mast, a convoy of leaping porpoises off our bow—an entire greeting committee of the creatures of the Marquesas appeared to welcome our sea-weary craft.

We tacked between the Sentinels—two towering rocks guarding Taiohae Bay—and, in the softness of the early day, rounded up and dropped anchor—2,906 miles over the bottom and twenty-six days out of Hawaii. Stillness settled over the *Morning Star*. As Shirl and I looked up at the barren mountains brooding over Taiohae Bay, she took my hand and quietly murmured, "We did it. It's hard for me to believe, but we made the impossible traverse. This makes everything all worthwhile."

CHAPTER TEN

THE FORGOTTEN ISLANDS
OF THE SOUTH PACIFIC

✍ Te Fenua Enata (the "land of men")—this was the name the inhabitants of these radiant islands called their home before the sixteenth-century European navigator Mendaña "discovered" them. Robert Louis Stevenson called the Marquesas Islands "the forgotten islands of the South Pacific." Tall, statuesque, strong, tattooed from head to foot, the Marquesan native was said to be the most attractive human being on the face of the earth. The group of six principal islands—Nuku Hiva, Ua Pou, Ua Huka, Tahuata, Hiva Oa and Fatu Hiva—along with six smaller islands, was populated in 1779 by approximately sixty thousand of these outstanding specimens of the human race.

But the introduction of diseases by the European and American scum of the South Seas—whalers, traders, beachcombers, deserters—during the nineteenth and early twentieth centuries decimated the population down to a low of twenty-eight hundred souls. Tuberculosis, leprosy, venereal diseases, flu, and the common cold, along with intertribal warfare and cannibalism, ravaged this proud breed of Polynesian aristocrats into near extinction.

As Britain, Spain, France, and America fought over the possession of these islands, incalculable harm was done to the

Marquesans by the introduction of opium. The Marquesan chiefs, incapable of maintaining order among their people amid the chaos swirling about them, entreated the French to assume sovereignty, and this group of islands was ceded to France by a treaty between the chiefs and a French admiral in 1842. The Marquesas Islands didn't live up to the expectations of the European colonists. Cotton plantations were established, and Chinese workers, along with their opium, were imported. With the collapse of the cotton industry, most of the Chinese workers left, but the insidious opium remained.

At the present time, the verdant islands, with natural resources to support a large population, are inhabited by only a handful of white men, Chinese, and about six thousand Marquesans. We cruised among these exquisitely enchanting islands, anchoring in every protected bay on each one, coming to know and respect the Marquesan people, learning their language and the history of their proud past.

On many of the islands, the Marquesans would take us on hikes inland to view the remnants of the ancient population. The *paepae*, the cleverly arranged unhewed stone foundations of their houses and meeting lodges, were scattered in the dense undergrowth of the jungle wherever we looked. We were shown their stone altars of human sacrifice called maraes. As our minds reeled back to what this all must have been like just a few decades ago, we imagined, through the vivid descriptions of our Marquesan friends, the *tauas* ("priests") appeasing their primitive Tikis.

But as we listened to the picturesque descriptions of the past portrayed by our Marquesan friends, we became acutely aware that the tales that they were telling us were, in the main, not handed down to them from generation to generation. There simply did not exist the unbroken oral history that we were to encounter elsewhere in Polynesia. What they had learned was largely picked up from the archeological expeditions initiated by, among others, the Bishop Museum scientists out of Hawaii.

The history of the transmigration of the Polynesian people— how, when, why, and from where they had populated these far-flung islands—is passionately interesting to the present-day scientist, anthropologist, archeologist, and botanist. Such preoccupation with the past, however, is of little interest to the Marquesan survivors of today. What they do know is that their race came close to extinction, and their culture simply did not survive the crushing effects of the invasion of the white missionaries, traders, whalers, and exploitative entrepreneurs.

But such is the way of the world. Everything is transient. The Inca, Aztec, American Indian, Babylonian, Roman, Greek civilizations—all began, flourished at a peak, declined, and finally burned out like a plunging comet being consumed in the atmosphere.

We heard occasional resentments expressed to us by some still-proud, educated Marquesans. "Our children are taught all about the glories of France, Napoleon Bonaparte, and European history, but they are taught nothing about the rich history of our own people." In the mid-nineteenth century, Herman Melville wrote the books *Typee* and *Omoo* and became America's literary discoverer of the Marquesas Islands and the South Seas.

During our prolonged cruise in the Marquesas, we became initiated into the intricacies of Polynesian gift giving. In almost every village of every inhabited bay on every island, we were invited into the homes of our inherently generous hosts. We shared the meals prepared for our benefit—apprehensively dipping our fingers into a common *poi-poi* bowl—eating baked banana bread, coconut dishes, fish, wild goat (*meny-meny*), mangoes, oranges, limes, wild birds' eggs, and all of the native foods which these lovely islands offered in profusion. We were given carvings, original stone adzes and war clubs, pandanus woven hats, cowrie shells (porcelain), and all manner of gifts springing from long hours of handiwork. The gifts were never proffered with a request for direct reciprocity or a quid pro quo. But the obligation for reciprocity was subtly created—not by guileful calculation but as a matter of ancient custom.

The most treasured of gifts that they accepted in return from us were "photo minoot"—snapshots—color Polaroid pictures of them, their children, their dwellings, their canoes. We would try to take these pictures in a candid manner, but each time the camera was pointed at them, they would stiffen into frozen, smileless, Bonaparte-like poses. We also reciprocated with gifts of clothing, blankets, canned goods, shackles, and tools.

A second gift, often asked for outright, was *cartouche*—.22 caliber rifle ammunition. The French authorities allow them a severely rationed number of these shells for their .22 rifles. With these shells, they are permitted to kill the wild goats, pigs, and cattle that exist in profusion on most of the islands. But illegally imported ammunition was contraband. The French gendarmes inflicted harsh punishment—jail terms—to foreigners caught supplying ammunition to the natives.

The gendarmes explained that if the Marquesans had an unlimited supply of ammunition, they would wantonly kill the wild animals of the islands beyond their needs. The Marquesans countered this argument with their own version— "Franay afraid we make revolution and kill them if we have enough ammunition." I was skeptical of both arguments.

After seeing the way the gendarmes had summarily clapped into the bleak jailhouse on Nuku Hiva the crews of two yachts merely suspected of dealing in contraband—drugs, liquor, guns, and ammunition—there was no way I would have risked breaking their laws. The French, along with officialdom of many other countries, are highly suspicious of visiting yachts. Human nature being what it is, we all have a tendency to generalize and to tar with the brush of the lowest common denominator an entire group or nationality by the conduct of only a few.

During the "permissive society" period of the 1960s and 1970s, cruising to distant, romantic islands of the world inevitably attracted some of the same rebellious element that was aggressively defying the established order of their own countries of the free world. A new breed of outlaw adventure seekers descended upon the unsuspecting peoples of the South Pacific. On any nondescript craft that would float, they brought with them their marijuana, cocaine, and "liberated" life-style.

But, quite different from the "do-your-own-thing and get-away-with-it" attitude of the ultralenient law enforcement apparatus that they left behind, they encountered swift and sure punishment meted out by the not-so-permissive police forces of the rest of the world. As they introduced young native people to the euphoria of pot smoking, trafficked in ammunition and liquor, freely helped themselves to limes, grapefruit, coconuts, and bananas growing "in the wild," they antagonized not only the gendarmes of Polynesia but the basically kind and tolerant native people who resented their discourteous, arrogant, and intrusive ways. All *citron* ("fruit") growing in these islands belongs to someone. If asked, the native people would cheerfully give, but they were greatly offended if anyone just helped himself without asking to their produce. Unfortunately, the conduct of only a relative handful of "yachties" of this type put every yacht under a cloud of initial suspicion, out of which they would have to extricate themselves by demonstrating that "they weren't *all* like that."

While the Marquesans wanted independence, they had to admit that the French had been good to them. They had brought them peace from intertribal warfare, free medical and dental care, free literacy and education for their children, and many amenities of the twentieth century that they otherwise would not have. There is no commensurate return for the millions of francs that the French taxpayers pour into Polynesia. There are no precious mineral, oil, or timber resources for a colonial power to exploit. Polynesia's only strategic value to the French is that it provides a military base in the southern Tuamotus for the highly controversial testing of nuclear weapons.

With their ancient culture and customs lying in shambles around their feet, the Marquesans have few options for the future. Having acquired a taste for whiskey, tobacco, rice, flour, candy, tools, cooking utensils, outboard motors, and transistor radios, the purchase of all of which requires cash, the nostalgia for going back to the simple life and the ways of their ancestors has virtually disappeared.

The cash can only be earned by the processing of copra (the meat of the coconut), which is very hard work. Unlike the process in the sun-baked Tuamotu atolls, copra in the moisture-laden atmosphere of the Marquesas can only be dried in roofed-over sheds with the meat lying on corrugated iron sheets over fires fueled by coconut husks. As the volatile copra market of the world goes up and down, so too do the fortunes of the Marquesans.

One of the most appreciated gifts we could make to the Marquesans was to take these fun-loving people day sailing—to extend to them the hospitality of our floating home. The big, powerful men were great sailors, and sailing around the islands on the *Morning Star* was a major treat for them. Oddly enough, the Polynesian women would almost invariably become instantly seasick. Most of the bays in the Marquesas group are "rolling anchorages." Quite often, visits to the yacht rolling at anchor would be blighted by the retching of the Marquesan women hanging over the rail.

We spent many tranquil days anchored in Hana Menu Bay on the island of Hiva Oa. A few steps down from the beach in a tropical forest glade was a bubbling freshwater pool where we would bathe and where Shirl would wash clothes. We were the only yacht there and became close friends of the sole occupants of this beautiful bay, Ozanne, his wife, Marie, and their beautiful children. Ozanne became as a son to us, and he spent countless hours on the *Morning Star*. I taught him how to use an electronic digital calculator. Although uneducated, Ozanne had a high I.Q. In no time, he was calculating the price of his copra crop and the proportionate revenues of his numerous relatives living in Atuona who sharecropped the land upon which Ozanne lived and worked.

He became so intrigued with the calculator that he begged to buy it from me "to give to his father for Christmas." I had two calculators, which I used for navigational problems, so I told Ozanne, "There is no way that I will take your hard-earned cash for this electronic gadget. As soon as I sail, it could fail in this saltwater atmosphere. Then you would feel your *ami*, Ray, had cheated you. I won't sell it to you, Ozanne, but I will give it to you. Here, it is yours." He was startled and tongue-tied with gratitude.

That night, Ozanne and two young Marquesan friends bumped alongside in their outrigger canoe. He said, "Ray, tomorrow before daylight, we go pig and goat hunting. I have gun and shells. You come with us."

Although I had been deer, bear, and elk hunting since I was

a small boy, the hiking-hunting expedition I was taken on the next day was the most grueling of my life. Up and down steep shale-covered mountains, the powerful young Marquesans effortlessly pursued the wild goats and pigs. Heavy leather boots protected my feet against the sharp shale as we climbed up steep slopes and slid down into deep valleys. The Marquesans were barefooted. But they had been barefooted all of their childhood and adult lives. Their scarred feet had toughened soles at least one-half inch thick.

The dogs cornered a fiercely snarling wild boar, and I shot him between the eyes. The other Marquesans, lacking guns, carried slingshots, with which they could propel a piece of shale with deadly accuracy. They killed a goat in this manner.

Burdened with these animals, we slipped and slid down the mountains we had so laboriously climbed. The Marquesans moved with long, sure-footed strides. Every once in a while, Ozanne would inconspicuously slow down thoughtfully to allow me to catch up with him, without causing me undue embarrassment in the presence of his rugged young companions.

We skirted foot-wide trails hugging the mountainside, with sheer drops to the boiling sea below, rounded bends with breathtaking views of the sea and mountainous terrain. My mind flashed back to a boyhood book, Melville's *Typee*, and its tale of two young sailors climbing the mountains of the Marquesas as they deserted ship.

As we came to a meadowlike plateau, Ozanne said, "We stop here, Ray, I want to ask you something." He began, "My relatives and I own all this land. They own most, but I do all the work and sharecrop with them. *Très difficile pour Marie et moi. Beaucoup de travail.*"

Ozanne continued, "When *enfants* old enough to go to *école*, we move around island to Atuona. They go to school with Catholic sisters there. We need *beaucoup* money to buy house in Atuona. A few months ago, *yate* come to Hana Menu. Full of young guys with beards and long hair. Plenty girls, too. *Yate capitaine* say to me, 'Ozanne, I give you seeds. You plant. We come back later when grass is grown. We buy from you for *beaucoup* money.'"

Ozanne went on, "Ray, they call seeds and plants 'grass,' but I know it is dope. I hear Americans call it pot. They tell me it grow real fast in my valley—plenty rain. I make fortune. Gendarmes never find out. Gendarmes in Atuona never come in mountains."

Abruptly, Ozanne stopped talking, looked me in the eye, and said, "Ray, you my friend. I trust you. What you think? Good idea, huh?"

I said, "No, Ozanne, bad idea. Sooner or later, gendarmes find out. Small island. Somebody maybe don't like Ozanne, maybe jealous, maybe want Marie, maybe want money from gendarmes for reward, who knows?

"Gendarmes catch you, *certainement.* You go many years in prison in Tahiti. You be old man when you get out. Children grow up without father. Best you forget about growing grass."

Ozanne thought for a few minutes, then replied, "I think you right, Ray. Bad idea. Let's go cut up goat and pig."

One Marquesan had the bloody goat slung around his shoulders. The other two were sliding down the mountain with the boar slung on a pole carried between them. With Ozanne and me trailing behind, we emerged into his settlement on the beach.

After a few days more, we said *kaoha* to Ozanne and Marie and sailed to Fatu Hiva, the southernmost island of the group. Here in Hana Vave Bay, with its spirelike pinnacles framing the sea, we anchored in one of the most spectacularly beautiful bays in the South Pacific.

Thor Heyerdahl and his young bride had spent a year living in Fatu Hiva with the Marquesans and wrote a Book-of-the-Month Club selection called *Fatu Hiva—Back to Nature,* which dramatically described his initial acceptance and subsequent rejection by the Marquesans of Fatu Hiva.

The people of Hana Vave befriended us and invited us into their huts for *kai-kai* ("food"). One old man said to me, "*Americain, bon mécanicien.* You fix my radio." Tracing the current with my voltohm meter, I found a loose connection. Much to my surprise, with a few squirts of WD 40, the transistor radio broke into the sounds of distant Tahiti. After that piece of sheer luck, every broken-down, rusted radio and outboard motor were dragged from the damp recesses of native huts, and the *Americain bon mécanicien* was asked to perform his black magic with his mysterious tools.

With the cash gleaned from their back-breaking copra work, the Marquesans would buy these gadgets from visiting trading schooners. Then, in short order the mechanical and electronic products of "civilization" would cease operating in the dank, saltwater atmosphere permeating their villages. I had mixed success in making these repairs, but whether I succeeded or failed, the gratitude of these kindly people for the effort extended was always there in abundance. We were showered with gifts of tapa cloth, *langoustes* ("lobsters"), intricately woven pandanus hats, and beautiful cowrie-shell headbands.

One young couple, Madeleine and Mathias, couldn't do enough for us. One day Madeleine asked Shirley to teach her how to use a Singer sewing machine for which she had paid 3,500 francs to an itinerant American sailor. The machine had been sold to Madeleine by the "snake oil" salesman with the assurance that she could operate it by hand. But it could only function with 110 volts of electricity, and, of course, there was no electricity on Fatu Hiva, so Madeleine had to continue to use the machine as a mere decoration in her pandanus-roofed house. It was a source of great embarrassment for us to have to tell Madeleine that she had been swindled.

When we ran across the occasional situation where these trusting, almost childlike native people had been taken advantage of, it made us wonder at not only how they could so stoically forgive and forget, but how they could continue to extend their simple hospitality to the vast majority of honorable "yachties" who would follow in the wake of the isolated few "takers" plying the South Sea Islands.

We heard on the ham radio that Bob and Nancy Griffith, along with their twenty-one-year old son, Reid, were in Taiohae Bay. In our estimation, the Griffiths were the greatest sailors of all time. They had sailed over two hundred thousand miles and always with a full crew. They are the only ones in history to circumnavigate successfully the Antarctic in a sailing vessel. Even the famous Captain Cook tried it and failed in the ice-bound deep southern latitudes.

Bob, Nancy, and Reid had, along with a crew of volunteers, hollowed two logs out of large redwood trunks in the Pacific Northwest and in California. They fashioned these logs into replicas of ancient Polynesian voyaging proas, and Bob, with his crew, set out to sail to the Marquesas, with Nancy—without a doubt the most formidable female sailor who ever lived—skippering their fifty-three-foot ferrocement cutter *Ahwanee II* as escort vessel. On their initial attempt, the first *Spirit of Nuku Hiva* had broken up and sunk on the rock-bound coast near San Francisco when her towline parted.

With characteristic determination, Bob set forth to hollow out tediously another log, build another proa. After extreme hardship, Bob and his crew sailed the second *Spirit of Nuku Hiva* to Taiohae, again escorted by Nancy in command of *Ahwanee II*.

We wanted to renew our friendship with the Griffiths and to hear of their most recent seagoing exploits, so we sailed back to Taiohae from Ua Huka. As we anchored in Taiohae Bay, we were met by Reid, who had rowed out to greet us. At age twenty-one, he had three circumnavigations under his belt. In his brief lifetime, he had been exposed to more raw adventure than most men will ever experience in five lifetimes.

Reid stayed aboard the *Morning Star* for dinner, and on into the night, Shirl and I listened to this quiet young man relate the story of the passage of the *Spirit of Nuku Hiva*. Bob and his crew had set out to live primarily on the fish they would catch on this passage. When they arrived in Taiohae, after weeks at sea, the crew, with the exception of one young man, were terrified and abandoned the venture. They were all encamped under tents of sails on the "no-no," fly-infested Nuku Hiva beach. As I listened to Reid describe the "crew problems" on the *Spirit of Nuku Hiva*, my former "crew problems" paled into insignificance.

We spent days with Bob, Nancy, and Reid. Among the numerous pictures that I took of them, the *Ahwanee II*, and the proa, I photographed Reid and his mother on the bowsprit of the *Ahwanee II*. This was the last picture ever taken of Reid Griffith. Tragically, he lost his life a few days later when he fell off a cliff while goat hunting on Nuku Hiva.

Reid and Nancy Griffith

But even this devastating tragedy didn't cause Bob and Nancy to give up and abandon their incredible venture. They were determined to sail the proa back to Hawaii. While attempting this last heroic feat, the *Spirit of Nuku Hiva* broke up—and sank in a storm. Nancy skillfully brought *Ahwanee II* about and fished Bob and his replacement crew out of the storm-tossed waters between the Marquesas and Hawaii.

Bob Griffith was one sailor whose advice I eagerly sought and respected. During our time together, I told Bob about an expedition that I had been planning to atolls in an area of the Tuamotus where yachts seldom, if ever, go. I told Bob how we had navigated through the Dangerous Archipelago in 1974 without a motor, and he told me how he, Nancy, and Reid shipwrecked their first *Ahwanee* in this region. They subsisted for sixty-seven days on an uninhabited atoll before being rescued by the French.

Although Bob and Nancy were very outspoken in their

opposition to shorthanded crews and most emphatically against single-handed sailors, Bob encouraged Shirl and me to go for it—to weave our way through treacherous current-bound reefs and atolls in search of adventure that was not available if we followed the lemminglike path of other yachts plying between the Marquesas and Tahiti.

It was now mid-November. We had lingered in the Marquesas for ten weeks. The Marquesas Islands do not experience hurricanes, but the Tuamotus have been devastated by them at this time of the year. Prudence dictated that we begin our Tuamotu expedition at once.

CHAPTER ELEVEN

TO THE LAND OF KON TIKI AND BEYOND

Almost imperceptibly, the skies behind the towering spires of Anse Hakaotu on the island of Ua Pou began to lighten. The protesting shrieks of roosting frigate birds fragmented the silence as the heavy plough anchor of the *Morning Star* reluctantly released its grip on the bottom.

We were underway. Heading SSW to Raroia Atoll. Raroia—where the Inca-type balsa raft *Kon Tiki* had crashed on the reef after its epic drift voyage in 1947 from Peru. Shirl and I had been enthralled with the classic *Kon Tiki* adventure of the courageous anthropologist Thor Heyerdahl and his five Scandinavian companions. As sailors, intimately familiar with the actions of prevailing winds and currents, we had been convinced, contrary to current scientific opinion, that it was quite possible that the Pacific Islands of Polynesia had been populated, at least partly, by the yellow-brown-skinned Indians of South America, as the *Kon Tiki* expedition sought to prove. Moreover, the presence of the South American yam in these islands, along with the similarities between the Inca and the Polynesian cultures, the tikis and petrographs found in Rapa Nui (Easter Island) and the Marquesas, made the Heyerdahl theory eminently sensible to us.

The night before we left Ua Pou, Marquesan friends had paddled over from Hakamai village and had given us four stalks of green bananas to deliver to the Paumotuans of the atolls where bananas do not grow. Stalks of bananas have a way of ripening all at the same time, so I was going to make an attempt to deliver them to what the French have named the Îles du Désappointement—Tepoto and Napuka. There is no entrance into the lagoon of Napuka. Landing can be accomplished only by standing off the island and unloading into local canoes.

Tepoto is a coral island that was originally an atoll, but it has become entirely filled up and lifted above sea level, possibly by some volcanic upheaval. The *Pacific Island's Pilot Book* description reads: "flat-topped and covered with coconut palms which give it an elevation of about 65 feet. There is no anchorage. Trading vessels which call once or twice a year, very occasionally, find a *precarious* berth on the western side of the island by anchoring off the reef and securing by the stern to the shore. Total population about 50." Lying almost in my path to Raroia, I decided to use Tepoto as a navigational challenge and, if possible, heave to and give the bananas to the natives, unloading into their canoes.

At midafternoon on the third day out from her position aloft in the rigging, Shirl spotted the smudged outline of the coconut trees of Tepoto dead off our bow—only six miles ahead of us! Having coped with a strong westerly current, frequent overcast skies, and shifting wind and sea conditions, I was particularly elated with this dead-on landfall. No matter how often repeated, we experienced again the electrifying thrill of making an exact landfall on a speck in the ocean. Celestial navigation continues to inspire in me feelings of awe, humility, and reverence for the genius of the ancient (B.C.) astronomers who studied, analyzed, and computed the movements of the heavenly bodies.

As our white sails became visible, the natives poured out to sea in dozens of dugout-outrigger canoes. A group of them strung out along an extending submerged reef to warn us of its presence. As we hove to under sail, three dugouts came alongside, banging into our topside in the open sea as the natives clambered aboard.

The ensuing minutes were chaotic. The language barrier

was almost total. No one spoke English or French. But by gestures and smiles and many *Iaoranas*, we knew that we were indeed welcome.

The "precarious perch" described in the *Pilot Book* looked to be too dangerous an anchorage—the reef shelves and plunges straight down into the sea. So I didn't want to remain. I wanted only to deliver to them the stalks of ripening bananas.

The husky natives on our deck were all jabbering at once, indicating to us that we should drop our anchor on the reef and count on the prevailing winds to hold us off. I decided to take this risk for a few hours, then leave before sundown. A sudden shift of the wind here in late November would put us on the jagged coral, and that would be the end of the *Morning Star.*

With the natives on the bowsprit, we maneuvered just short of the reef and, at their signal, let go the anchor. I was astonished to watch the seventy-five-pound plough anchor and chain plunge into the crystal-clear water, down and down, before I braked the windlass to a halt. As the natives argued among themselves, I brought in the anchor and put our bowsprit right up to the coral ledge, where this time the anchor hooked into the reef. While backing off, I suspended a stern anchor straight down 300 feet, so that if the wind fell calm or shifted, it would, I hoped, catch on something as we swung parallel to the reef.

When we came surfing in over the reef in our new rubber Zodiac, the entire village was on the beach to greet us—all fifty of the total population. Smiles, *Iaoranas*, shell *heis*, hugs, and kisses—it was as though long-lost relatives had dropped in from Mars.

As the chief helped us lift the dinghy off the reef, he slipped and fell, cutting his legs on the razor-sharp coral, causing blood to stream down his leg. Everyone laughed—the chief most of all. This is the way of these good-natured primitive people. They laugh at the petty misfortunes of life.

Everything pales into insignificance as they are confronted with the harshness of their primordial way of life. Fish, turtle, and coconuts form the backbone of their diet. Although there are two wells of brackish water, they drink coconut water from the young, green drinking nuts.

They escorted us to an area under the coconut palms, brushed clean and paved with gleaming white-coral pebbles. Here they insisted that we sit on a wooden bench, while they all squatted in a semicircle around us. We couldn't communicate effectively until the schoolteacher shyly stepped forward to admit that he spoke French *un peu.*

We responded then to their barrage of questions. Where did we come from? How could we sail across the ocean to see them without a crew? What nationality were we? Franay ["French"]? As we answered their questions, Manaia Tamatoatauto, our interpreter, told us that we were the first yacht in the history of this island ever to call there.

At this, I apprehensively glanced out at the *Morning Star* pitching and rolling in the swell off the reef. We gave them clothing and canned food, which the chief tried to disburse equitably among them. They had closed the school during our visit, and we stayed in Tepoto two days and two nights, standing anchor watches during the night. We were ready to get out fast at the slightest shift in the wind.

Our visit had been something of an event in their lives, and, as always, we were saddened to leave these kind people whose lives brushed ours in our travels, but we were bound for Raroia, lying 130 miles south-southwest of Tepoto.

We carefully timed our landfall off Raroia's sister island, Takume, allowing for an approximately two-knot west-setting current. While we were in Tahiti, our friend Bengt Danielsson, an anthropologist who had been with Heyerdahl on the *Kon Tiki* expedition, dramatically told us how they had almost lost their lives in the crashing breakers on the submerged windward reef of Raroia.

A three-star position fix—Sirius, Canopus, Jupiter—shot at dusk caused us to change course and reduce sail to slow down to three knots. The current was propelling us at a faster-than-anticipated rate. At the first light of predawn, there was Takume only three and a half miles ahead of us. Notwithstanding the current allowance cranked into our navigation, we were too close for comfort.

The windward side of these particular atolls is awash. The noise of the sea around the boat drowns out the sound of the downwind breakers. Despite the full moon, around which we had planned our Raroia expedition, it is almost always impossible at night to see the breakers until you are in them—and then it is too late. Had I not shot the star fix the night before, we might have gone on the merciless reef at Takume during the night.

Our radar was of some aid, but it can't see a submerged reef. It could booby-trap us into a reef by targeting the above-the-surface atoll on the *opposite* side of the lagoon. So we used it with suspicion. We eyeballed our way along the Takume coast, across the channel to Raroia, searching for the pass into the lagoon. A snapshot of the brilliant then morning star-planet, Venus, told us where the pass was far more accurately than counting the scattered motus along Raroia.

We hove to off Passe Ngarue, waiting for an eight-knot ebbing current to abate. Then, with Shirl directing me while wearing Polaroid sunglasses that enabled her to see the coral heads beneath the surface, we entered the radiant lagoon of Raroia Atoll. Wending our way among the coral heads, we anchored off Ngnarumaova village. Men, women with babies, children and barking dogs clustered on the dilapidated jetty as we tossed them the painter of the dinghy.

In Nuku Hiva, the part-white, part-Marquesan trader Maurice McKittrick had asked me to bear a letter of greeting to his friend, the chief of Raroia. This message assured us profusely elaborate hospitality, extended by the forty-two Paumotuans living on remote Raroia.

It was Sunday, and we were the guests of honor at a memorable dinner in the chief's home. We carefully listened while one Paumotuan tried to outdo the other in the eloquence of his oratory. The Polynesians love to give long speeches, and we were deeply touched by their references to how God had brought us to their lonely atoll.

Of course, the major event in the history of Raroia was the landing of the *Kon Tiki*. All Polynesians love to sing and play the guitar, and many evenings were spent while they serenaded us with the ballads that they had composed describing the romantic legend of *Kon Tiki*. With the decks of the *Morning Star* teeming with Paumotuans, including Tehau and Pai, who had aided the *Kon Tiki*, we sailed across the lagoon to the windward reef where *Kon Tiki* had landed. Looking out over the smashing breakers, we were in awe of the bravery of Heyerdahl, Danielsson, and their shipwrecked mates as they crawled over the slashing coral to the safety of the white-sand beach.

Balsa wood from the *Kon Tiki* had been salvaged, shipped, and painstakingly reconstructed. The raft now resides in its original form in a museum in frigid, faraway Norway, so remote from this translucent atoll of the South Pacific that it may as well be on another planet.

As we said good-bye to our friends in Raroia, we told them that we were going to Taenga. They replied, "Stay here. Taenga no good. *Très dangereux.*" We had noted with interest how the natives of one atoll are sometimes critical of the natives of another atoll, so we took their warnings with a grain of salt.

Back in Hawaii in 1973, I had met and swapped war stories with Guido, a German World War II ex-U-boat officer. He and his crew, Lydia, had just sailed their sloop *Kis-Ky-Hei* from the South Pacific. Guido told me about a remote atoll, Taenga, which he had accidentally discovered—a place where the natives told him that never in their history had a yacht called there. While Guido and Lydia were ecstatic in their description of Taenga, they warned us of the great difficulties with the currents and the narrow pass. I respected Guido, his navigational abilities, and his seamanship, so I mentally stored his information.

While not named on our American charts, Taenga was clearly identified and located only twenty-four miles west-southwest from Raroia on the more reliable French charts that we had obtained in Tahiti. I assured Shirl that visiting there would be a "piece of cake." (A phrase she had come to hear with uplifted eyebrows and deep suspicion.)

The seas enter the lagoon over the windward reef, and there is a continuous outgoing stream in the pass. As we warily crawled up to Pass Tiritepakau on the northwestern side of the atoll, we hadn't seen a sign of life. Guido had told us how he had stayed offshore until the Taengans came out in high-powered outboard-motor-driven boats and towed him against the current into the pass.

Aloft in the ratlines, Shirl shouted over the wind, "The pass is too rough! I see white water in the middle!" The current overfall was creating the white water, so despite her apprehension, I decided it was now or never! As the outgoing river of current began to reduce in velocity, with cotton in our mouths and white knuckles we shot into the main pass at full power, past the settlement, through the coral-toothed eighteen-foot wide mouth of the lagoon and safety. In retrospect, I would never try an entrance like this again. We had been very, very lucky.

Taenga was indeed the "tropical paradise" of the movies. The lagoon swarms with edible fish. Curiously, unlike some in other atolls, none is poisonous.

The handsome young chief, Tuarira Taharagi, made us part of his family. We dove in lucid-clear water. We speared fish and moray eels. We photographed the sharks underwater in the pass. Even they and the manta rays we photographed were benign as the natives and I swam along with them. Taenga is alive with marine life. There are so many fish that the sharks never go hungry. The native people had never been attacked by them, so we felt quite safe in our underwater photography.

One cloudless day, the chief paddled his canoe out into the lagoon and told us, "Faarua ("northeasterly storm") coming. You must leave the lagoon and tie up in the pass in front of my maison." Our barometer was up—the weather reports from Tahiti carried no warnings, but I deferred to Tuarira's instincts and decided to follow his advice.

As I maneuvered the Morning Star, Tuarira dove repeatedly to depths of forty feet, unwrapping our chain tangled around the coral heads on the bottom. With Tuarira piloting with hand signals, we had to exit the narrow pass and go back out to sea in order to turn around and effect the tie-up to the jagged coral outcropping in front of his house. Placing kedge anchors out in all directions in order to stabilize our position two feet from the coral ledge, we firmly secured the boat and settled down to await the Faarua that the chief had so positively predicted.

We had noticed throughout the Tuamotus that the Paumotuans fervently believed in tupapaus ("ghostly spirits"). They were afraid of the dark, when the spirits would roam freely, so each night a dim light was left to burn to ward off the *tupa-paus* while they slept.

Roaring across the lagoon that night came a northeasterly fifty-knot gale. Anchored in the turbulent pass, Shirl and I were awakened by the tearing and grating noises against the coral made by our fender boards protecting our topsides. With the wind howling through a large purau tree to which we had lashed one hawser, we struggled to windlass in the cables secured to kedge anchors in the middle of the pass. We were only twenty steps from the chief's front door and could see through the horizontal rain the *tupapau* lantern dimly flickering behind his shuttered window.

As we pushed against the twenty-ton hull of the *Morning Star*, I yelled for Tuarira to bring some men. Reluctantly he appeared with three Paumotuan men who started to push the boat while I tautened the lines leading to the kedge anchors that were holding us off the jagged ledge.

The winds, now gusting to sixty knots, were setting up an eerie howl in the limbs of the giant purau tree. In one massive gust, the wind shrieked to an ear-piercing tone. At this, Tuarira and the other men ran in terror into their huts and abandoned us and the *Morning Star* to our fate. Crouched at the rail in the coal black, rain-swept darkness, Shirl and I spent the rest of the night jamming coconut logs vertically between the *Morning Star* and the razor-sharp coral.

At dawn, the storm abated. Tuarira and his villagers sheepishly appeared. They conspicuously grunted their approval of the *popaa* and his wife and asked why we weren't afraid of the *tupapaus*. No apologies. No regrets. A new day had arrived in Taenga. Last night was the past. Tomorrow may never come. "Now we catch fish for breakfast. What kind you and 'Jurlee' like?"

We found two twenty-year old American Mormon missionaries stranded on Taenga. These fine young men desperately wanted to get to Tahiti for Christmas, but until the next copra schooner arrived, no transport was available from Taenga. After listening to the entreaties of their superior on the ham radio in Tahiti, we violated our long-standing policy of *no passengers* and took them with us to Makemo.

In Makemo, the Mormons asked us to take still another

member of their church—a Paumotuan named Babu—to Tahiti, so now the *Morning Star* was getting crowded. But we managed, and en route stopped to see Babu's relatives on Katiu, where, with the fluent Paumotuan-speaking Mormons and Babu aboard, we could barely cope with Polynesian hospitality.

On December 13, we left Katiu, sailing between Faaite and Fakarava. We were enormously relieved to be out of the Tuamotus, bound for Tahiti. A storm had delayed our departure from Katiu, so with only two hurried snapshots of the sun as it broke out of the dark overcast, we navigated to Tahiti—three hundred miles west of Katiu. Our passengers, including the Paumotuan, were violently seasick all the way, so it was with great relief that Shirl and I deposited them on the Papeete wharf.

We sailed out to the west coast of Tahiti and placed the *Morning Star* under a custodial arrangement while we flew home to be with our family over the Christmas holidays. When we deplaned in Los Angeles, we were impacted by a reverse cultural shock. Thoughts flooded our minds. "Everyone is in such a hurry. Where are all these people dashing to? Why all the hectivity? Everyone is so uptight. Hurry up and wait. For what? What do they do with the time that they save?"

After another year in the South Pacific, it all seemed so strange. Our perspectives and values had subtly changed. Our perceptions of what *is* reality had heightened. We noted the preoccupation with trivia. We had been living in an ambience where our mental and physical preoccupation was with earthy things. Day-to-day survival, weather and its direct, proximate effect on us and on our plans. Nature—pure, undistilled, raw nature—manifesting itself in the uncaring, remorseless, boundless heaving open sea. The primitive, mountainous Marquesas—the sun-scorched glittering atolls. The star-filled heavens of the tropics.

"Here we are back in civilization. This is where the *action* is? This is where *really* important things are happening? This is where we were destined to live life to its fullest?"

As we watched television for the first time in a year and

heard the seers and prophets of our day who call themselves newsmen relate their editorialized views of the news of the day, our thoughts turned back to lonely Tepoto. As we heard about the "religious" wars in Ireland and Lebanon and saw the killing, the terrorism—man's inhumanity to man—our thoughts rolled back to Taenga. In Taenga, they have short-wave radios. But they are listened to only because they convey messages for every possible family occasion—birthdays, weddings, deaths among the Polynesian people, whose multitudinous interrelated family ties are very strong, deep, and affectionate. In Taenga, the people are "deprived." No automobiles, no television, no movies, no newspapers. They don't really know what is going on in the world. But the mystery of all of this is that they don't seem to *feel* deprived, nor do they feel that their lives would be uplifted if they only knew more about the killings, rapes, assaults, or the latest Mideast crisis.

We neither saw nor heard of any evidence of ulcers, coronary artery disease, or nervous breakdown among the natives of the atolls. All of this made us ponder and appreciate our changed life-style more deeply. At the end of a month in the "real" world, we began to long for the *Morning Star* tugging at anchor in the azure lagoon of Tahiti, beckoning us to direct her beyond the western horizon into new adventures.

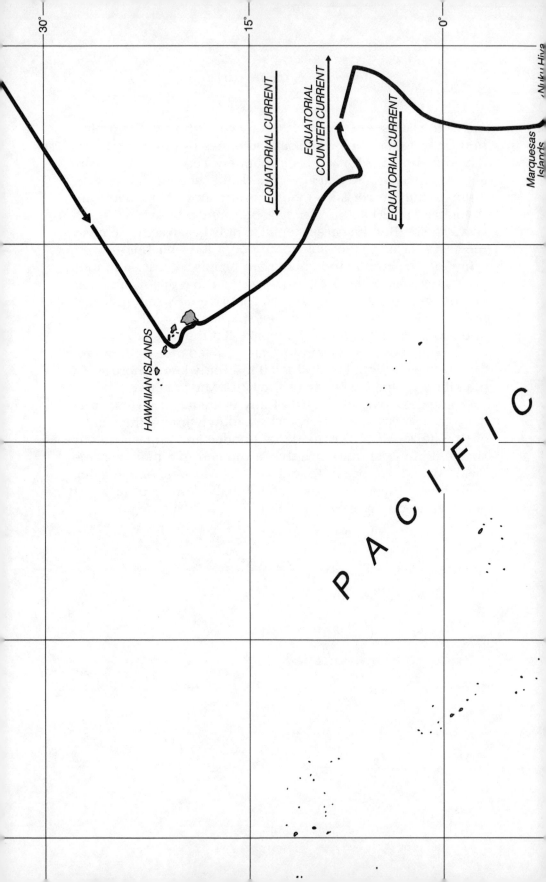

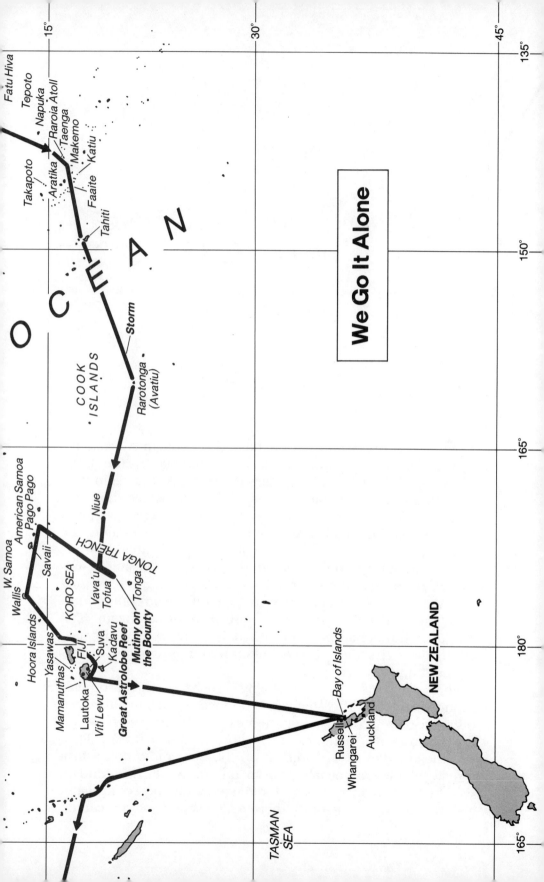

We Go It Alone

CHAPTER TWELVE

STORMS AND COPING WITH FEAR

As the hurricane season neared its end in March, we sailed WSW from Tahiti to Rarotonga in the Cook Islands—six hundred miles before the wind. At the beginning, we had an ideal fair-wind passage, running before the trade winds with our boomed-out twins—exhilarating sailing, and vastly preferable to our beat to windward from Hawaii to the Marquesas for twenty-six days. The feel of the motion of our small vessel at sea, the solitude under the stars, the smells and sounds of the sea, the song of the trade winds in our rigging revitalized our souls and blew the cobwebs from our minds. With jubilant high spirits, we were back at sea again! The month at home had been just enough to make us appreciate all the more the life-style we had chosen for ourselves, voyaging on the high seas.

The euphoric sense of well-being vanished as the barometer plunged and a southeasterly gale pounced on us one hundred miles east of Rarotonga. For the next ten hours, we rode out the storm, hove to under storm jib and storm trysail. Fleet Weather in Hawaii had told us on the ham radio that a fast-moving front was bearing down on us. While this kind of weather information is useful to have, when you are at sea in a slow-moving sailing craft, there isn't a whole lot you can do

Reaching across the Trades

Salt water shower

Greeting committee of dolphins

Fatu Hiva

except batten down and prepare for the worst. Our storm-survival technique began with shortening sail and heaving to.

Depending upon sea and wind conditions, we had a number of alternative sail settings: back the staysail and reef the main, back the staysail and allow the mizzen to draw, or back the storm jib and allow the storm trysail to draw. Our storm trysail was always in position on its separate track, to be hoisted with the mere switch of the main halyard. We think lying ahull in curling, breaking, large seas is dangerous and may cause a 360-degree rolling capsize.

Once while doing so with a deep-keeled sloop that I owned in the 1960s, we endured a knockdown that put the mast in the water, and that episode taught me an unforgettable lesson. Although we carried a cargo parachute sea anchor, it would only be used to keep us off a lee shore. We do not believe in pinning down a sailboat in heavy seas in any way.

Our worst storm at sea was a hurricane northwest of the Gulf of Tehuantepec on the maiden voyage of the *Morning Star*. We had ample sea room—thousands of miles between us and the Galapagos, so we ran off before the storm with bare poles, dragging two Volkswagen tires chained and attached by swivel shackles to three hundred-foot-long, one-inch nylon drogues streaming astern out of each quarter. The winds, at seventy-two knots—gusting to eighty—were not that unmanageable, but the confused sea conditions set up by the revolving storm superimposed on a large northwesterly swell were intimidating.

There is nothing more awesome than a storm at sea in a small craft, but Shirl and I had long since learned to face them with the following reasoning process: "What is the worst thing that can happen? The worst thing is that we die. We have to die sometime anyway, and if we die out here, we die together."

We feel that it is inconsistent to believe that we are in the palm of Almighty God and at the same time cower in fear of anything. Long ago we had surrendered to the will of God and accepted whatever dangers we had to confront, with the idea that only without fear could we live life to its fullest. Fear, or the fear of fear, is at the root of most of our problems. The only antidote we know for fear is faith in God.

This doesn't mean that we enjoyed these storms at sea; but we did, in some respects, behold them with childlike wonderment as we realized how great and powerful were the raging forces around us. There are no atheists in foxholes, and there are no atheists in a small craft caught in a heavy storm at sea.

The sea will quickly destroy an overinflated ego. It is remorseless. It is terrifying when it is angry. It doesn't care who you are, or who you think you are, or how much fame or fortune you may or may not have. The sea is neither benign nor malignant. *It is just indifferent.* If you defy it and its rules, it will kill you. If we went down in one of these storms, within seconds there wouldn't be a trace of our having existed, and the uncaring sea would eternally continue to crash and roll along without leaving the slightest sign of its act of violence.

As the storm blew itself out, an obscured sun shot revealed that we had drifted only twenty miles while riding it out. When we arrived in Rarotonga through the narrow slit in the reef called Avatiu, the officials expressed surprise at the earliness of our visit. They told us that the storm had blown down wires, torn off roofs, and uprooted many trees on the island. They said that the winds on the airport anemometers had gusted to eighty-five knots. They looked at our unscathed vessel with wonder.

The 300-foot interisland ship *Manuvae* came into Avatiu Harbor. The captain, Don Silk, told me that they had been in the same storm and said that it was the worst he had experienced in years. He said that as thirty-foot seas reached as high as his bridge, the ship was "standing on end," and all of the passengers and crew became seasick. Our confidence in our rugged little wooden craft continued to grow.

We were the first yacht of the "season" to arrive in Rarotonga, so we anchored stern to the wharf with our bow facing the entrance to the harbor, totally exposed to the north. We experienced two northerly gales while at anchor here; but our lengthy chain scope and plough anchor held fast. The *Yankee*, Irving Johnson's former steel vessel, was wrecked at Rarotonga, and her rusting hulk, lying on the reef, bears mute testimony to the unforgiving treachery of a South Pacific coral reef.

Yankee on Rarotonga Reef

Our five-week stay in Rarotonga was prolonged and blighted by one—only one—mosquito, which bit my face. It was a dengue fever mosquito. The dengue fever was a new phenomenon on Rarotonga and Tahiti. It was a particularly virulent strain and had caused the deaths of two children. Dengue fever is very debilitating, and the doctors told me that I would feel as if I were one hundred years old for three months. They were right.

Sailing from Rarotonga, we had another six-hundred-mile dead-downwind, five-day run to Niue Island. Niue (Savage) Island is a ten-by-twelve-mile lump of coral limestone with thickly wooded hills about two hundred feet high.

The Polynesians (Niueans) here are believed to be descended

from a combination of Maori, Samoan, and Tongan ancestry and are a fiercely independent lot. They speak a language of their own and had just been granted independence from New Zealand. Now a Third World nation with a population of approximately five thousand, they enjoy a seat in the General Assembly of the United Nations equal to that of any country in the world. But with a ten-to-one unfavorable trade balance, it is difficult to anticipate how a tiny nation like this can survive economically.

An intelligent, articulate Niuean official told me that a delegation from the United Nations had come to Niue and urged them to demand "independence." He asked me rhetorically, "Now that we are 'independent,' what do we do?" He told me that the Tanzanian member of the U.N. delegation, agitating most strongly for their independence, had gone back to Tanzania, where he was later assassinated.

On Niue, Shirley and I were interviewed for a local radio program by a very talented young Niuean. With mixed emotions, we heard ourselves on a Saturday night giving extemporaneous answers to questions regarding our sailing alone across the Pacific. We could only say that we are never less alone than when alone with God and his mighty sea and creatures abounding about us.

From Niue, we sailed off our mooring with twins set while our cruising friends, Bill and Betty Whipple, filmed the action from their sleek yacht *Tyee*. We were heading for Vava'u in the northern Tonga Islands—240 miles to the west.

The easterly winds were really piping up in the Tonga Trench area, and we were running fast in confused seas. It was 1800 ship time. Shirl had just stepped out to the cockpit to check the steering vane. I was below on the radio. For some reason, she turned to look over her left shoulder just in time to notice an out-of-phase, towering rogue sea curling up over the quarter. I looked up from below, amazed to see this wall of water coming at me through the companionway. Shirl was hurled against the mizzenmast, where she hung on for dear life. I streaked forward to strip down one of the 450-square-foot twins.

For the next two hours, Shirl sat out in the darkness of the cockpit, wet and shivering, hand-steering the boat while I, in water up to my calves, manned the pumps. The diesel-driven clutch pump jammed, so I laboriously pumped the boat with the large manual navy pump, assisted by the electric bilge pump, which was going as well. When the boat was dry, we hove to for twelve hours, forty miles east of Vava'u. We worked half the night cleaning up the incredible mess—electronics, tools, drawers, charts, books—all were swimming in salt water.

At no time during this episode did we feel an overriding sense of danger. We were simply too busy to panic. Cautions from "harbor stallions" had led us to wonder what would happen if we filled the large cockpit with water beyond the capacity of the self-bailing scuppers to drain. Now we knew. The grates floated to the top! Bill Garden had designed the *Morning Star* with so much reserve buoyancy aft that she just charged along after shipping the sea with her cockpit abrim and a ton or more of water sloshing around in her belly.

The Tonga Trench area is one of the deepest parts of an ocean anywhere in the world. We were hove to in three thousand fathoms of water—eighteen thousand feet, or over three and a half miles to the bottom! Also there is great live volcanic activity in this region, with submarine volcanoes erupting on the floor of the sea.

I had blamed this event on my faulty seamanship—running too fast in steep following seas, a common error of small-craft sailing. But months later in Fiji, while we were with the famous British circumnavigators and authors Eric and Susan Hiscock, they told me that a similar episode had happened to them in the Tonga Trench area. It was Hiscock's theory that the great depth of the ocean and the volcanic activity may affect the surface sea under certain conditions to bring about the disturbance that we experienced. Our attitudes toward our ability to cope were nourished by this incident, and the whole event caused us to feel very humble in the grand scheme of things.

After arrival in Tonga, we spent one week laboriously cleaning the saltwater residue off everything below. There followed five unforgettable weeks cruising among the islands of Tonga

Tonga landfall

and living with the kind Tongan people. Captain Cook called Tonga "the Friendly Islands."

We sailed down to Tofua Island to relive the experience of the mutiny on the *Bounty*, which occurred within sight of Tofua. It was here that Captain Bligh when attempting to land was stoned by the Tongans. The loss of the life of a crewman at Tofua caused Bligh to forgo any further attempts to land during his epic thirty-six-hundred-mile open-boat passage to Timor.

Tonga is a constitutional monarchy and has never really been under direct colonial control, albeit closely allied with England. Thus, the ancient Tongan customs are still very much a part of their everyday life. Their daily meals are cooked in the umu ("earth oven").

We gave away our sea-soaked carpeting, and the Tongan women wove for us pandanus mats, custom fit to our cabin.

We lined the bulkheads with Tongan tapa cloth (mulberry-tree-bark cloth) pounded and painted for us by the few *nima potos* ("clever hands")—Tonga women specializing in this art form.

Tongans would paddle out to see us, singing out their greeting, *"Malo le lei, malo e folau!"* ("Good day. Thank you for sailing here.") We enjoyed numerous meals in their pandanus *fales* ("homes"), where we always felt uncomfortable with their custom of serving their guests first while they smilingly watched us chew every bite. We were the *papalangi* ("white men") and, as guests of honor, we awkwardly abided by their customs.

We were particularly attracted to a young Tongan couple, Lupe and Lau. The Tongans are desperately in need of employment and cash wages, so I hired Lupe and Lau for such projects as painting, polishing, and varnishing. They would paddle out from their village on Utangahe every day, Lau usually bringing a fish. They worked with tender, loving care on any task assigned to them. We took them sailing to Kapa Island and a spectacular cavern called Swallows Cave.

The tapestry of the lives of Lupe, Lau, and their four-year-old boy quickly became interwoven with our lives. One evening while Lau and I were sitting in the cockpit under the stars, talking about the timing of the work on the boat, he spontaneously said, "You know, Ray, here in Tonga, time is *our* servant. We are the *master* of our time. It seems to me that with most *papalangi*, it is the other way around. Time is their *master* and controls and regulates their lives. You ask, 'When can we get this done?' I say, 'I don't know. All I know is that I will do what I can today.' We Tongans don't think to worry about tomorrow."

As I pondered Lau's homely philosophy, I realized how extremely difficult it was for me to effect the transition from a totally structured life-style to an unstructured one. Procrastination is contradictory to the American work ethic. To adopt a life-style where we can just *be* without the obsession to validate every moment by appraising what we are *doing*—what we are achieving—is extremely difficult. For me, the rearrangement of value systems is a painful process, and one not easily made overnight. I was learning much more from Lau than he was learning from me.

As I told him about the Great Depression that traumatized Americans and the world of the *papalangi*, he couldn't believe what he was hearing. "How could American people go hungry, be cold, have no clothes, or be without shelter?" Lau said, "Here in Tonga, we are poor, but we always have food, fish, coconuts, bananas, chickens, pigs—plenty. We can make tapa clothes from tree. We make our houses from pandanus. We make fires at night from coconut husks. Sometimes *afa* ("hurricane") come—blow down all houses, but everyone help and we make new houses. I guess, God plenty good to Tongan people."

The Tongans are a deeply religious people. Tupou, a young Tongan woodcarver who had befriended us, said to me, "Morning Star name of Mary. I carve for you statue of Mary to put in bow of yacht. She protect you and keep you safe."

He led me into the jungle and carefully chose a pua tree. He said, "I make *telie'* ['statue'] from this tree—its wood will marry the sea."

From the time Tupou cut down the tree to the emergence from its trunk of Tupou's sculpted rendition of Mary, I was fascinated with the skills of this primitive young sculptor. After weeks of work, Tupou was ready to bring the statue to the *Morning Star* and affix it to the bowsprit—like the figureheads of the sailing ships of old. When Tupou's work was completed, Father Philip King-Turner, a young New Zealand missionary in Tonga, came out in a native canoe and, fully robed, appropriately blessed the boat and its new pilot in the centuries-old tradition of the Catholic Church.

Freshly oiled, painted, and varnished, the *Morning Star* sailed from Vava'u bound NE into the tradewinds for Pago Pago, American Samoa. We wanted to be in the nearby American possession for the bicentennial Fourth of July celebration. Picking up a day as we recrossed the date line, we entered Pago Pago harbor on July 3, after three bruising days hard on the wind. Weeks of downwind sailing had spoiled and softened us. Beating to windward again gave us a taste of what it would be like to head from this far west against the trades, back to Hawaii. One thought like this was enough to bolster our resolve to continue to circumnavigate the globe.

The American Samoans went all out for the bicentennial celebration with Samoan war-canoe races, brass bands, marches—the whole works. Everything from stones and coconut trees to buildings and buses was painted red, white, and blue. The Samoan *matai* ("chiefs" or "heads of families") were just showing their rich Uncle how much they loved the annual gifts in excess of $100 million in outright cash given to the *matai* for distribution to their constituencies via the U.S. Department of the Interior. This was the most shocking waste of the dollars of the American taxpayers we were to encounter anywhere.

American Samoa is an unincorporated territory of the United States with seventy-six square miles and approximately twenty-seven thousand Samoans. The United States proclaimed this part of the Samoan Islands as an American territory in 1899. At that time, it was useful as a coaling station for U.S. vessels. The U.S. Navy abandoned its base in 1951, and the territory has absolutely no strategic value to the United States. As "American nationals," the Samoans can come and go freely to Hawaii or the U.S. Mainland. We, as American citizens, however, must go through Samoan customs and immigration procedures. American Samoa is administered by the Department of the Interior, and until the Samoans recently decided that they wanted only our money, not our governorship, the governor was appointed by the "in" politicians in Washington every four years. Millions in cash gifts to the *matai* are disguised from the surveillance of the American people within the bureaucracy of the Department of the Interior. Samoa's dependence on America exists mainly for the convenience of the Japanese, Taiwanese, and Korean tuna boats that deliver their catches to the two canneries polluting Pago Pago Harbor. New Zealand cast off Western Samoa's dependence on their taxpayers, and now the citizens there are doing well running their own independent country.

The Samoan people are like other Polynesians, innately kind and fun-loving, but the corrupting and demoralizing influence of the United States throwing the taxpayers' money at them, with no strings attached, has had a profoundly detrimental effect. After a month in the Samoas, we sailed away with no regrets from this brush with Western civilization to as off-beat an island as we could find—back to true Polynesia, Uvea, or Wallis Island, three hundred miles to the west. This was a two-and-a-half day passage with the only casualty a broken twin boom.

As we were running before the wind, with the large Western Samoan island of Savaii in sight, we accidentally backed the twin while I was aloft in the ratlines. The boom crimped around the shroud like a wet toothpick. All of a sudden, I had the backed sail and boom stub flogging away at me while I came down the ratlines like a monkey. Down with the unboomed twin. Aloft to lower the boom stub. Lots of action and many words flying in all directions. But there was no way we would go back to Pago Pago to repair the boom. So, flying on one wing—one twin boomed out—we oscillated downwind to Wallis and arrived ahead of our ETA.

Wallis is an overseas territory of the French: chief industry, copra; population, about eighty-three hundred Polynesians. The few French people on the island were extremely cordial to us, inviting us to dinner in their homes. The islanders were lovely, and no tourists come here. It was refreshing to learn that they remembered with affection the American troops who occupied the island during World War II. We could have stayed in Uvea much longer, but the pressure of the approaching hurricane season was upon us. It was now late August, and we wanted time to cruise Fiji before heading out of the tropics for New Zealand. We stopped at Futuna and Alofi in the Hoorn Islands. The harbors do not offer safe anchorage, so we remained in these majestic high islands for only three days.

Heading SW to Fiji, we heard on the ham radio that one of the yachts that had been with us in Pago Pago had smashed on a reef three days earlier. The captain's navigation had gone awry in the submerged-reef-infested waters of the northeastern Lau Islands, and the vessel was a total loss. They had a crew of four, but stated that no one was on watch when they struck the reef. The reefs of the Fijis are littered with ships, fishing vessels, and yachts. These are dangerous waters in which to navigate at night.

This was the most fatiguing passage of this leg of our voyage because in addition to navigational hazards our call at Futuna had put us west to a point where we had to tack against strong southeasterlies. On one tack northwest of Wailangilala Island, we, all of a sudden, saw the *bottom* coming up—in the middle of the blue Pacific! We jibed around in a hurried 180-degree turn just as a breaker exploded twenty yards off our beam. The charts call these events "breakers reported or occasional breaker," but this shoal was uncharted. Later, in the hydrographer's office in Suva, I showed the officials this area, and they said, "Yes, this has never been surveyed, and the charts originating with Captain Bligh are quite inaccurate, you know."

Picking our way through the reef-strewn Nanuku Passage into the Koro Sea, we entered rain-obscured Suva Harbor on August 31, 1976.

For the last three years, we had been immersed in the culture of Polynesia. Now we were eagerly looking forward to experiencing and learning about the culture of the Melanesian people of the western Pacific.

Welcome to Fiji

CHAPTER THIRTEEN

MEN FROM UNDER THE SKY

One day in the year 1643 the astonished Fijians glimpsed the white topsails of ships of the Dutch navigator Abel Tasman on the horizon. There was nothing in their legends to explain these curious strangers or the land from which they came. They only knew that from a place where their empty horizon met the sky there suddenly appeared white-skinned men who would transform their destiny forever. The Fijians called them *kai* Vavalagi ("men from Vavalagi"—the land from under the sky).

Over a century went by before Captain William Bligh, cast adrift from the *Bounty*, sailed his lifeboat through the Fiji Island group in one of the most remarkable feats of seamanship in maritime history. On this, and on his second voyage in search of the *Bounty* mutineers, Bligh drew the first charts of the Fiji Islands. He charted thirty-nine islands, the largest of which was Viti Levu. Because the Fiji Islanders had a reputation for savagery and cannibalism, the islands were known as "the Cannibal Islands" and were avoided by European navigators.

Fragrant sandalwood was in large demand in Europe. The European firearms traded with the chiefs of Fiji for the precious sandalwood altered the balance of power among the fiercely warring tribes, and the result was murderous chaos. Finally, in 1874—only a century before the arrival of the *Morning Star*—the great chief of the Bau tribe, Ratu Cako Bau, accepting cession to England, picturesquely stated, "If matters remain as they are, Fiji will become like a piece of driftwood on the sea and be picked up by the first passerby. The whites who have come to Fiji are a bad lot. They are mere stalkers on the beach. The wars here have been far more the result of interference of intruders than the fault of the inhabitants. One thing I am sure of, if we do not cede Fiji, the white stalkers on the beach, the cormorants, will open their maws and swallow us."

Fiji became independent from Britain in 1970—ninety-six years from the day the Fijian chiefs ceded the islands to Queen Victoria. The Dominion of Fiji is a member of the British Commonwealth, and now has all of the problems of a "developing nation." There are about 320 islands in the group with about 150 of them inhabited.

We found Fiji to be a fascinating crossroads of the Pacific, with a total population of 560,000—250,000 Fijians (Melanesians with Polynesian mixtures) and 288,000 Indians. A scattering of Whites, Chinese, and other races make up the balance.

The British brought the Indians here up to 1916 as indentured servants to work the sugar cane plantations. They multiplied rapidly and now numerically dominate the country. Racial tension between the hardworking Indians and the easygoing native Fijians lies explosively beneath the surface of this society. The Fijians rigidly retain ownership of all of the land and control the armed forces and the police—the guns. But the educated and industrious Indians have quite naturally become established into the bureaucratic infrastructure and control customs and immigration and administer the multitudinous rules and regulations that were part of their heritage from their British mentors.

In Suva, for the first time, we encountered less than a hospitable reception. As the *Morning Star* warped up to the dock in Suva, we were boarded by a bevy of white-uniformed, unsmiling Indian officials. They searched the vessel from stem to stern—clumsily pawing through drawers of clothing. Their demeanor was rude and arrogant. As they confiscated our fire-arms, they meticulously counted every bullet.

One particularly pompous Indian inspector said, "You, Americans! Why do you carry guns?"

I replied, "My wife and I alone are very vulnerable in many primitive parts of the world—places where there are outlaws and pirates—not like Fiji. Also we use one gun to shoot large fish like sharks—which we sometimes catch. But you must understand that with Americans, the right to own and bear firearms is an integral part of the freedoms contained in our Constitution and Bill of Rights. It was only with guns that we were able to get rid of our colonial masters, and we haven't forgotten it."

His querulous look showed me that it was simply impossible for him to comprehend the American concept of liberty. But he didn't really want an explanation. This particular official merely wanted to strut the petty power conferred upon him by his uniform. It was our first brush with this degree of surly officialdom, but as we continued to encounter the Eastern mentality, it was not to be our last. Kipling was right when he said, "East is East and West is West and never the twain shall meet...."

Shirl and I were determined not to let isolated hostility like this perpetuate resentment within us. We reasoned that the Indians elsewhere on Fiji couldn't *all* be like this. The beauty and adventure that we anticipated awaited us in the Fijis far offset brief annoyances such as this one encounter with unfriendly officials.

Suva, the capital, is a fascinating place, with Indians in their brightly colored saris blending into Fijians wearing their tra-ditional sulus (wrap-around skirtlike cloths—lavalava or pareu in other island cultures). Although we sailed into Suva during the dry season, it rained torrentially almost every day, so after a week we decided to move to the dry side of Viti Levu to spend our remaining time in the tropics in hot sunshine and clear water.

Preliminary to leaving, however, we reprovisioned in Suva's pulsating open-air market. These daily expeditions always offered us fascinating encounters with the vibrant people of

Fiji. Shirl purchased an intricately woven pandanus hat at a stand owned by a big, jovial, sulu-enwrapped Fijian woman. As Shirl tried on the hat, she asked for a mirror. The smiling Fijian said demurely, "You don't need a mirror, missy. Just look into your husband's eyes." How could anyone not be attracted by such childlike guilelessness?

Fully reprovisioned, we sailed from Suva bound for a remote village on the island of Mbengga—the home of the Fijian fire-walking tribe. We saw the Fijians of this cult—young men, old men, and boys—leisurely walking on beds of stones heated with open fire to over seven hundred degrees. They eagerly asked us to examine the soles of their feet after their fire-walking demonstrations. No burns whatever! Medical science has no conclusive explanation for this mind-over-matter phenomenon. Despite our tendency to deify science, there is much of this world and its creatures about which scientists simply have no answers.

In the village of Mbengga, Shirl and I had our first intimate contact with the Fijian people. As we were hospitably received into their community life, we were intrigued with the customs of these jovial, gentle, and fun-loving people. *Kere kere* ("the right to the property of others") and the sense of joy *(meke)* still is part of the Fijian village life. Fascinated, we watched outrigger canoes being adzed out of tree trunks and women making pots or tapa cloth. We thought, "How very different—how much more attractive are these warm, gentle Fijians than the few dour Indian officials who had been so rude to us in Suva." Seeking to become still more immersed in Fijian culture, we set sail for the island of Kadavu, surrounded by the Great Astrolabe Reef, lying forty miles south of Viti Levu.

It is the ancient custom for a visitor to a Fijian village to present the chief with a gift of yaqona or kava roots. In the huge market of Suva, we had purchased a large supply of these roots to be used for this purpose. We had first become acquainted with the ceremonial custom of kava drinking in Tonga. Yaqona is ground into a fine powder from the roots of the pepper plant, then dissolved in cold water and strained through a piece of shredded bark of the vau tree. It is not an alcoholic beverage. Part of a welcoming ceremony performed when a high-ranking chief visits another village is the gathering of men only in the *yaqona bure* ("thatched-roof house") to exchange stories as they drink the kava from the *bilo* ("half coconut shell").

Tui, the chief of Solotavui village on the island of Kadavu, along with the villagers, met us at the water's edge as we waded ashore through the soft mud of a mangrove swamp. When the Polaroid camera began to perform its magic, the women emerged from their *bures* with their babies all dressed in their finest. Their reaction to the studiously examined color pictures of themselves and their babies was so ecstatic and gave them so much laughter-filled, unalloyed joy that I continued to present them with their pictures until my film was gone.

As Tui graciously accepted my gift of yaqona roots, he commanded that "Now we have welcome ceremony for you, Ray." Although at a similar ceremony in Tonga, I had not acquired a taste for kava, there was no way I could refuse Tui's invitation.

The women of the village vied with one another to hostess "Jurlee" in their *bures,* while Tui hustled me off to the ceremonial *bure.* Kava drinking is always a men-only affair. Tui solicitously directed me exactly where to sit cross-legged on the earthen floor in the circle of men surrounding the *tanoa* (a three-foot-in-diameter wooden bowl skillfully carved from a single piece of a special hardwood). The *tanoa* bowl was carved in the shape of a turtle.

The complex, centuries-old ritual of yaqona mixing is always performed in the presence of the guest of honor. Protruding from the *tanoa* is a coconut fiber rope decorated with cowrie shells. It is called the *tui-ni-buli* and is always pointed at the guest of honor. Tui explained that it is strictly taboo for anyone to come between me and the *tui-ni-buli.*

Finally the ceremonial mixing was completed to the accompaniment of chanting and the pounding of small wooden drums. Then Tui directed a cupbearer to present to me the first bowl, with more ceremony and much respect. Custom dictated that I drain the entire bowl with one series of gulps. When the last dregs of the muddy substance had trickled down my throat, all of the men shouted *"Maca"* (meaning "it is drained") as they clapped their hands. Then the *bilo* was passed to Tui and, in the carefully designated order of rank, to the other men in the circle.

Amid politely suppressed gales of laughter on their part and wan grins on my part, this process was repeated five times. Squatting in the dimly lit hut in this circle of black men, I wondered at their generosity of spirit in granting to me—a white man from "under the sky"—their highest of ceremonial honors. I also mused, "If only my friends back in distant America could see me now."

After five large cups of kava, I felt none of the euphoric effect supposedly attributable to this vile-looking potion. But when Tui accompanied me back to our dinghy, Shirl said, "You may not feel anything, but the expression on your face looks to me like you think you can walk on water." Our remaining days in the Great Astrolabe Reef were spent in constant dread that I might be again similarly honored.

Now we were headed NW for the warm western side of Viti Levu. When we checked in with the Indian officials in Lautoka, they were so cordial and helpful that we radically revised our opinions formed by our initial encounter with Indian officialdom in Suva. Then we met an Indian businessman, Uday Singh, who invited us into his home, where his lovely wife, Nirmala, and charming daughter, Shaleen, prepared a traditional Indian curry dinner for us.

Uday insisted that we meet a medical doctor friend of his who was intensely interested in our adventures. The doctor friend prepared kava, and we had an Indian version of the kava-drinking ceremony right in his office. They went out of their way to make right our initial, unfortunate experience in Suva. We, in turn, entertained them on the *Morning Star* and formed a close friendship with Uday and Nirmala.

Similar to the Chinese of Hawaii, their diligent and thrifty forebears had worked hard, lived a Spartan existence, and invested their small wages in the education and training of their children. By dint of the exhausting work and rigid discipline of these sugar cane field workers, their children and grandchildren attained positions of prominence in the business and professional life of their adopted country. Again we learned the lesson how wrong it is for human beings to judge and negatively generalize about a whole race, nationality, or group of people by the actions of just a few. People all over the world share much the same aspirations and are more ready to extend friendship and warmth to their fellow human beings, if given the chance.

For many days, we cruised the Mamanuthas and the Yasa-was of Nadi waters. The water is translucent blue and green in color, and a warm eighty-five degrees. As we swam, dived, and snorkeled the reefs, we were getting into physical shape for our passage out of the tropics to New Zealand.

We had invited an official of the American embassy—an old friend from Hawaii—Harlan Lee and his wife, Mary Jane, an American Peace Corps nurse, for an overnight sail with us to Malolo Lai Lai. We had a marvelous time, and as we disembarked them in front of the Regent Hotel back in Viti Levu, Harlan said, "The *Morning Star* is the only American-flag vessel in these waters, so if you remain anchored here, I will arrange a pleasant surprise for you. Senator Mike Mansfield and former astronaut Senator John Glenn are stopping here for a few days for a rest en route back to Washington from a fact-finding mission to China." For the next few days, Shirl and I found ourselves in the company of these distinguished senators and their staff people.

John Glenn and his lovely wife, Annie, were intrigued with the adventures of two middle-aged Americans sailing alone around the world. In 1962, Glenn was the first man to orbit the earth, and I was *more* interested in his stories of this historic experience.

John Glenn is a wholesome, open-visaged type of man who radiates integrity. He makes you feel proud to be a fellow American. He is an aeronautical engineer, and at lunch one day with him and Annie, John drew sketches on a napkin, showing me how I could, by altering the underbody of the *Morning Star*, make her go faster. I was interested, but I said, "If we wanted to circumnavigate the world in a hurry, we could simply do it in a plane." I continued, "For example, as you wing your way back to Washington on *Air Force One*, every fifteen minutes you will travel the same distance that it takes us on our fastest day to cover in an entire twenty-four-hour period."

With his computerlike mind, John responded, "Yes, and in just thirty-six seconds, I covered that same distance in *Friendship Seven*."

I thought to myself, "So much for trying to impress an astronaut."

During our extended stay in Tonga, we had become close friends with Philip King-Turner, S.M., a thirty-nine-year-old Catholic missionary priest. Father King-Turner, a New Zealand citizen, had been in Tonga for thirteen years on his mission. He had a three-month vacation, beginning in November, and he had asked us if he could sail with us to New Zealand from Fiji.

In almost every port, we are asked to take passengers, guests, and/or crew but decline these requests as a matter of firm policy. The reason is that most people making these requests simply do not realize what they are getting into. They romanticize how pleasant it would be—how luxurious it must be—to sail over the blue Pacific to lush tropical islands with swaying palm trees and uncluttered white-sand beaches. Then, when they find themselves pitching about in the open sea in rough weather, confined in a tiny living area with no way to get off, they get sick, irritable, and, in some cases, frightened.

But as we came to know Father King-Turner, who had been in love with the sea and boats all of his life, we decided to take him with us to New Zealand. The son of a fisherman, Phil had grown up on boats in the rough seas off the South Island of New Zealand. As a missionary, he was accustomed to the lack of creature comforts, and he is a deeply spiritual, companionable, warm, and dedicated human being.

So promptly, on October 30, there was Father Phil, with his shock of flaming red hair, wildly waving to us from the wharf at Lautoka, Fiji. He boarded the *Morning Star* with all of his worldly possessions contained in a small cardboard suitcase. Within an hour, we weighed anchor, exited the pass from the sheltered Nadi waters, and were on the heaving open Pacific Ocean, bound southward for Aotearoa ("the Long White Cloud"), the Maori name for New Zealand.

CHAPTER FOURTEEN

THE LONG WHITE CLOUD

Armed with weather information obtained in Fiji, our strategy was to get west as fast as possible. When we crossed the Tropic of Capricorn, out of the southeast trade winds, we would pick up the hoped-for southwesterlies, which would give us a favorable slant of wind to New Zealand—lying eleven hundred miles south.

The first few days gave us warm, ideal trade-wind sailing—saltwater baths on the foredeck, shorts, bare feet, and moderate seas. Strumming his guitar in the cockpit, our passenger, Phil, was "bubbling with joy," as he described his feelings.

Then, as the *Morning Star* left the tropics for the first time in three and a half years, the nights began to get cold. Out came sweaters, jackets, and layers of long-unused clothing, buried in the lockers below. But we still shivered through our night watches as we became exposed to south-southwest winds sweeping up from the Antarctic across the stormy Tasman Sea.

With the hoped-for southwesterlies superimposed on the Tasman southerly swell, we encountered steep, confused seas, with winds ranging from calm to—minutes later—forty knots. This involved a lot of sail changing, and the storm trysail came out of its bag for the second time in its career.

Although he had never before been on the high seas in a sailing vessel, Phil King-Turner took all the sea and weather threw at us with serenity and good cheer. Never once did a complaint or negative comment leave his cracked and blistered lips. A redhead, with a fair skin, is particularly vulnerable to sunburn and windburn. Though aware of this, he exulted in standing for hours on the weather side of the cockpit or on the gyrating bowsprit, mesmerized by the huge Tasman seas curling and breaking toward us. As the *Morning Star* lifted to allow the seas to roll under her, Father Phil saw, with some wonder, the stability, seaworthiness, and relative safety of a properly designed sailing craft in action.

As we neared New Zealand, we were struck by a fifty-knot gale with thirty-foot seas. Stripped down to spitfire jib and storm trysail, we sailed through the gale. The only good thing to say about the treacherous weather around New Zealand is that the storms quite rapidly pass over or blow themselves out.

During this brief period of heavy weather, Father Phil, upon seeing a particularly mean-looking sea roaring at us, asked "Aren't you going to turn into it?" That instinctive reaction was born in his powered-fishing-boat youth.

As the rogue sea drew near, I said, "Turn into it? No way, Phil! This is a *sailboat!* That is where the wind is coming from." As I spun the wheel, the wave, larger than the rest but in phase, broke and rolled harmlessly under our hull. Phil just looked over his shoulder at me and silently shook his head.

On the eleventh day out, just at noon, Shirl and I were thrilled to hear Phil cry out "Land—I see land!" He had sighted the North Cape of his motherland for the first time in years. He was enraptured!

All of the mumbo-jumbo arithmetic that he had observed me doing had produced *New Zealand* after days of guidance sought and gathered from the heavenly bodies. So we hove to that night off the Bay of Islands, and exactly twelve days to the hour from leaving Lautoka, we tied up to Opua Wharf near Russell, New Zealand. We had sailed 1,296 miles over the bottom—fastest day, 160 miles; slowest, 70 miles.

In the intimacy of a sea passage such as we had just shared, human beings can quickly become either mortal enemies or

loving friends. Rarely is there an in-between. In accompanying
us on this passage, Father Phil gave far more to us than we
could have ever given to him.

The New Zealand officials and the people on the wharf displayed the genuine feelings of kindliness and hospitality that
so characterizes New Zealand and many of its people.

I prepared a chart of our track, rolled it into a diplomalike
parcel, and with due ceremony presented it to Father King-
Turner, granting him the title of "Sailorman Extraordinaire."
When he said good-bye, a sense of emptiness descended on our
cabin as we realized how much he had come to mean to us.

A country the size of California, with only 3 million people,
New Zealand here in the Bay of Islands radiates an atmosphere
of cleanliness and tranquility. The clean, small towns are rem-
iniscent of rural, Midwestern America fifty years ago.

During the remaining weeks in November and early December—midsummer there—we cruised in the scintillating Bay of
Islands. This bay of Prussian blue water encircled by jade
green hills covered with fresh-smelling pine and shrubs must
rate as one of the finest cruising areas in the world.

Captain James Cook sailed his ninety-eight-foot long
Endeavor here in 1769 and gave the Bay of Islands its name.
He was the first European to discover this area, and now, just
a little over two-hundred years later—less than three life-
times—it was an enormous thrill for us to sail our forty-six-foot
Morning Star in this great navigator's wake.

But we had sailed to New Zealand for two principal reasons—to get out of the hurricane season of the Tropics and to
drydock and refit the *Morning Star* before taking on the Indian
Ocean crossing.

For many years, Alan Orams's boatyard in Whangarei had
enjoyed an outstanding reputation among American yachtsmen. Orams was known for its skilled shipwrights and honest
dealings. Errol Flynn had brought his famous yacht *Sirocco* to
Orams years ago for a refit.

The *Morning Star* had been sailed hard since leaving the
Golden Gate in 1973. We had a list of projects that had been
accumulating since we left America. Heading it was a revised
system of sail handling, incorporating a design for reefing

headsails that I had formulated over the years. With just two of us, sail handling had increasingly become a tiresome chore.

There were many black nights at sea when I would be shaken out of a sound sleep by Shirl's gentle voice saying, "Ray! Wake up! There is a squall bearing down on us!"

My adrenaline would surge as I clambered from my warm bunk, made for the cockpit, evaluated the situation, strapped on a safety harness, and began my clutching, grabbing, walking, crawling trip to the foredeck. I would have to uncleat the jib halyard, then creep out onto the pitching bowsprit to muzzle the falling headsail. Sometimes the motion on the bowsprit is like that of a superfast elevator, or that of a light airplane dropping in an "air pocket."

One night while out there on the foretip of the boat, hanging on and harnessed to the forestay, the bowsprit fell into a trough, and as a sea swept over me, I was momentarily submerged. When I came back up, sputtering like a walrus, I resolved that this folly had to end. If I went over the side, two lives could be lost. A couple of years ago, a friend of ours in Hawaii was lost at sea while dropping a headsail at night without a safety harness attaching him to the boat. His wife, on their yacht alone, was found alive forty days later between Japan and Hawaii by a Japanese fishing vessel.

When we arrived in Orams's yard, I met Alan, and he quickly explained to me how he had recently sold the entire operation to his young foreman, Ray Roberts, and no longer had anything to do with its operation.

An American yachtsman setting out to accomplish a major refit in New Zealand is extremely vulnerable for two reasons. One, he is operating against a rigidly enforced time frame—his six months' visa. He is forced to leave, with few exceptions, when his visa expires. Second, if any work performed is unsatisfactory, the defects in workmanship or materials usually show up after he is at sea. Unlike the New Zealand yachtsman, he cannot come back and seek remedy.

I, along with other American yachtsmen, was soon to find out that the new owner's basic business philosophy in dealing with Americans was quite different from that of the highly ethical and conscientious Alan Orams. It could be summed up by "let the buyers beware—they are here today and gone tomorrow." Already letters published in the Seven Seas Cruising Association bulletin had indicated the dissatisfaction of other American yachtsmen with Roberts's work. When he took over, Alan's crew of skilled shipwrights quit en masse. The friendly tradesmen of Whangarei—sailmakers, mechanics, and specialists in other areas—told me, in bitterness, how Roberts was charging an exorbitant fee for any work performed on a foreign yacht in his yard. This unjust toll, they explained, had to be passed on to the foreign yachtsman. They openly resented these tactics, but there wasn't much that they could do about it. As our voyage continued beyond New Zealand, we were later to find the true extent of the shoddy materials and poor workmanship that caused the projects performed by Orams's yard to fail dismally one by one.

The reefing headsail project, however, was an unqualified success due to an independent machinist, Jim Bates, whom I sought out in his shop in McLeod Bay. I had read a book called *High Adventure* written by the famous New Zealander Sir Edmund Hillary, who was the first man to scale the summit of Mount Everest and the first man, after Scott, to reach the South Pole overland. Jim Bates had been chosen by Hillary to become a member of these expeditions because, as Hillary described him, he was the most innovative, versatile mechanic Hillary had ever known. When I explained to Jim what I wanted— reefing, not merely furling, headsails—he set about to design and custom-make the stalwart equipment that, working with him, we installed at anchor in McLeod Bay.

Jim and I rowed the fifty-foot stainless steel spars, stretched between two dinghies, out to the *Morning Star*. The tedious installation could have been performed much more efficiently with the crane in Orams's yard, but the fiercely independent adventurer Bates would have no part of Roberts's extortion scheme.

Sailmakers had told me that this system wouldn't work because of the distortion of the reefed headsail. But I had been working with Noel Lloyd, a saddlemaker cum sailmaker, in Whangarei, and between Noel and Jim, they designed a genoa that, with altered sheet leads, would reef down to a storm jib. Noel insisted that we give these innovations sea trials, and I was so impressed with his conscientious approach to the development of this system that I had Jim and Noel design a genoa forestaysail, that would prove to be our salvation three years later in the Pacific as we neared the end of the circumnavigation.

Despite our disappointment with the way things were going with Orams's work, we enjoyed our stay in New Zealand and made many friends in this beautiful country down under. The first New Zealander I had met was in the British Eighth Army in North Africa during World War II, and I had always liked and respected this rugged breed. Our visit to their country generally enhanced this high regard for its people.

Following the war, New Zealand had outdone the British in their headlong plunge into socialism. While we were there, the newspapers and television contained daily accounts of labor problems. In a country of 3 million people, with an annual trade deficit of $1 billion, there are 290 labor unions. At any given point in time, there is one form of strike or another.

By maintaining rigidly restrictive immigration policies, the New Zealanders, heretofore, had enjoyed relative prosperity and full employment. They imported cheap labor from Tonga, Samoa, and other South Pacific islands. These Polynesian people had lived in New Zealand for years.

Now, as synthetics began to replace wool, and the experiment with the welfare state began to collapse, unemployment (minimal by American standards) began to rear its ugly head.

The New Zealanders threw out the left-wing labor government and set about, as Britain is now doing, to unscramble the eggs of socialism, already deeply embedded in their system—to reinvigorate the private enterprise system.

In the process, the South Sea Islanders, called "overstayers," were rounded up and summarily deported back to their places of origin. As this process disrupted the lives of many of these Polynesians who had been in New Zealand for years, it caused great resentment and hostility among them, not only in New Zealand, but in the islands from which we had sailed. This fact was to have an important bearing on the adventure that awaited us north of New Zealand.

New Zealand to Egypt

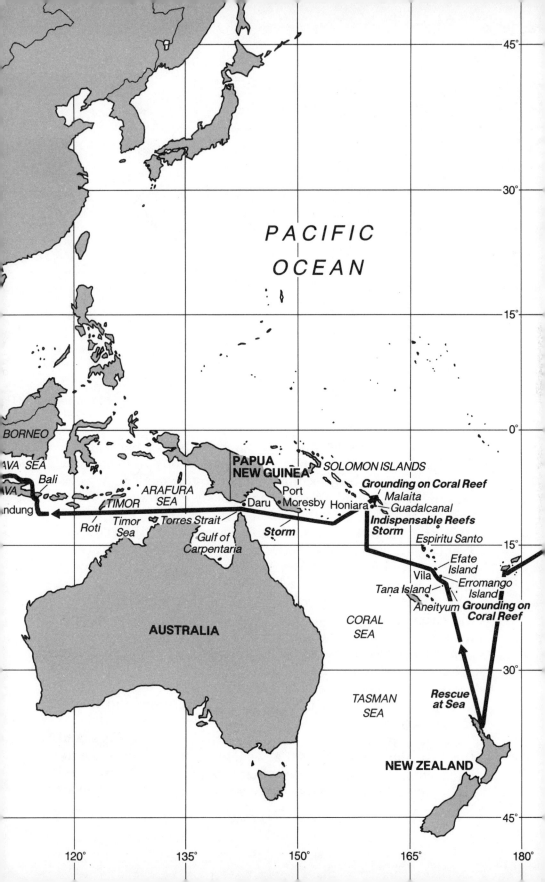

45°

30°

15°

*PACIFIC
OCEAN*

0°

BORNEO

JAVA SEA

JAVA   Bali

Bandung

Roti   Timor
Sea

TIMOR

*ARAFURA
SEA*

Torres Strait

Gulf of
Carpentaria

**PAPUA
NEW GUINEA**

Daru   Port
Moresby   Honiara

SOLOMON ISLANDS

Grounding on Coral Reef

Malaita
Guadalcanal

**Indispensable Reefs
Storm**

Espiritu Santo

15°

AUSTRALIA

*CORAL
SEA*

Storm

Vila

Tana Island

*Efate
Island*

*Erromango
Island*

Aneityum   **Grounding on
Coral Reef**

30°

*TASMAN
SEA*

**Rescue
at Sea**

NEW ZEALAND

45°

120°   135°   150°   165°   180°

CHAPTER FIFTEEN

RESCUE AT SEA

⚓ The sun was 17° north of the equator. We were at latitude 35° south. Winter was setting in down under. The mid-May days were becoming shorter and colder. We had been living in lovely New Zealand for six months, and it was time to set a course north, back into the Tropics. The weather systems around New Zealand, influenced by the Antarctic, the Tasman Sea, and the Pacific Ocean, are notoriously fickle and treacherous. Gales off North Cape come up with little warning and great ferocity.

So, on May 9, with a low-pressure system moving in from the Tasman, we decided that the weather could only become worse before it became better. We left Whangarei with mixed emotions. We regretted leaving the many new friends we had made in New Zealand and somewhat dreaded the cold passage north. At the same time, we looked forward to cruising again in warm water among islands with coconut trees and white-sand beaches.

After a prolonged stay ashore, we both lose our sea legs, and the first night out is one that usually must be unpleasantly endured. But, as the Cape Brett Lighthouse slowly disappeared below the horizon, the seas were smooth, and a chilly fifteen-knot southwest breeze, put us on a broad reach—a comfortable point of sail for the ketch-rigged *Morning Star.*

The next morning, after our nighttime watch standing— four hours on and four hours off—we listened to the weather from Radio New Zealand. At the end of the broadcast came a routine notice to all ships at sea to be on the lookout for a New Zealand sailing vessel that had sent a Mayday distress call eight days earlier.

Her name was *Hau Moana.* She had been an entrant in the annual Auckland-Suva yacht race, which had its start on May 1.

The second night out, the fleet of racing yachts had been caught in a North Cape southwesterly gale. The *Hau Moana* radioed that she had been dismasted, as had ten other yachts. A large section of her deck had been ripped off, and she was flooded. She had managed the single distress call, then—radio silence.

The RNZAF Orion patrol planes had been conducting an extensive search, but no trace of the yacht or its six-man crew could be found. As I listened to the radio warning in the morning, I had an indescribably overwhelming premonition that we would find these people.

At 1330, we were gliding smoothly along in clear weather; Jonathan, our wind vane, was effortlessly steering our proper course; and Shirl was sleeping in her bunk below. I, too, was tired from the interrupted sleep of the first-night-out routine, so I decided to go below and catch a couple of hours' rest as *Morning Star* took care of herself. But, before I did this, I routinely stood on the top of the cabin and scanned the horizon for ships.

Far off our starboard bow, I saw a fleck of white appear and disappear in the troughs of the undulating sea. While I continued to watch, the appearance of white became constant. The object was closing on our course! When I laid the binoculars on it, I could see a tiny rag of a sail hoisted on a stub above a hull that was now taking form. Just then, an orange smoke flare went spiraling up from the craft. I shouted below for Shirl to wake up and get into her woolens, boots, and oilskins. Within minutes, she was in the cockpit, wide awake and alert.

We altered course and rapidly closed on the vessel. We learned later that she was using her last ten minutes of fuel to get near to us. Soon I could make out the name—*Hau Moana*—and see four men and two teenage boys jumping up and down, yelling, screaming, and hugging each other.

When we came within shouting distance, I asked them, "Any injuries or sickness aboard?"

"No," they answered.

"Do you need food or water?"

"Not now," they cheered.

While Shirl circled them, I got on the ham radio and instantly found an Auckland ham operator routinely calling "CQ, CQ, CQ. This is ZLILT." He was just looking for someone to have a "bit of a chat." When I came back to his call, I gave him our coordinates—obtained from advancing a dawn three-star fix, sun lines shot at midmorning, along with a meridian passage noon sight, and another high-angle sun sight shot while warily circling *Hau Moana*.

I asked ZLILT to phone the New Zealand authorities and the skipper's wife.

The skipper, Ernie Maddox, and his fifteen-year old son rowed over to us in their dinghy as we hove to, three boat lengths from the crippled vessel. He told us that in the storm their mast had pulled out at its base, tearing with it a six-foot-square section of their cabin top. They had to cut the mast rigging free to prevent it from holing their hull, but they salvaged the boom. The seas flooded them below, and after their first distress call, their radio went dead from saltwater immersion.

The crew of six husky men had rigged the boom as a mast and stretched plastic tarps over the gaping hole in their cabin top. The jury-rigged sail on the boom was ineffective. They couldn't make progress back towards New Zealand—eighty-six miles to the southeast. They had burned up all but ten minutes of their fuel supply trying to power against head seas.

Several nights after the dismasting, they had spotted a ship's lights. They fired distress flares, and a Tongan freighter came alongside of them. They thought that they had been rescued. From the freighter's bridge, it was quite obvious that here was a vessel in distress. They had fired distress flares. Yet, the captain of the freighter, claiming later at an inquiry that he didn't understand their English, steamed away over the horizon, abandoning these desperate men without so much as a radio call advising their position. When we found *Hau Moana*, she was inexorably drifting into the vicious Tasman Sea. They were quite naturally frightened. The next gale would have swamped them for certain.

Moreover, the Orions were searching over two-hundred miles from where we found the disabled craft, although it had drifted only twelve miles from its original Mayday position. We reassured Maddox that there was no way that we would leave them until we were certain of their safety.

At midafternoon, the U.S.-made Orion patrol aircraft came roaring out of a cloud-flecked blue sky. They buzzed us just above our masthead and took the aerial photo that, we later learned, appeared on the New Zealand front pages and national television.

We arranged with the New Zealand Coast Guard Orion for them to send out a surface tow craft for *Hau Moana*. I told the Orion radio operator that I would send a key-down signal every five minutes on 2182 kc. to enable the surface craft to home in on us with his radio direction finder.

As the Orion continued to circle us, I decided to risk getting a line onto *Hau Moana*. The problem with this procedure was that two vessels joined on the high seas can collide unless one or the other has sufficient maneuverability and crew to keep clear. But if we couldn't attach to *Hau Moana*, we were certain to lose them during the night, just a few hours away.

I maneuvered the *Morning Star* in the swell alongside, and Shirl deftly threw a coiled line, which their eager hands seized at the first toss. Our line was secured to their anchor line with a sheet bend, forming an umbilical cord of safety. After experimenting, we found the only way in which the vessels would lie dead in the water attached together without colliding was for *Hau Moana* to be placed stern to the *Morning Star*, with their jury headsail set and drawing.

The Orion left with the promise that a surface craft—the *Lanakai*—would arrive at approximately 0130. I requested that *Hau Moana* hoist a small kerosene lantern in her rigging. After

Aerial photo from RNZAF Orion

Tepoto chief

Tonga friends Lupe and Lau

Author with Senator John Glenn and his wife, Annie

Hove to in Tasman Sea

the blackness of night had closed in, the pinprick of light from *Hau Moana* rose and fell, barely visible only three hundred feet astern of us. We took aboard their two coolest heads, one a paratrooper named John, to keep a chafe watch on the attachment line.

Now we just waited. John said that he had 600 jumps to his credit and that he had been on many simulated survival exercises, but this one was for real, and as they drifted out of the shipping lanes he told of the fears that haunted the men aboard their helpless craft.

Although he was serving in the New Zealand paratroopers, John was an Englishman and was quite outspoken about his attitude toward New Zealand. When Mike, the big New Zealander, told us about the Tongan freighter that had abandoned them, he was quite bitter. I commented that it was a real mystery to me why the Tongan captain hadn't rescued them.

John said, "I'll tell you what, mate. It ain't no mystery to me! The Tongans hate the bloody Kiwis so much because of their being rounded up and deported that once the captain saw we were a bloody Kiwi lot, he and his crew said, 'To 'ell with 'em. Let 'em drown.' That's what I think, mate."

His Kiwi shipmate didn't say anything. In New Zealand, the feelings toward the English run rather high. They derisively call their fellow Commonwealth members "Pommys." Quite often, we saw New Zealanders wearing T-shirts with the legends Pommy Go Home or Punch a Pommy Today.

John went on, "Look at me, mate. I've been down here ten years, training bloody Kiwi airborne troops. Would you believe that for me to go on this bloody race to Suva, I had to get a bloody exit permit—just like a bloody foreigner they treats me."

On a lighter note, they told me how they had loaded the *Hau Moana* with duty-free liquor. The custom was that after the race, the racers' families would join them in Fiji, and there would be a succession of parties and liquid celebrations. They lamented that "now that they were rescued, they would have to pay duty on all the booze they brought back." Mike said the only sensible Kiwi solution was to drink it all.

At about 2100, I had been up almost twenty-four hours, so I told them to sit in the cockpit and keep an eye on the chafe guard I had wrapped around the attachment line. I explained that I wanted to catch a couple hours' sleep before the *Lanakai* got there. At midnight, I was awakened by the thumping of their wooden dinghy against our rolling hull. When I came into the cockpit, I saw that they were slugging at a bottle of duty-free Scotch, smuggled aboard on a trip to *Hau Moana* while I slept.

Not knowing what the rest of the night might hold for us, I said, "I don't want to be a hard-nose, but you guys aren't rescued yet. Toss the jug over the side." Without a moment's hesitation, John, the tough paratrooper, with a flip of his wrist said, "Okay, skipper, over she goes." Judging from the sounds coming from *Hau Moana*, they were trying as fast as possible to consume the duty-free booze.

I said, "Now one of you take that damned dinghy along the attachment line back to *Hau Moana*. When and if *Lanakai* ever shows up, you can come back and get your mate. I need only one guy to watch that line."

So, off into the night went Mike—back to his prison of the last eight days.

At 0200 there was still no sign of the *Lanakai*, but I could hear intermittent bursts of static on our VHF radio. Someone nearby was trying to send a signal.

Our masthead aircraft strobe light was flashing furiously. I figured that *Lanakai* must be close, so I loud-hailed on our PA system, instructing *Hau Moana* to fire their last parachute flare. Someone yelled back, "Fire our last flare? What the 'ell for?" By this time my patience was wearing a bit thin, so I yelled over the loud-hailer, "Fire the damned flare—now!"

Without another word, the night turned to daylight as the parachute-suspended burning magnesium brought out in stark relief the two vessels and the heaving sea around us. We carry a commercial 50 mm. Very pistol. But the flares are almost impossible to replace, except in major seaports. We cannot have them shipped to us because the airlines won't carry explosives. Had *Hau Moana's* flare supply been exhausted, I would have fired one of my own. But once free from this res-

cue operation—the sooner the better, the way it was developing—we were outward bound to places where no flare car-
tridges would be available.

In another ten minutes, the VHF broke into a jubilant *"Morning Star, Morning Star,* this is *Lanakai.* We saw the flare. We
see your strobe light. We ETA you in fifteen minutes."

As *Lanakai's* lights came up over the horizon, she bore
straight for us, made a sweeping turn toward *Hau Moana,* now
illuminated by our twelve-volt searchlight, and hailed, "Thank
you, *Morning Star."*

Out of the night, pulling himself along the attachment line,
Mike reappeared to collect John. He said, "Ernie says to thank
you, Ray, and to thank Mrs. Triplett." He asked, "Shall I cut the
line when I get to the knot?"

I simply said, "No, Mike, just untie the sheet bend and we'll
haul in our line when we are sure you are safe. We'll keep the
searchlight on you. Good luck. And tell Ernie he is most
welcome."

With that, our two friends—the Kiwi and the Pommy—
pulled themselves through the seas along the attachment line.
When they came to the sheet bend, they untied it, and our line
went slack. We kept the searchlight on them until they
crawled aboard *Hau Moana,* rolling in the troughs. In thirty
minutes, it was all over.

Lanakai radioed, "We have *Hau Moana* in tow. Bon voyage,
Morning Star."

We were groggy with fatigue, but had a sense of deep relief
and gratitude that God had used us as his instrument in saving
these six lives.

We set sail and resumed our course for the New Hebrides,
lying seven hundred miles north-northwest of us. I stayed on
watch until dawn to shoot Venus and figure out where we
were, after drifting with *Hau Moana* for twelve hours.

As we charged along for the next few days, reefed down in
fresh to strong winds, we gradually recovered from the
exhaustion brought about by the preparation to leave New
Zealand, the *Hau Moana* rescue, and six months of life ashore.
Soon, the giant albatross began to become fewer in number,
and the Southern Cross appeared lower and lower in the sky

astern of us. Off came the down underwear and the hot-water bottles draped around our necks during our night watches. The sliver of the last phase of the old moon hovered in the star-studded sky above us. The sea was beautiful.

We were broad-reaching north to the Tropic of Capricorn in ideal sailing weather. The reefing headsails were working perfectly. No more changing headsails on a pitching bowsprit for me. The New Zealand–installed deep freeze was full of steaks, and life seemed great again.

Then, on the fifth day out—as we neared the variables— where the trade winds begin and the southwesterlies end— we were hit by squalls packing forty-five knots of wind kicking up rough beam seas. Shirley's entry in the log on May 15 during her watch, 0100–0400: "Rough seas, several in cockpit. I think I smell copra." My entry: "I hope not."

Other log entries on this passage: "Winds NE 25–30 knots. Reefed headsails. Reaching at 6 knots. Beautiful sailing—getting balmy. Crisis of the day—vane line broke—replaced while hanging over stern. Water pump alternator belt broke while charging freezer. Replaced in nasty seaway in 30 minutes. Slamming into seas. Calms."

Then, on the seventh day out of New Zealand, we crossed the Tropic of Capricorn, and we were back in the tropics, where we and the *Morning Star* belonged.

We were elated at getting out of New Zealand unscathed by weather, and our general feeling of well-being was marvelous. Cruising was wonderful—the only way to go. Everything looked bright, but we had no idea what the next few days had in store for us.

CHAPTER SIXTEEN

NEAR DISASTER IN THE NEW HEBRIDES

On the morning of May 17, our position was latitude 22° 33′ south, longitude 170° 12′ east. We had a twenty-four-hour run of 141 miles. The log entries bubble with joy and enthusiasm.

Then at 1300, while running the engine to accommodate our new deep-freeze compressor, all hell broke loose! With a muffled roar, the boat filled with oily black smoke. At first I thought we were on fire. While I tore apart the engine housing, Shirl stopped the engine. As the smoke disappeared, I saw the problem. The brand-new exhaust pipe installed in New Zealand had ruptured at the manifold. Our former exhaust pipe had lasted nine years. The Orams's installation had lasted forty hours.

In prior years, we have had engine failures that could not be repaired at sea. We had sailed, in the aggregate, over five thousand miles without an operating engine and regarded this as of no great consequence because we are voyaging on a sailing vessel.

Now, however, engine failure was important! Why? We had to hurry and get it running again so that the 200 steaks in the deep freeze wouldn't thaw! This is what happens when wants become needs and a dependence is built upon the luxuries of life.

We changed course from Port Vila to Aneityum—the southernmost of the New Hebrides Islands—lying black and unlit—practically uninhabited, sixty-three miles north-northeast from our position. We had fresh east-northeast winds, so we close-reached along as I spent four hours jury-rigging the broken exhaust pipe with tin cans and chemical muffler bandages.

The steaks would last three days. Our landfall at Aneityum would be at dawn the next day. The plan was that we would sail into a bay called Port Aneityum and drop the anchor. I would then make more permanent repairs to the exhaust pipe so that the steaks would remain frozen until we reached Port Vila—180 miles farther north up the New Hebrides chain. The bay was exposed to the west, but the British *Pilot Book* solemnly told us that the winds were rarely out of the west this time of year.

At predawn on May 18—eight and a half days out of New Zealand—we made our landfall squarely on the western point of Aneityum Island. Coconut trees, "lush tropical paradise"—we were in heaven again.

At 1045, the seventy-five-pound anchor plunged down to the coral bottom in five fathoms in front of a mission station called Anelgauhat. After days of constant motion, the *Morning Star* was now lying benignly still. We had the peaceful feeling that comes over us when we drop anchor in such a place after a high seas passage.

Melanesian natives came paddling out in their dugout canoes. They were friendly and brought us bananas and papayas. Aneityum is not a port of entry, so we didn't want to have undue contact with the natives, nor did we want to go ashore. The British and French, who jointly control the New Hebrides,* are very sticky about the formalities of entering their colonies.

We ran the engine with the jury-repaired exhaust, and it held together for the two hours it took to drop the freezer tem-

*The New Hebrides have recently become an independent country called Vanuatu.

perature to zero. After eight hours of motionless, uninterrupted sleep, we were ready to dismantle and repair the exhaust pipe more permanently. The log shows that on Thursday, May 19, we spent the entire day replacing the broken exhaust section with a spare section that we fortunately had with us.

The next day at 0830 the wind suddenly came up strong out of the *west!* The seas in the bay started to break, and our anchorage and access to the open sea became dangerous.

So, I made a stupid (in retrospect) decision. I decided to work our way around a point of a reef between the main island and a projection of a reef from an islet called Inyeug. Here we hoped to find protection from the breaking sea. The British chart from a survey made in *1853* (the most recent chart available) showed a seven-fathom passage between these reefs.

In maneuvering around coral reefs, I am aloft in the mizzen ratlines—about fifteen feet up from the deck. From there, with Polaroid glasses, I can see the ugly brown discoloration that signifies submerged coral heads. I can then con Shirl with steering directions—"Come left five degrees. Come right ten degrees"—while she concentrates on the compass and the depth finder.

With the breaking seas churning the water on either side of us, we slowly proceeded between the clearly visible reefs. The fathometer, shooting its signal thirty degrees ahead of us, indicated the charted seven fathoms—forty-two feet. Suddenly, the fathometer went to *four* feet!

As I shouted "Reverse" to Shirl, we struck an invisible, submerged coral head. With a sickening, grinding, tearing, rending crash, the *Morning Star* impaled herself and listed over to port.

By the time I got down from the ratlines and to the controls, Shirl had full power astern. The seas were lifting us from astern and dropping our twenty tons with a pounding thud onto the sharp coral. It looked as though our beloved little ship, which had safely transported us one-third of the way around the world, was finished. She was listing heavily to port, and water was pouring in below.

We couldn't back her off, and there was a visible reef close to starboard, so on a purely instinctual hunch I throttled full power forward with the rudder hard to port—the direction in which she was lying. With the seas lifting us from astern, we literally wrapped her around the coral head, and with more tearing and rending noises, we spun free, heading back into the bay.

With the electric and engine-driven pumps going, and with the water level below ominously rising, we searched for sand upon which to beach her. But there was no sand not fronted by coral, and we were running out of time. The only way to save the boat was to reanchor, despite the rough seas pounding into the pass. So we maneuvered into seventeen feet of water under our keel, getting a little protection in the lee of Inyeug. Here, if she sank, we could easily swim ashore and possibly even salvage her later.

As soon as the anchor with 300 feet of chain went down, I free-dove with mask and snorkel and a handful of pillows and towels. The water was gushing into the boat right behind the main fuel tank on the port side, so quick access from within was impossible. I rammed the pillows and towels into the hull where one plank was stove in and another had a depression fracture. As I surfaced and kept free-diving with more bunched-up rags, Shirl had miraculously dragged out of our disorganized storage system the sheet lead, scuba gear, caulking gear, and roofing nails.

The stove-in plank was just above the garboards—a rather awkward place to punch a hole in a boat. As the pumps kept working and the pressure of the water helped to compact the mass of material I had stuffed into the hole, the water coming into the boat slowed to a small stream that could be easily handled by the pumps.

By this time, I had the scuba gear on, sheet lead patches cut, and had punched the roofing nails into the sheet lead and wound them with caulking cotton laced with underwater epoxy putty. I rigged a hammer to my wrist with a lanyard and jumped into the sea. Shirl then handed me all of the material, and with the hammer in one hand and the sheet lead in the other, I sank to the level of the holes. The hull was pitching into the seas breaking into the bay, so it was a bit difficult to lie on my back, bashing away at the roofing nails with the hammer while molding the sheet lead over the hole. The lead was very malleable and very effective. Once the patches were in place, I could get the crook of my arm around the pitching keel and with more accuracy pound the roofing nails into the hull. I had worked, along with everything else, a mixture of white lead and tallow into the cloth-stuffed hole. Every time the hammer struck, the white lead would send out a cloud that would obscure my mask. Then the hammer came off my wrist, and I watched in some dismay as it spiraled to the bottom. So, down I had to go to get it.

The leaks were now down to a mere trickle. By then it was noon. The wind had backed into the southwest, which was a bit of luck. Three natives came paddling out. They had seen the whole event. They had watched us go on the reef and get her off the reef. Only now did they come out with fruit and offers to help. In some of these places, when a shipwreck occurs, it is considered fair game, and the natives will strip a yacht bare right before the owner's eyes. This happened to a yacht we knew at Sumbawa, Indonesia.

But these three New Hebrideans were all smiles now. I explained the problem. That if the patches didn't hold, I would like to know of a place where I could beach the boat on sand. They pointed to a place near their village. So we weighed anchor and followed them as they paddled their dugout in front of us to an opening in the reef with a clear sand channel.

Then they took me ashore and *gave* to me—wouldn't let me pay for—a piece of three-eighths-inch plywood that they had salvaged from the famous South Sea Island schooner *Tiare Taporo*, wrecked on the Aneityum reef a few years ago.

Back to the *Morning Star* we went with this prize. I sawed the plywood into patches about twelve by twenty-four inches in size. Then over the side again with the scuba gear. With these plywood patches nailed over the sheet lead with bronze serrated boat nails and imbedded in underwater epoxy, we felt that we could safely travel the 180 miles to Vila.

The next morning the wind was out of the northwest, so we sailed away from Aneityum. We had been extremely lucky, and were grateful that we weren't leaving the *Morning Star* to bleach her bones on the reef. There is a saying among professional seamen in this part of the world. "Until you have been on a reef at least twice, you are not a real seaman." At that moment, we were exquisitely uninterested in qualifying for this dubious distinction.

With the wind out of the northwest, I didn't want land in my lee, so we sailed up the east coast of Tana Island, right under a live volcano belching and smoking and sending volcanic ash with the wind far out to sea.

As night fell, the wind switched into the east, so we sailed up the west coast of Erromango Island, where we would have an offshore current if the wind and engine quit. The next dawn, there was Pango Point, Efate Island, right where it belonged, thanks to a Venus and Port Vila RDF fix.

It was a glorious Sunday morning—balmy, breezy, and sunny—as we sailed into the lovely harbor at Port Vila with the Stars and Stripes fluttering from our stern, the British flag under one spreader, and the French flag and our Q flag under the other. You choose in this way which jurisdiction you prefer to clear through and be under in the New Hebrides. We preferred the French for a variety of reasons.

On the way up from New Zealand, I had been in contact with a French ham in Vila—Jacques Sapir. What a great break for us! Jacques owns a shipping company and the one and only "slipway" in Vila. He and his wife, Robin, met us as we sailed in; had us to their home for showers and a meal and over the weeks that followed became two of the best friends we had made in our cruising life.

Jacques had arranged clearance in with the French on Sunday and had everything organized for me. We examined his decrepit, worm-eaten marine railway to assess its ability to haul the *Morning Star's* estimated twenty tons of deadweight. Yachts can be and are wrecked on slipways, too. Jacques left it up to me. I weighed these options.

We haul tomorrow at the highest tide of the month, or we sail almost two hundred miles to Espiritu Santo, where there is a slipway but dubiously qualified shipwrights. More open sea with a patched-up stove hull. What would a storm do to those patches? Next option? Sail to Tulagi in the Solomons—

nine hundred miles away, good haul-out facilities and ship-wrights. I decided to risk hauling on Jacques's slipway the next morning.

At daylight, Jacques and I were measuring everything. With a crew of natives, we beefed up the worm-eaten sleepers with sections of railroad tracks and lowered the slipway into the water. Because of broken railway wheels, it derailed. We strained to get it back on the track before the tide fell, and finally, with the aid of a fork lift, the slipway was in the water and ready to embrace the *Morning Star*. We drove the boat onto the slipway with six inches to spare under the keel, and, due to Jacques's great skill, got her safely out of the water.

Shirl and I excitedly surveyed the underwater patch job. I had to remove the patches with a crowbar! Except for the fact that the teredo worms would have devoured the plywood, the patches would have endured all the way around the world.

There were no shipwrights in Vila to replank the boat, so I got on the ham radio and located the yacht *Kraka*, owned by a Dane named Lars, whom I had met in Tahiti and again in New Zealand. *Kraka* was in Nouméa. Lars had built his strip-planked yacht in Denmark with his own two hands and was a highly skilled shipwright. He grabbed his tools and flew over to Vila.

We replanked her with vasa wood—tough, oily, rotproof, and wormproof—a Solomon Island cousin of the teak in the rest of the boat's 1 1/4-inch planking. In one week we were back in the water in as-good-as-new condition.

After all of this—the rescue of *Hau Moana*, the northward passage from New Zealand, near shipwreck—I said to Shirl, "Just think, grandmother, you could be home in a rocking chair." Her answer? "No way." I just looked at her and said, "Incredible."

CHAPTER SEVENTEEN

SHARK WORSHIPERS AND THE REEF AT FALAMBULO

⚓ On June 8, we reluctantly left the New Hebrides with a course laid off for Port Moresby, Papua New Guinea, lying fourteen hundred miles to the west. The winds were southeast, ten to fifteen knots, the weather clear—ideal trade-wind sailing.

As we entered the Coral Sea, a lightning storm put on a spectacular display all around us. We have a lightning rod at the masthead, but every time we have chain lightning in the vicinity, we keep our fingers crossed, for lightning has been known to strike the tall mast of a sailing vessel at sea.

On the fourth day out, the winds came up to thirty knots out of the south-southeast. The seas rose and one wave swept our taffrail section, tearing loose the fifteen-foot-long dan buoy man-overboard pole, snapping the fiberglass pole like a match and carrying it overboard.

For months, we had been vacillating about whether or not to go to the Solomon Islands. Our course to Port Moresby put us then 310 miles south of Guadalcanal. The seas were rough and confused, and several were breaking into the cockpit, so we decided to turn north, run with the wind off our quarter, and head for Guadalcanal.

Sailing through the area where the Battle of the Coral Sea was waged, I thought of the thousands of American boys whose lives were lost in these waters. It was this battle, fought by the Americans against a large Japanese task force, that saved New Zealand and Australia from Japanese conquest. In Australia, they commemorate the day of this battle as a national holiday.

In overcast conditions, we sailed past Indispensable Reefs, the islands of Bellona and Rennell, and on June 4 sighted the ominous, cloud-enshrouded tip of Guadalcanal. Between rain squalls, we groped our way into Wanderer Bay on the southwest tip of the island. Natives by the dozens came out in their dugouts to welcome "Joe"—the name they give all Americans. Here on Guadalcanal, the chief topic of conversation is still World War II. These Solomon Islanders not only remember the Americans here, but they remember us with affection—a rare thing nowadays.

The next day we worked our way around the west and north coasts of the island, past Savo Island to Honiara at Point Cruz on Guadalcanal. Here we entered and were slapped with a $100 "light fee," concocted by a yacht-hating, Yank-baiting, petty little British customs officer, John Green. We thought how bizarre it would seem to many of our friends who fought and died here that one day, Americans would have to *pay* to come to this island, the only place in the world where such a "fee" is levied against yachts.

We cruised Guadalcanal and the Solomons for six weeks. Today, the import of the Battle of Guadalcanal has faded from memory, but this campaign was one of major importance. Here the Japanese suffered their first defeat, and Guadalcanal marked the first ebbing of the tide of fortune, which had been running in their favor since Pearl Harbor. Japanese Rear Admiral Tanaka wrote after the war, "There is no question that Japan's doom was sealed with the closing of the struggle for Guadalcanal." Admiral Mitsumaso Yonai, Japan's naval minister, commented, "When we had to retreat from Guadalcanal, taking the whole situation, I feel that there was no further chance of success." And when, after the Japanese surrender,

Wrecked war plane on Guadalcanal

an interrogator asked Admiral Kurita, "At what stage of the war did you feel that the balance had swung against you?" Kurita simply answered, "Guadalcanal."

During the time Shirl and I roamed the island of Guadalcanal and sailed back and forth across the Slot and Ironbottom Sound, the historic battles of Bloody Ridge, Cape Esperance, and Savo Island came back to our minds. It was hard to believe in this beautiful setting that just a few years ago incredible violence took place here. The savagery of the night naval engagements off Savo Island was beyond imagination. In one night the Americans suffered the loss of three cruisers. Two additional cruisers—one American and one Australian—were severely damaged.

After all of this, today the Japanese have a fish cannery at Tulagi, and their fishing boats illegally poach in Solomon Islands waters. Their products dominate the import scene in the Solomons. It makes one wonder who really won the war.

The war hadn't touched primitive Malaita, so we decided to sail from Florida Island north to Malaita to see what these people were like. Our studies had indicated that the British always had problems with the Malaitans, and the natives of the other Solomon Islands fear these people. For centuries, the tribes in the Solomons and on Malaita have been feuding, killing, head-hunting, and warring with one another. They say to the missionaries, "We are grateful to you because the most important thing you brought us was peace."

To protect themselves against attack from their hereditary enemies who live in the highlands of Malaita, the lagoon people, over the centuries, built a series of artificial islands on the outer fringe of Langa Langa Lagoon. These islands are built of coral blocks. The people subsist on fish and coconuts, and they trade and barter with the mainland Malaitans.

Their principal activity is the making of shell money. The men dive for the shells, and the women string them into intricate patterns with established denominations and a set value throughout the Solomons and Papua New Guinea. Shell money is the medium of exchange for the purchase of brides, a centuries-old custom, and for many other transactions. Shell money and its "minting," or manufacture, are the chief sources of international hard currency for the tribe of pagan shark worshipers living on Laulasi Island off Malaita. The shell money in Malaita and Papua New Guinea bears a distinct and direct relationship to the rates of exchange of Australian dollars, and as worldwide inflation set in, the price of brides became so prohibitive as to cause the Australians to attempt to influence these primitive tribes to abandon this curious tradition. Many young men simply could no longer afford to buy a bride.

These people swim and dive with sharks in the vicinity and worship them as their ancestors reincarnated. The hill tribes are afraid of the water, sharks, and all of the other evils of the sea; so they do not know how to operate a canoe or swim; thus affording the lagoon people a moat of protection between them and their enemies.

All of this intrigued Shirl and me, so we sailed into Langa Langa Lagoon and dropped anchor off Laulasi Island on July 20. We went ashore, met the chief—Bosikoru—circulated among the half-naked, tattooed natives in their village, took pictures, gave handouts to the kids, and, in general, seemed to be getting along with them without any problems.

We left Laulasi after a couple of days and visited the dedicated missionary staff at Mbuma mission, south of Laulasi. After a few days at Mbuma, we decided to stop off again at Laulasi to see Chief Bosikoru. This time, as we anchored, we were met by a menacing native in a dugout canoe who demanded money from us. He was drunk on methylated alcohol, which the Chinese sell to the natives. I finally got rid of him, and Bosikoru came out to apologize to us and explain that this man was a "problem" with his methyl-spirits drinking. Bosikoru told us that some of his people go blind from drinking methyl alcohol.

We went ashore to Laulasi village later in the day. This time we were asked for money to take pictures of the sacred skulls in their skull houses, so we paid them. But out of nowhere came two ugly-looking thugs whom we hadn't seen at Laulasi during our prior visit.

They demanded more money from us, and I told them we would leave their island, but that I wouldn't pay them. From the British days, they still refer to the "white skin" man as "mahstah," and they don't know just how far they can push him as yet. But they are learning fast. I walked over to Chief Bosikoru with these two hoodlums close on my heels. But Bosikoru was intimidated by them and had nothing to say. He was genuinely afraid of them.

I rounded up Shirl, whom they called "missy," and we literally backed off the island into our dinghy with the "Malaita Mafia," as we later learned they were called, glowering threats at "mahstah" all the way. Before there was a chance for them to put any more ideas together, we had raised the anchor and were around the point out of sight of Laulasi, headed back to Mbuma.

We were advised *not* to report this to the police in Honiara because of fear of reprisal against us or the boat in Honiara Harbor. The Malaitans have *One-Tok* ("relatives") in the police, and they would be made instantly aware of our complaint. By this time, we decided that we had "had" Malaita and would leave, going north in the lagoon to Malaita's principal village, Auki.

Normally, we try never to move in coral-infested waters until the sun is well up, and there is a ripple on the water. But I had a Solomon Island's Marine Department Chart that I had bought in Honiara, and it showed that the channels through the reefs were well marked with numbered beacons—diamond- and square-shaped—denoting starboard and port hand marks.

We left Mbuma at daylight, working our way carefully through the marked channel. We passed Laulasi, but gave it a wide berth to port. Just two miles north of Laulasi, still in the lagoon, and in the marked channel, we went between the indicated marks at a coral village called Falambulu, headed directly toward the next set of marks, and struck a clifflike coral reef squarely in the middle of the marked channel! We had done it again! This time there was no hope of getting her off, as it was one hour after high tide and the water was going out the pass fast.

Dozens of natives came pouring out in dugouts from Falambulu and other islands in the area. As the dugouts approached and the *Morning Star* began to list, I felt utterly defeated. I put my head down on my arms and said to Shirl, "We have lost her this time, but I can't let these people see me like this." She touched me on the shoulder and said, "Come on, honey, you will think of some way to save the boat." Just a little touch. A little support. A little expression of confidence. That was all that I needed to galvanize me into action!

One big guy was obviously a leader, so I took him aside. First, I told him about our experience at Laulasi. He said, "Laulasi people, very bad. They pagans. We Christians—Melanesian church." He told me that two months ago a government ship had gone on this same reef, while following the channel marks, and six months before that, a Chinese trading vessel had also done the same thing, following the same stupid chart.

Now what to do? The tide was going out, but *Morning Star* was still standing upright on her keel. I told him that if he and his men helped me, I would pay them each five dollars Australian and him ten dollars. This was more money than they could earn in a week, so he cheerfully and enthusiastically agreed.

First, I told him I wanted his best diver to go down deep in the pass and set an anchor imbedded in the coral. From this anchor, I led a line to a bridle I rigged at the masthead. Then I rigged anchors out from the bridle to the port side, and two more from the bow and from the stern. The trick was going to be to prevent *Morning Star* from falling over onto the sharp coral when the tide was way out. The chief told me that the reef dried out at low tide.

I then asked him to get me all the logs he could scare up. Within thirty minutes, out of nowhere came dugouts with coconut logs, which we then embedded in the coral and wedged against the hull. They even brought half coconut shells into which were placed the butt ends of the logs to protect the hull where they were wedged against it.

Next we lashed the tires and cushions that we had aboard, along with the two-by-six planks that we carry, to the coral heads projecting up on both sides of the hull. As the water receded, I could see how incredibly lucky we had been. We had driven our twenty-ton boat squarely onto this cliff of a reef, passing neatly between upraised pointed coral heads on either side of us. It was as though we had driven it onto a slipway.

Everything was fine if only the wind and the seas would remain calm. The next high tide was at 1800, just before dark. The boat was crawling with natives—men, women, and children. It was pouring rain and the skies were black with ominous peals of thunder rolling over the spectacle. Just then, the anchor from the masthead broke loose from the coral and the boat sagged over, against the coconut logs. With two men on each log adjusting them as necessary, we kept the boat from falling all the way onto her side. The natives in the water were squatting down below the surface to get protection from the cold rain.

With the boat canted over at thirty degrees, Shirl had managed to prepare hot coffee and chocolate bars for everyone involved—served in shifts. The natives were friendly, laughing, and indispensably helpful. They wanted to stay on the boat until 0500 the next morning, stating that the next high tide, due at 1800, would not be high enough to float *Morning Star* free. But I wanted to make every effort to get her off before dark because if the wind shifted and the seas came into the pass, there would be no hope whatsoever. She would break up for sure.

Leaving Shirl and the chief in charge, I scrounged a dugout with a fast outboard and loaded it with gasoline I had on deck. Then two natives and I took off for the twelve-mile round trip to Mbuma Mission. I had seen a mission boat there and was going to try to recruit it to pull us off at dusk. When we got to Mbuma, the missionaries told me that the boat's engine was disabled, but that an interisland ship was due in the lagoon at 1600.

After borrowing some large iron picks and bars, we made the trip back to Falambulu. The natives took the bars and chopped and picked away at the granitelike coral surrounding the *Morning Star*.

As the afternoon wore on, the wavelets started to slap against the hull. The tide was coming in! Gradually, ever so slowly, the *Morning Star* began to straighten up. We took all of the chain out of the boat and lightened her in every way, short of pumping out her fuel tanks and water tanks. I was saving this last procedure until I was certain that there was no way to get her off the reef. Much to the derision of fellow yachtsmen, we carry seven anchors, and six of them were in use as we struggled to save the boat.

At 1400, the interisland ship had not appeared. At 1700—one hour before high tide, a small interlagoon cargo-passenger vessel came by. I had given up on the ship the missionaries had thought might help, so I got word to the skipper of the passing vessel that I would pay him twenty dollars Australian if he tried to pull us off and *if we succeeded.*

In excited Pidgin English, he agreed. As the tide slowly started to reach its maximum height, the little 155-h.p. vessel strained and pulled a single line out our stern, then double one-inch nylon lines crossed. He jockeyed back and forth for over an hour with his passengers enjoying the show and not at all worried about their interrupted schedule.

It was now 1815 and dusk was falling over Langa Langa Lagoon. The natives thought we might get one more inch of water before slack. At 1830 with full power astern and the native boat churning up a mighty wave, the *Morning Star* scraped free, and in minutes we were safely anchored in front of Falambulu village.

We handed out clothing, dishes, and gifts of all sorts, and promised that we would spend the next morning in the village. With that, the natives all boarded the dozen or so dugouts around our boat and paddled off into the darkness. At that moment, our love for these people was overwhelming. They had so cheerfully spent ten hours working with us in this crisis of the day. They had enjoyed every moment of the episode as a major event in their lives. We learned a lot about patience, fortitude, and laughing acceptance from the simple Malaitans of Falambulu.

The next morning, we rowed in and had to visit each hut. We gave them *Morning Star* T-shirts, which they cherished and wore with great pride. At noon, we hoisted anchor and, with misty eyes, waved good-bye to these kindly, primitive people as we made our way back to Mbuma Mission.

At Mbuma, we hauled the boat on their mission-boat slipway, the best, most carefully engineered haul-out we have ever had any place in the world. Because of the tide, we had to go onto the slipway at 2200 at night. At 2100 it was pouring rain. High tide was due in one hour. No lights appeared on the shore, so I rowed in through the darkness to try to find Brother Stan, one of the missionaries there.

Floundering through the jungle with a flashlight, I stumbled onto a coterie of hill people huddled under a tree. They had just walked into the mission station with a freshly killed crocodile skin to sell. These fierce-looking people were the most primitive in appearance and manner of any natives we had ever seen. Brother Stan was well aware of what the tide was doing, and promptly at 2200, flashlights and lanterns appeared, and a crew of ten or so natives dove repeatedly to make sure that we were well chocked on the cradle.

The next morning, we discovered that we had sustained no substantive damage. Incredibly, the propeller, rudder, and hull were unscratched. Only a few gouges in the keel and deadwood had to be epoxied, and we were back in the water by late afternoon. By now, we had earned the doubtful distinction of being "real seamen" by having been on at least two reefs.

When we returned to Honiara, we were astonished to find tied to the wharf a large white Soviet cruise liner with a load of Australian and New Zealand passengers. As we circulated among the passengers, we noted the Soviet officers and seamen distributing packets of printed material in English extolling the virtues of Marxism and Leninism to the black citizens of the Solomon Islands.

The Solomons were scheduled to gain independence from the British within the year. As elsewhere in the world, the vacuum caused by the collapse of the British Empire and European colonialism was being filled inexorably by the new imperialists—the Russians.

CHAPTER EIGHTEEN

BALI—THE LAND
OF 1,000 TEMPLES

While in the Solomons, we had been tormented with indecision whether to remain another year in the western Pacific or whether to make the Indian Ocean crossing to South Africa in 1977. It was getting late in the season to cross the Indian Ocean, so we finally decided to leave the Solomons on July 30. We would head for Port Moresby, New Guinea, Thursday Island, Christmas Island, Cocos Islands, Mauritius, and arrive in Durban by November 1—just before the typhoon season off Madagascar was due to begin.

From Honiara, Guadalcanal, through the Coral Sea, around the Louisiade Archipelago, we ran into the worst weather we had experienced in years. With solid overcast precluding celestial sights, we operated on dead reckoning alone. Strong wind warnings came out of Thursday Island. The RDF at Port Moresby had broken down. The log is replete with entries: "Shipped big sea over boat. Squalls, thunderstorms, heavy rain, 40 knot SSE winds. Reefed down. Dropped main. Mizzen and reefed staysail only. Hove to. Riding out storm for 16 hours." Off the coast of Papua New Guinea, we had several birds—gannets and other seabirds—land on the boat. Exhausted by the strong winds, they sought shelter with us.

This is the first time in all of our years at sea that we have had this happen.

With black/white racial problems developing in Papua New Guinea, we decided to bypass Port Moresby altogether and continue straight for Bramble Cay and the Bligh entrance to the Great Northeast Channel of Torres Strait ... This is the route Captain Bligh took in his open-boat voyage following the mutiny on the *Bounty*, and he named many of the Torres Strait islands during this epic voyage.

When the storm blew out, celestial sights revealed that a northwest-setting current had put us thirty-six miles ahead of our log and dead reckoning position. I had intended to pick up the light on Bramble Cay, a small spit of sand surrounded by a reef, at 0400 the next morning. Now a fast snapshot of the fuzzy sun at twenty degrees put Bramble dead ahead of us three miles. We couldn't see it on radar, but I told Shirl it *had* to be right ahead of us. Just then, she saw the thin spire of the light-tower, right off our bow.

Just at dusk, we skirted Bramble with the wind steady at thirty-five knots, gusting to forty. It was too wild to try to anchor, so I had three equally hazardous choices: proceed until 2300 to Daru, Papua New Guinea, where I could pick up a light—maybe; do a 180-degree turn and go back out into the rough Gulf of Papua, littered with huge logs from the Fly River, and heave to all night; or turn down Torres Strait and try to pick up reef-encircled Stephens Islet on radar and fathometer.

Thursday Island radio continued to report strong wind warnings. I chose the last course of action, and when I told Shirl, her raised eyebrows caused me to wonder a bit.

Shirl steered, huddled in her oilskins, with seas breaking over her. I had my eyes glued to the radar screen below. By 2300 I had the pimple of land surrounded by a reef called Stephens Islet on the screen. There was another prominent target, a *ship* at anchor sheltering until dawn in the lee of Stephens.

Crawling toward the radar target sitting in the middle of the submerged reef, Shirl was to yell when the fathometer registered thirty feet. Inching toward the reef, she screamed,

"Twenty feet!" "Reverse!" I ordered. Down went the anchor, and we pitched behind this reef throughout the rest of the night. In the morning, we found a row of uncharted rocks one hundred feet off our bow, so we had stopped just in time.

We day-sailed the rest of the way through the reef-strewn Torres Strait—a narrow passage between Australia and Papua New Guinea. On August 9, we arrived at Thursday Island, a pearl-diving center, where we provisioned, fueled, and watered.

On August 13, we left Horn Island, Australia, bound for Christmas Island, South Indian Ocean. Sailing dead before the wind in the Arafura Sea, we had one gorgeous day after another: southeast winds, fifteen knots; no squalls—not even a rain shower. Day after day, we ran across the Gulf of Carpentaria, Australia, out of the Arafura Sea, into the Timor Sea.

Log Entry, August 15: "Best first three days at sea ever. 35 fathoms. Cool breezes. Clear starlit night. Latitude 9° 57′ South, Longitude, 135° East, 132 mile run. This is trade-wind sailing at last. Caught large barracuda, but shark bit him off right behind gills before I could land him."

Then, 175 miles from Timor, 890 miles out from Thursday Island, the generator exhaust pipe broke, and the autopilot quit—both at the same time. We hove to all night, and the next morning I had the exhaust pipe silver-soldered together and the autopilot repaired. On the tenth day out from Thursday Island, we entered the Indian Ocean, standing well off from war-wracked Timor and fifteen miles south of Roti.

One evening, Shirl and I were having dinner below when we heard a bumping, scraping noise on the hull. Startled, we jumped up as another grating noise echoed through the hull. We both thought, "It's got to be a whale!" We saw nothing, but I started the engine to frighten any whales in the vicinity. Several sailing vessels have been sunk by whales in recent years, and we wanted no part of a romance between *Morning Star* and a whale equally her size.

The next morning on our radio schedule, our faithful friend and daily ham radio contact, Bud Alvernaz, in distant San Jose, California, asked me if I had felt the large earthquake that had struck Sumba Island, Indonesia. We were just south of Sumba in 2,700 fathoms (16,200 feet) when it struck, so we felt no tidal-wave effect. However, we wondered later if the strange noises heard through the hull could have been related to this giant quake.

We had been getting continuous progress reports about Shirley's mother from Bud. On August 24, Shirley's sister reported that her mother was critically ill. We were 280 miles south of Bali, Indonesia, and 800 miles from Christmas Island. Bali has an international airport. We could abort our Indian Ocean crossing in 1977, head north for Bali, and fly home so that Shirl could visit her mother. But we had no visas for Bali, and the Indonesian officials were notoriously unpleasant about this. We could continue on to Africa and fly home from Durban in November.

The next morning at 0545, I obtained a perfect four-star fix on Venus, Sirius, Canopus, and Capella. Just then, two beautiful snow white tropical bosun birds flew at our masthead, then headed off north toward Bali. They returned and did the same thing again and again. I felt that these frantic birds were trying to tell me something.

I changed course to 342 degrees, awakened Shirl to relieve me, and told her that we were going to Bali and fly home from there. A few minutes *later*, I had my scheduled radio talk with Bud, and he told us that Shirley's sister had called to ask that we try to get home. This was *after* we had changed course.

On August 26, we were in the rough waters of Lombok Strait, heading for Benoa Harbor, Bali. While working against the strong current pouring out of Lombok, the alternator bearings froze and burned up the water-pump belt. As Shirl tacked the boat off the reefs at Nusa Dua, I replaced the alternator and got the engine going in time to enter the tricky channel at Benoa Harbor. Behind us lay a thirty-two-hundred-mile passage, completed in twenty-seven days.

We overcame all the visa problems; lined up a trustworthy custodian for the boat; set up a double anchor mooring; scheduled a twenty-three-hour flight from Bali to Guam, Honolulu, and Los Angeles; and on September 9 were winging our way

back to California. Shirl's one-month visit with her mother was
a tonic, and her health improved.

Before leaving Bali, we had recruited two woodcarvers from
Mas village. They had been living on the boat, working full
time—seven days a week—while we were gone. When we
returned, we were delighted with the intricate, exquisite carvings of Balinese legends that adorned the *Morning Star's* interior. We had come to Bali quite by accident and were completely enthralled with the fascinatingly different culture we
found there, which has remained relatively intact throughout
the centuries.

Indonesia, with its 130 million people, is the fifth most pop-
ulous nation in the world. On the small island of Bali alone,
there are 2.5 million people. Like most Indonesians, the
Balinese are an evolutionary mixture of races. In the main,
they are descendents of the Malayo-Polynesians, ancient deni-
zens of the three thousand islands comprising the archipelago.
Along with their eastern Javanese ancestors, Indonesians have
traces of Indian, Chinese, Polynesian, and Melanesian blood,
resulting in a variety of features among the Balinese. By western standards, the Balinese are a most attractive race.

The Balinese-Hindu religion dominates the daily lives of
these people. Eighty percent are adherents to this religion on
this island of one thousand temples. Another 10 percent are
Muslims, and the balance are Buddhists and Christians. Every
action of the day is preceded by an offering to their god or
gods. Every rice paddy, every home, has a small minitemple
for the offering of incense and floral gifts. Lives are centered
on the dictates of a power greater than themselves. Woven
throughout this tapestry is the central thread of all ancient civilizations—the family.

Every family event is an occasion for celebration. The end of
the first three months of a child's life is a festive event, followed by another family gathering at the end of six months of
life, when the child's feet are allowed to touch the ground for
the first time. Prior to this, it is always carried when awake by
a parent, grandparent, brother, or sister. Betrothals, weddings,
funerals, cremations—all are occasions for feasts, ceremonies,

pageantry, and a reunification of the family. A man's riches are measured in terms of the number of children he has, children who will venerate and care for him in his old age. The aged are functional and needed—an essential part of the fabric of the family. They are not put on the back burner as their "productivity" declines.

The wood-carvers continued work on the boat while Shirl and I lived in a tropical thatch-roofed bungalow on Sanur Beach. The white-sand beach began at the stone wall surrounding our courtyard and unfolded down to the sea inside the barrier reef.

Each morning during breakfast, we looked at a scene of breathtaking beauty as the sun rose over the Indian Ocean. The seas, driven by the southeast monsoon, geysered up on the reef with the sound of distant thunder. Inside the reef, the Balinese prahus (outrigger-dugout canoes) with their spectacularly colorful lateen-rigged sails on bamboo masts and booms ghosted along over the calm water. Balinese fishermen waded in groups, spreading their nets to gather their fish needs of the day. We continued to marvel at the industriousness and infinite patience of these people. Each day begins and ends pretty much as did the day before and the days before that, centuries ago.

As we toured all of Bali, we observed the people stooping from the waist down in the centuries-old terraced rice paddies, wading in mud to implant or harvest each precious shoot of rice. They work ten hours a day—0500 to 1200—two hours to rest in the thatched shelters dotting every field—then another three hours until 1700, as the evening begins. Everyone—men, women, children—works at some communally assigned task. The women, right along with the men, are engaged in manual labors of all descriptions—construction work, building roads and irrigation dikes, animal tending, fetching heavy containers of water and river-bottom mud in pails and baskets atop their heads. Bali was far and away the most interesting and vastly different place we had ever visited.

It was now late October. There was no way we could risk the Indian Ocean crossing at this time of year. The typhoons off Madagascar and the cyclones in the Bay of Bengal would tear us to pieces. So, the only place to sit out the typhoon season was in Singapore, lying one thousand miles north of Bali. On October 27, we sailed from Bali with Benoa villagers escorting us out the pass in their sailing canoes.

We proceeded through Bali Strait to Pang Pang, Java, then to Djangkar, Java. We anchored there and watched the spectacle of hundreds of picturesque sailing vessels with their lateen rigs and colorful figureheads returning to their village with their catch at dusk. A Javanese fisherman luffed up alongside of us, and we bought a ten-pound tuna from him for eighty cents. Late into the night and long before dawn, we listened to the wailing chants of the Muslim worshipers praying to their god of Islam.

Before we left Bali, the police had warned us about piracy in the Java Sea and cautioned us about stopping at Madura. They said, "They kill you with knives." But anchored all night in an open roadstead off Madura, we stood watches and had no unwelcome visitors.

As we cruised along the coasts of Java and Madura, we learned a lot about this fascinating part of the world. There are 80 million people on Java and Madura in an area of one hundred thirty thousand square kilometers, representing a density of more than 600 per square kilometer, which is almost twice that of Holland and England, the most densely populated countries in Europe, and more than twice that of Japan. There are more than 5 million people in Jakarta, and over a million each in Bandung and Surabaya. Eighty-five percent of Java's enormous population lives in rural areas, and around 70 percent is engaged in agriculture.

When Sir Francis Drake sailed the *Golden Hind* to Java in 1580, he logged, "The Javans were sociable, full of vivacity and beyond description, happy. They were likewise hospitable to strangers." Although there are exceptions, these words generally still apply to the Javanese of today. All white men here are called *belanda*, which originally meant "Hollander" when the Dutch controlled the then "Dutch East Indies," but the term now applies to all white men.

As in Bali, there are dozens of ancient temples and monuments, most of them older than Europe's great cathedrals, all of them completed long before the first colonists set foot on North American soil.

Leaving Madura at dawn, with all of the ominous warnings about piracy in this part of the world well imbedded in our consciousness, our Java Sea passage to Singapore began.

CHAPTER NINETEEN

PIRATES

⚓ The word *pirate* conjures up in the mind swashbuckling romance of novels and Hollywood, eye-patched cutlass-wielding duelists, captives walking the plank, three-masted galleons, Captain Kidd, and Jolly Rogers. But Webster simply defines a pirate as "one who robs or commits illegal violence at sea or on the shores of the sea."

Today, worldwide lawlessness—international terrorism, aircraft hijacking, or the everyday assaults, murders, robberies, and muggings—is commonplace in many of the large cities of the "civilized" world, particularly of America. We are so inured to this criminality that it only rarely attracts more than superficial attention from the media.

Several years ago, a friend of mine, aboard his boat in a marina in Southern California, surrounded by harbor police as well as county and city police, was accosted at night, kidnapped in his boat, taken out into the Santa Barbara Channel, and murdered. The killers were caught when they sold the stolen yacht in Santa Barbara. On other occasions two expensive sailing yachts were hijacked right out of Ala Wai Boat Harbor in Honolulu. One has never been found. The other was later recovered after the hijackers had put the crew adrift. In another tragedy, two friends from Hawaii were murdered while at anchor in paradisical Palmyra Island. Yet, in relating to friends our risks of pirate encounters—particularly in Southeast Asian waters—I invariably encounter either an upraised eyebrow of sheer disbelief or expressions such as "What! Pirates in this day and age? You've got to be joking."

For centuries, piracy and smuggling have been a way of life in the waters off Indonesia, Malaysia, Borneo, Thailand, and in the Java, South China, Sulu, and Celebes Seas, and in the Strait of Malacca. The pirates of this area just happen to find themselves in the twentieth century.

In a bulletin published by the Seven Seas Cruising Association, we read a letter written from Malacca, Malaysia by Peer Tangvald, a veteran Norwegian sailor, tragically describing how pirates in this area of the world had murdered his young wife.

Paraphrasing Peer's description of this horrible event: "We saw a boat steering straight for us with the apparent intention of coming alongside. Lydia [his wife] suggested we shoot a warning shot over them to prevent them from coming any closer. I thought it was too late. Most likely they were just fishermen wanting to trade fish for cigarettes or whiskey, but at worst, should they be pirates, let them take what they want without resistance—our best chance of not being harmed. Lydia went quietly below, but, to my dismay, she reappeared through the forehatch with the gun just as the boat was coming alongside. She shouted to them, raised the weapon quickly, and fired.

"Immediately, they shot from their wheelhouse, and Lydia's bullet-riddled body tumbled backwards into the sea. The man aimed his gun at me, but when he saw my little blond-haired boy clinging to my leg, he didn't shoot. They boarded me, robbed me, and left in a hurry.

"The Malaysian police later told me that there were several hundred attacks in these waters each year. 'They spared you because they love children and felt sorry for the little boy. Lydia's idea of firing a warning shot would have been good from a distance—to leave them a possibility of turning away.

But your idea of no-resistance would only work with less hardened pirates. The hardened ones kill everyone, strip the yacht, then sink it to eliminate all evidence of the crime.'"

In March, 1980, Peer wrote again about a second attack while at anchor in Tunisia in the Mediterranean. This time, he and his crew were severely beaten and robbed while his female companion furiously fought off attempts to rape her.

Excerpts from an Associated Press report of October 17, 1978, state:

> The only thing romantic about modern sea brigands is the area in which they still plunder; old spice routes in the Straits of Malacca between Malaysia and Indonesia, the waters off Borneo. Fishermen, yachts, and even refugees fleeing Communist Indo China are the victims.
>
> Sometimes the sea gangs show a dash of gallantry and send their victims off after filching valuables. But they have also shot innocents down in cold blood or forced them to swim for it on the high seas. . . . Rival gangs clashed in early August in the Straits of Malacca. . . . Fishermen reported seeing at least one headless corpse in the area after the fight in which long spears and other weapons were reportedly used. . . . In March off Sabah in East Malaysia, a boat opened fire and gave chase to a yacht occupied by a German couple and their five year old son. The Germans hauled up a white sheet to surrender . . . later without explanation the pirates fled. The German yachtsman said, " . . . few people in Europe will believe that there are still pirates around."
>
> While the pirates usually attack small craft in remote areas, they have ventured to the doorsteps of the regions' modern cities. . . . Raids occur in Singapore, the world's fourth busiest seaport.

Time magazine on July 31, 1978, reports:

> Few men live to tell tales of the marauding buccaneers who currently infest the sea-lanes of Southeast Asia. . . . Sumatran pirates constantly harass coastal freighters and fishermen in the Straits of Malacca. . . . The greed of the pirates is unbelievable, says a Malaysian official. . . . One ruthless pirate tradition of yore prevails: walking the plank. Of 500 victims attacked by

Jury rig mast on *Hau Moana*

Underwater patched hull

Laulasi, Solomon Islands

High and dry on reef at Falambulu

buccaneers last year, more than 300 drowned. . . . Some pirates have even tried attacking big ocean going ships. . . . Malaysia plans to buy 31 additional patrol boats and four special aircraft for pirate detection.

" . . . Few pirates have been caught so far, and authorities fear that it could take years to find most of them. Unlike the days of Captain Kidd, 1978's pirates do not announce themselves. . . . A police lieutenant lamented last week, "It would be much easier if they still flew the black flag."

When we were in New Zealand, we had been visited by a friend who owned a large tugboat-and-barge operation in Singapore. When we first asked about what he thought of our sailing to Singapore, he told us about the piracy problem in the area. He said, "If I were you, I wouldn't sail through these waters—and if I did, I wouldn't just be armed. I would have a full crew and be *heavily* armed."

Shirl and I, sailing alone in remote corners of the world, are quite vulnerable. We move from place to place on a whim— no sail plan is filed. If we fail to show up at a certain place at a certain time, there will be no one to go out and conduct a search. By the time we are missed, a search would be too late to be helpful. We are on our own. Alone with God.

Sailing up the Java Sea, we kept going night and day, literally slaloming through the small sailing-fishing vessels that would light a dim lantern only when they saw our lights. We would have preferred to run without lights, but because of the dozens of unlit small craft drift-fishing in our path, we had to keep our running lights going. One night, I saw something dimly in the darkness off our starboard quarter. I flipped on our twelve-volt searchlight, and there, silently sailing across our starboard quarter, only seventy-five feet away, was a full-rigged topsail schooner showing no lights.

Each day I checked into the daily amateur radio Maritime Mobile net reciting my latitude and longitude. Gary was an American radio operator who had lived in Tokyo for years. As a regular member of the net, Gary and I had been talking on the radio for the past four years. He had been enormously helpful in expediting shipments of parts from Japan to me in

Tahiti in 1973. As I reported my coordinates one day, Gary excitedly broke in and said, "Hey, Ray, you are right in the middle of a flock of pirates!" He said, "Just a minute, and I'll read to you a story in today's Tokyo English language newspaper." Gary read to me the news account of how five pirate vessels had attacked a *freighter* just north of Jakarta. In response to a Mayday distress call from the captain, Indonesian patrol vessels had sunk four of their boats, killed a number of pirates, and captured seven.

When Gary signed clear, I decided to head toward Borneo with the strategy that our chances of escaping observation would be better north of the shipping lanes in which Gary's pirates were searching for prey. There was no way to tell the good guys from the bad guys, so we kept loaded guns at the ready throughout this passage. An American oil man who had lived in Sumatra for eight years had flatly told us that if we were boarded, they would kill us. So he advised that we fire guns into the water to let it be known that we were armed. The sailing pirates off Indonesia and Borneo are generally armed with only knives and machetes, and the petroleum engineer had said that if they knew that we had semiautomatic weapons, they might leave us alone.

We kept going, dodging fishing stakes and sailing vessels until we came to an uninhabited island named Kebatoe, west of Borneo, where we anchored in a cove and had a solid night's sleep.

Ten days out of Bali, we entered Bangka Strait between Bangka and Sumatra. The haze and smoke from burning rice fields in Sumatra was so dense that visibility was down to one-eighth of a mile. It had been an almost windless passage, and we were low on fuel.

We came to a place called Rede Muntok in Bangka and entered a small harbor which did not appear on our charts. As the eight-foot shallow harbor opened up, we were amazed to see a dozen large Indonesian sailing schooners rafted up. A ragged assortment of people began beckoning us. Screaming, naked kids came swimming out to meet us. The collection of scruffy, rough-looking people clustered on the jetty, along with the general appearance of the place, made us feel that we had blundered into a veritable pirates' lair. We beat a hasty retreat out of the narrow entrance and anchored well offshore.

I rowed the dinghy back into the harbor and encountered a surly Indonesian official. After he had pawed through my papers, I crossed his extended palm with an extorted bribe and arranged to have two drums of fuel brought out to the *Morning Star*. At dusk, as soon as we had pumped the diesel aboard from the Indonesian fishing vessel, we weighed anchor and left this dubious area.

On the eleventh day out, we were cruising along the murky coast of Sumatra, thinking of the elephants, tigers, pythons, water buffalo, and other creatures inhabiting the dense, steaming jungles of this mysterious land. Just at dusk, in dense haze and low visibility, we were heading for an uninhabited anchorage off the coast of Sumatra. Out of the murk ahead of us loomed a full-rigged topsail schooner. It is only in this part of the world that commercial fleets of these big engineless sailing ships still operate. We had seen dozens of these picturesque sailing vessels on this passage—they haul teak logs and general cargo between Sulawesi, Borneo, Celebes, and Java. If we sighted them in time, we always tried to give them a wide berth; again, not knowing what their intentions toward us might be.

But here we were, with Sumatra only one mile to port, and the large schooner close on our starboard side. I was motor sailing in light breezes, trying to get to an anchorage off Sumatra before night fell. Rather than show fear, which could be dangerous, I chose to maintain our course. As we literally paraded past them, I counted through the binoculars sixteen rough-looking, gesticulating men, silently staring at us—no waves—no smiles.

Shirl and I would go below, change hats and shirts, and keep reappearing, to create the impression that there were more people aboard. I instructed Shirl to dress in men's clothing with her hair tucked up into a man's hat. The last thing I wanted them to know was that there was a woman on board.

But, so far their course was unchanged. They were close-reaching in five to eight knots of breeze. Night was coming fast, and they began to disappear from sight. I gradually started to close on the Sumatran coast. Using radar and fathometer, we slowly crept up to the jungle and anchored in fifteen feet of water. I reckoned that there was no legitimate reason for them to come that close to shore.

As I cocked our guns, I felt as if I were in a John Wayne movie. It was now pitch dark and the schooner had disappeared from visual contact. But I was watching them on radar. Suddenly, they radically changed course—heading right for us! Now we began to worry a little. Spotting us, the schooner could anchor, quickly put a longboat over the side, and sixteen of these rough seamen could overwhelm us in minutes. It was small consolation that I could shoot some of them in the process. The radar showed them to be less than a half mile away and closing on us fast.

We hurriedly windlassed in the anchor and powered straight into the wind up the Sumatran coast with no lights showing. Crawling along the dark jungle coast with eight to ten feet flickering on our fathometer, we rounded two points and reanchored in a deep cove one hour and six miles farther north.

The schooner disappeared from the radarscope as we rounded the points of land. I hoped that not finding us, he might scour south down the coast, figuring that we would beat a retreat back to the direction from which we had originally come. Sitting there in the pitch darkness with my eyes glued to the radarscope, I heard only the sounds of the night noises of the jungle. Lacking radar, there was little chance he could find us for hours. He would have to tack endlessly to make the same distance we had made with our motor into the wind.

Two more hours dragged by as I stared at the blank radarscope. Then, a blip—a moving target—appeared from behind the points of land. It was the schooner—now on an offshore tack, four miles out and heading away from the Sumatran coast. He had given up his search for us and must have thought that we had been swallowed by the jungle. After dinner with one dim cabin light burning, no more seaward radar targets appeared, but we took turns sleeping and standing watch through the black, moonless night.

This episode shook both of us. While we felt little apprehension in dealing with the forces of nature, somehow we had more of a sense of foreboding when we felt threatened by crude, primitive, and lawless men.

Armed and ready to ward off pirates

CHAPTER TWENTY

WE ALMOST GIVE UP

In early November, we sailed from Rembang Island, Indonesia, and entered Singapore Strait and the Republic of Singapore. We were astonished at the hundreds of ships—freighters, supertankers, container ships—vessels of all kinds, clustered at anchor over dozens of square miles in Singapore Roads. Singapore! The fourth largest seaport in the world—after Rotterdam, New York, and Yokohama. Singapore! The giant, overflowing cash register of Asia. An independent island republic since 1965, Singapore was once a British colony and briefly a part of Malaysia. With 2 million people—80 percent Chinese—Singapore is a green, clean, fascinating city.

We were boarded by a horde of officials—immigration, customs, health, and police. The fact that a middle-aged American couple had sailed out from California, across the Pacific, and through the Java and South China seas aroused genuine interest in these Singaporean officials, who were quite friendly as they searched our vessel. Numerous questions were asked along the lines, "Weren't you aware of the piracy problems in these waters? Weren't you afraid of pirates?" The newspaper publicity and the police information that they received regarding increasing acts of piracy in the surrounding waters seemed to make them almost obsessively curious about why on earth we would sail our boat to Singapore rather than take a plane or cruise ship to visit their tiny country.

From its skyscrapers towering over ancient back streets buzzing with traffic—Rolls-Royce limousines weaving among rickshaws and trishaws drawn by Chinese coolies—to its canals and rivers cluttered with barges, junks, and sampans, Singapore defies ordinary description.

We had suffered so many failures of the work performed during our unfortunate refit in New Zealand that we placed the *Morning Star* in a commercial shipyard owned by a friend of ours from Hawaii, Bill Conklin. On our arrival in Singapore, Bill and his staff extended to us the most elaborate hospitality that we have ever received anywhere. Bill insisted that we bring the boat to his shipyard, where it was guarded twenty-four hours a day. He loaned us his flat, transported us, and simply overwhelmed us with his kindness.

After the series of misfortunes that had occurred to us in 1977, capped by the pirate scare off Sumatra, we seriously thought about giving up in Singapore and shipping the *Morning Star* home on a freighter, the way she had come to California from Hong Kong, where she had been built in 1968.

While in Singapore, the news was sprinkled with references to pirate activity in the area around us and in our path. Even if we could surmount this problem, the formidable Indian Ocean crossing yawned before us in our imagination. Then, the warnings of the American consul in Singapore concerning the political situation in the Red Sea didn't do much to bolster our faltering courage and determination.

But, as we thought it through—imagined ourselves standing on the wharf at Alameda as a freighter slung our beloved *Morning Star* over the side, boxed in a cradle, with masts drooping on the deck, the thought appalled us with feelings of failure and self-disgust.

I didn't want to give up, but a thread of guilt had been running through my thoughts over the past few years—especially in heavy weather and storms at sea. "Is Shirley out here just to please me? If so, it is wrong of me to involve her any further in this venture. We should quit while we are ahead."

The process of rationalization, leading to surrender, had begun. If not confronted, it could snowball amidst the creature comforts and safety of Singapore. These negative thoughts could trigger impulsive actions on my part. Actions that we could spend the balance of our lifetime regretting. We would be quitters in our own minds. Never having set out to prove anything to anyone, we could not care less what anyone thought about our quitting. But we would care what *we* thought about our quitting. While no one likes a quitter, what is most important is that the quitter doesn't like himself. And even worse than being a quitter is never being a starter.

Shirl put it to me straight. "Honey, I am here because I *want* to be here with you, involved in this adventure of a lifetime. I consider myself lucky to have this chance. Please believe me! Compare our life-style and the adventures that we have had to date to anything we have ever done or will do again. Naturally, I am afraid of the pirate stories and what I have heard about the Indian Ocean; but if you think you can get us through, then God will do the rest."

So there it was. The ball was back in my court.

However, playing doubles with me at the net was God. How could we lose with that combination? But no clouds opened, nor did any messenger from on high descend to assure me that all would be well. While Shirl's confidence in my ultimate abilities was gratifying, it carried with it the same awesome responsibility for someone else's life that is a daily ingredient in the interrelationship of a man-wife crew of two at sea.

It seemed to both of us a question of the maintenance of basic self-respect. As we, along with all human beings, faced the inevitability of our personal mortality—the finiteness of all life on earth—we then simply *had* to carry on. We just could not give up without reckoning with the very real psychological inner discomfort that our lack of determination would inevitably produce in the waning years of our life.

As we talked these things out together, we also realized how the four-year confinement and danger could unduly stress the very best of marriages. Character defects and personality traits not normally exposed come out glaringly under severe stress.

Our childhood backgrounds, the Depression, wartime experiences—had taught us that stress lays bare the best and the worst in us.

Bill Conklin, a professional merchant marine captain, encouraged us to continue our voyage around the world. He said, "You have come so far, it seems a shame to give up now." As Bill surveyed the problems connected with the boat, his jovial "it-ain't-no-big-thing" attitude gave our spirits an enormous lift. Bill owned a three-masted, 100-foot Garden-designed sailing yacht in Hawaii. It seemed strange to us when he said one day, "I only wish that the circumstances of my life permitted me to do what you two are doing."

When we had flown home from Bali, we had both had complete physical examinations. The doctor told us that "whatever you are doing, keep on doing it because it certainly agrees with you both." By all criteria our health is better now than it was five years ago. The maintenance of priceless good health alone is sufficient reason for us to sail on while we have the never-to-be repeated opportunity to do so.

As we were tormented by the demons of the temptation to quit, we analyzed how the last few years had been years of growth and learning. Standing back from our former lives, we had learned to reorder our priorities and values. Plagued by the uncertainties that beset us in this life, we had learned to live each day—twenty-four hours at a time. We had learned not to project too far ahead, not to have overriding anxiety and fears about the morrow. As with all creatures living this fragile, tentative life, for us there may not be a tomorrow. So we were gradually learning to suffer, enjoy, savor, and cope with the circumstances of the moment more deeply. The *"Now"* is what is important. Our sometimes seemingly harsh experiences had imbedded into our consciousness the wisdom of ancient axioms such as "First things first," "One day at a time," and "Live and let live."

With the war between Somalia and Ethiopia raging in the Red Sea, our State Department advised that this would be a precarious place for an American yacht to go. With the Soviets and their East German and Cuban puppets totally in control of

Aden, it would be folly for an American-flag vessel to enter what is now called the People's Republic of Yemen. As we looked ahead, with some apprehension, on the many thousands of miles of open sea still to cross, the sheer magnitude of this undertaking sometimes crushingly came in on us. A Chinese friend in Singapore told us of their ancient axiom, "The longest journey begins with the first step."

We thought that when we had completed our odyssey, we would be more mature and better equipped to live the balance of our lives with a measure of equanimity. With this altered perspective, we believed that we could be of greater service to and be able to offer increased understanding and compassion for our fellow human beings, walking the daily path of life with us. Recently we read someplace that old age can be a state of mind—a self-fulfilling prophecy.

We had analyzed ourselves and our reactions after the reef episodes and the pirate scare and had gained increased self-respect as well as gratification that we had been determined enough to rescue ourselves and *Morning Star* from the perils of the reefs of the New Hebrides and the Solomons.

With all of this introspection and analysis, along with a great deal of prayer, we had an electriclike renewal of resolve and set all thoughts of quitting aside as we looked forward to what new adventures awaited us.

CHAPTER TWENTY-ONE

ACROSS THE INDIAN OCEAN

⚓ The leaden skies over Singapore disgorged sheets of chilling, drenching rain. Two figures huddled in yellow oilskins were slowly rowing through the heavy chop in a small orange dinghy. Barely visible through the blinding rain was the sailing ketch *Morning Star*, straining at her mooring off Changi, the infamous World War II Japanese prison camp.

With last-minute provisions purchased, and our firearms recovered from the Singapore marine police, we were clearing Singapore for the Strait of Malacca, the main seaway used by vessels from Europe and India bound to Malaysian ports and the China Seas. It provides the shortest route for tankers trading between the Persian Gulf and Japan.

The British *Pilot Book* states: "Navigational aids are difficult to maintain and in Indonesian waters are reported to be unreliable. A considerable amount of shipping uses the Strait, and in addition, many local fishing craft with nets may be encountered in this area. Since passage through the Strait entails a run of more than 250 miles, long periods of considerable vigilance are necessary in order to maintain safe standards of navigation."

Despite the ancient superstition "never sail on a Friday," we sailed with the tide from Changi, Singapore, at 1030 on December 30, 1977. In order to do everything possible to avoid any hostile encounters, I had planned to be anchored at an uninhabited island named Pulau Kukup off the Malaysian coast shortly after nightfall. We would have between one and two knots of current to help us all the way the first day.

With heavy rain squalls all around us, we swept around Raffles lighthouse and into Malacca Strait. The police in Singapore had told us that there were pirates in Kukup village, so we gave it a wide berth—barely visible in the rainy murk of approaching dark. Working north of this village until the island of Pulau Kukup was between us and the village, we turned into the lee of the island anchoring off fish stakes in eleven fathoms of water. There was a three-quarter moon due to rise at 2200, so I thought that if we hadn't been seen through the rain from the village, we could escape detection before moonrise. By that time, I figured any self-respecting Malaysian pirate would be ashore drunk. It worked! We had a good night's sleep, although I had first locked all doors and hatches from within and had loaded guns in instant readiness.

As we left this anchorage at predawn, we saw boats pouring out of Kukup village behind our island hideout. We made directly for the center of the strait, where the heavy volume of ships going each way would, I thought, make the presence of pirate vessels in broad daylight unlikely.

We were pushed up the strait with the current, making eighty-two miles in twelve hours. At 1230, a Russian ship, the *Kapitan Dostenko*, bore down on us deliberately, and I had to swerve to avoid him. As the hammer and sickle on his stack went by within feet of us, I was angry enough to salute their bridge with the Communist balled fist. Balled that is, except for one protruding finger. Later in the Indian Ocean and the Gulf of Suez, we were to have this Russian-vessel performance repeated, so we are convinced that it is by design. The bullies of the high seas!

There is no such thing as a private citizen of the Iron Curtain countries taking off in his personal pleasure craft to sail around the world. So we supposed that this conduct of Soviet ships could only be explained by their preformed notion that any yacht had to be from a Western bloc country and was vulnerable fair game. Had we survived being run down, which would have been highly unlikely, to whom would we protest? The Soviet captain could always say it was an accident. They hadn't seen us. Although under international maritime law, a sailing vessel has the right of way, as a pragmatic matter, the final right of way belongs to these mammoth ships. Avoiding shipping is always our problem under the best of circumstances. When a huge freighter or tanker alters course and attempts to ram you, the only recourse is to execute a quick evasive maneuver and head for shallow water.

It was New Year's Eve as we approached the Water Island group of islands off the historic port of Malacca. Again, we were probing for a bay where we could feel secure and wouldn't attract attention.

Just as night was falling, we spotted a high-speed cutterlike vessel tucked back into an inlet called Pu Besar. As we changed course to come closer to him, I was aloft with binoculars to try to determine if this could be a Malaysian patrol boat or an "unfriendly."

As we studied their activities, we saw them putting a rubber boat over the side and uniformed men climbing in along with a girl. So we turned right toward them, hoisted the Malaysian flag, and with cotton in our mouths, passed close enough to see that it was a Malaysian armed patrol boat. What a welcome sight! They waved at us as we anchored fifty yards from them. We were secure for another night with protection from a heavily armed "friendly."

Malacca is a town with a great and glorious past. For centuries, it had been a rendezvous for every seafaring nation. Indian, Javanese, Chinese, Arab, Siamese, Portuguese, Dutch, and British—all ventured to the harbor town in search of profit through trade, piracy, or plunder. And each, in turn, left something of his own culture behind, to be forged and blended into what had never been before.

It was the rich port of Malacca—the key to controlling the spice trade—that caused some of the early East-West power struggles. In 1511, Malacca fell to the Portuguese, and for more

than 100 years they made the city their fortress. In 1641, the
Dutch took over and held the city for 150 years, until they
ceded it to the British in exchange for Bencoolen in Sumatra.

After a few days in Malacca, we calculated the tides and currents so that by leaving Pu Besar at 0500, we could be in the
major Malaysian seaport of Port Kelang, free of any pirate wor-
ries for that leg of the journey. Again, swept north by the current, we had a fast passage in the main shipping lanes.

At dusk, we entered Port Kelang and were amazed to find
dozens of ships at anchor. We had come 220 miles over the
bottom at an average speed of 6.9 knots since leaving Singapore
and had safely transited one section of the strait where pirate
activity was reputedly heavy. The *Morning Star* moored in
Port Kelang for two weeks under guard. We drydocked and
antifouled the bottom to prepare for the long Indian Ocean
crossing lying ahead of us. Shirl and I went to Kuala Lumpur
and toured Malaysia, saw its wildlife, visited rubber plantations, and studied the history of this incredibly wealthy country of 10.5 million Malaysians.

The Malays were kind to us. The hospitality of these attractive yellow brown people was extended to us at every turn.
There are many Chinese merchants in Malaysia, and, as in
other places, there are strong animosities directed toward
them by the *Bumiputras* ("native Malays"). The Chinese, with
their habits of thrift, industriousness, and sharp dealings in
money matters, as well as their exclusivity, bring down upon
their heads the wrath of the more relaxed, playful Malays.
Racial tension is explosive.

With a freshly antifouled bottom, we sailed north from Port
Kelang assisted by a two-knot current to resume the hide-and-
seek game with Malacca Strait pirates. We spotted another
patrol cutter and a suspicious-looking motorized Chinese junk,
but with a light breeze and slight swell, we ghosted up to an
anchorage in an open roadstead off Kuala Bernam. Although
we felt somewhat vulnerable here, we had the reassurance
that at 1600, we had seen a Malaysian patrol boat sweeping
these waters.

The next day, we worked our way up the jungle on the

Dingdings River to the village of Lumut, where we felt totally secure from weather and pirates. It was the best anchorage in Malaysia.

While in Singapore, I had been on the ham radio with an American yacht, the *Crusader*. She was skippered by an American named Don Sortie with a crew of six. During the time I talked to Sortie, *Crusader* was in Galle, Sri Lanka (formerly Ceylon). She was heading back to Thailand, Malaysia, and Singapore. It was November, 1977, the worst time of the year to cross the cyclone-ridden Bay of Bengal.

On November 16, a cyclone packing two-hundred-knot winds came roaring up the Bay of Bengal, toward the southern coast of India. This storm caused twenty-five-thousand deaths in India. It also caught *Crusader* squarely in its devastating path, and she disappeared with all hands aboard.

While in Lumut, I talked on the ham radio to an Australian whose only son had been aboard the *Crusader*. This distressed father had flown to Galle to talk to the people who had last seen his boy alive—a pathetic grasping for any straw.

When he learned that we were setting out to cross the Bay of Bengal in late January, he implored me to keep a sharp lookout for any "uncharted" island where his son might be stranded. Although I was reasonably certain that there are no uncharted islands in the Bay of Bengal, I told him that we would be vigilant for some trace of *Crusader*. No small craft could survive a two-hundred-knot cyclone, but it would be cruel to say this to the distraught father, clinging to any vestige of hope. There is such a senseless loss of life at sea brought about by lack of preparation, experience, and the ignoring of weather systems, seasons, and patterns. When, for example, we had gotten into the tail end of a seventy-two-knot hurricane aboard the *Morning Star* in 1970, we had had no business being in southern Mexican waters in June. The fact that it was the kids' summer vacation was a feeble excuse for our recklessness, and we learned our lesson.

From Lumut, we worked our way back down the Dingdings River out into the strait, dodging fishing stakes and floating deadhead logs. There was no wind, so we powered to arrive at Penang Island at 1800. We anchored amidst a flotilla of Chinese junks and trading vessels. The Malacca Strait was behind us. No pirates, no problems.

From Penang, we cruised through the wildly exquisite Langkawi Islands, standing twenty miles offshore along the Thai-Malaysian border. From the sea, these islands appear to be solid land with a saw-toothed silhouette. The cliffs plunge precipitously into the sea, forming intricate multiple channels that fragment the land into countless islands and coves. Deep, labyrinthian fjords provided a hidden lair for the many pirates who for centuries preyed on the trading vessels in the Malacca Strait. The maze of hiding places made it almost impossible for expeditions of British warships to trace these buccaneers to their refuge.

Cruising through these seldom-visited Thai waters to the island of Phuket, we made an overland trip to Bangkok. Buddhist Thailand—ancient Siam—is friendly toward Americans, and we were so enchanted by this country and the beautiful Thai people that as we returned to Penang, we hoped that someday we could come back to spend months cruising these fascinating waters. Working against this hope, however, was the harsh reality of modern-day pirates, tin smugglers, and drug smugglers operating out of the "Golden Triangle" of Southeast Asia. A private yacht with but two people aboard is particularly vulnerable in these attractive but dangerous waters.

We were fascinated with Penang Island, the Pearl of the Orient. We trishawed around the narrow, congested, clean streets of George Town and its pulsating waterfront. George Town is unmistakably a Chinese town, from crowded streets with Chinese characters spelling out mystic logos to the thriving port where Malaysia's rubber and tin find their way to the world's markets.

We visited the Snake Temple (the "Temple of Azure Cloud"). After climbing the 100 steps to the ornate temple, you see poisonous pit vipers everywhere—on altars, shrines, incense burners, candlesticks, vases, tables, and overhead. The Chinese say, "Not worry, no bite." Although I had shot pictures of Shirl with a nine-foot boa constrictor draped around her neck in Bangkok, she wouldn't do any similar posing with these "no-bite" pit vipers. We became good friends with a Chinese guide. He was a convert to Buddhism and was a profoundly interesting philosopher.

It was late in the monsoon season, and ahead of us awaited the Indian Ocean. The only month of the year when the Bay of Bengal is supposed to be free of cyclones is February, so we decided that all odds were in our favor. As January drew to a close, we maneuvered our way around Penang through myriads of fish traps and headed west—the first step across the Indian Ocean. Penang Island slowly disappeared below the horizon.

With sails set before the wind, our course was 270 degrees—rhumb line due west to Sri Lanka. It was the northeast monsoon season. We were rolling along with fifteen-to-twenty-knot winds off our starboard quarter in moderate seas at latitude 6° 14′ north, longitude 95° 01′ east. Our course was to take us thirty miles south of Great Nicobar Island. India has leased these islands to the Russians, and we had been warned that to go there would cause confiscation of the yacht. A Russian ship approached from starboard across our bow and passed very close. He must have come from the Nicobars.

A school of porpoises played around the bow. The moon was full, we felt great, and we were leaving our concern about piracy behind us. The dangers posed by murderous men were, in our minds, much more frightening than were the three-thousand miles of open sea lying before us.

We were on the ham radio to Guam daily. Dixie, the lovely lady ham in Guam, worked us each day—getting the weather for us from the navy in Guam—relaying our position and messages to our faithful contacts, Bud and always enthusiastic Ernest "Jeff" Jefferson, our original ham radio contact, in far-away Pebble Beach, California.

On the fourth day out of Penang, we had heavy waterspout activity off our port beam. Then squalls and spouts all around us. The Indian Ocean was trying to live up to her nasty reputation. A waterspout is a small tornado at sea—a twisting, violent segment of wind that sucks up water in its narrow path. While these spouts pack a tremendous velocity of wind and could probably wreck us if we were struck by one, we would change course to avoid them when we could and trust in God when we couldn't.

Our emotions, as reflected by the log entries, were bouncing around like a yo-yo:

Fifth day out: Heavy seas. Squalls, thunder, lightning. Oil-skins worthless. Soaked to skin. Shorten sail. Don't care about course. Just heading WNW to close reach with vane steering. Anxiously awaiting dawn. Shirl brave but exhausted. A night like this is no fun.

Sixth day out: Entry 0300 Lovely watch. Peaceful. No ships. Entry 0500 Thunder, lightning storm, violent squall. Changed course to avoid ship. Seas chaotic with frequent wind shifts. Motion atrocious. Rewards of cruising not worth punishment like this. No sights for two days. Estimate 1¾ knots WSW current. 330 miles from Galle.

Seventh day out: Fleet weather in Guam asks us if we have had waterspout activity. Bilge pump broken. Boat taking excessive water. Using portable whale gusher pump, 10 gallons per hour. Everything is going wrong all at once. Just to keep her afloat to Galle. 150 miles to go. Repaired bilge pump. Reefed main again. Guam weather warns heavy thunderstorm activity. On soundings 50 fathoms. 0700 LAND HO! Sri Lanka coastline perfect landfall with Rigel Kent and Alkaid fix. Strong current south coast of Sri Lanka. Up all night again, but will be in Galle Harbor by noon.

At 0930 on the eighth day out of Penang, we encountered friendly, waving Ceylonese fishermen. Then, slowly under sail, we made a majestic entrance into the beautiful harbor of Galle. Sunlight. Blue water. Ancient fortress and walled city on our port side. Spectacular!

It is strange how the human mind works. Until reviewing the logs and journals of the passage, we had completely blocked out all of the negatives, as registered in the log. Upon being asked months later, we probably couldn't have recounted what really happened on this record-breaking (for us) eight-day passage. But the logs' stark testimony indicate that it was a dreadful passage—cluttered with heavy shipping across the Bay of Bengal, contaminated by heavy weather and fatigue most of the way.

Our original plan had been to go to the Maldives and Seychelles from Sri Lanka. "No way would I ever go up the eleven-hundred-mile blowtorch of the Red Sea." I had complete charts of the Indian Ocean via the Seychelles, Madagascar, and Cape of Good Hope. And no charts for the Red Sea. Also, conventional wisdom had it that we might miss the northeast monsoon for the Arabian Sea crossing.

If this weren't enough, the wars raging between Somalia and Ethiopia and Ethiopia and Eritrea were assuming full-scale proportions. Our advisors in the States were fearful that Djibouti might be taken by the Russian-Cuban-led Ethiopian troops. Aden in South Yemen was completely dominated by the Soviets. North Yemen's political allegiance was precarious. At any rate, the advice received from all quarters—ships returning from there, State Department people—had been to "stay away from the Red Sea." Also, January was supposed to be the only month of the year when it was reasonable for a sailboat to beat against the prevailing head winds in the northern seven-hundred miles of the Red Sea, and here we were already approaching March.

But after resting in Galle, we began to consider other factors. The Mediterranean and all of its ancient countries were thirty-six hundred miles away, compared with a vastly greater distance around South Africa. A cholera epidemic had broken out in the Maldives. The Seychelles government had been overthrown in a left-wing coup. We would have to sit out the typhoon season off Madagascar in the Seychelles, while, if we could brave the Red Sea in March, we would be entering the Mediterranean in the spring.

So after a few days in Sri Lanka, we made the final decision.

We would head for the Mediterranean with the first leg a non-stop twenty-five-hundred-mile passage from Galle to the Hanish Islands in the Red Sea—a group of uninhabited islands off the North Yemen coast. We began then to gather all the charts and tracings of charts we could get. We got some from a yacht, some from ships in Colombo, and some from a chandler there. But we couldn't get all of the detailed charts we normally would have sailed with, so we made do with what we had.

With the new excitement of our revised plan, we savored all the more our stay in Sri Lanka, an enchanting, primitive, beautiful land of tigers and elephants, Buddhists and precious gems. It lies 22 miles from the nearest point of southern India, 400 miles north of the equator. A former British colony, it is a teardrop shaped island 270 miles long and 140 miles at its widest point. From tropical white-sand beaches to eight-thousand-foot mountains, the contrasts are breathtaking.

It was heart-wrenching for Shirl and me to travel through the countryside and see the poverty prevailing there. Somehow, developed countries like Japan and West Germany must be persuaded to contribute more to the abolishment of hunger and poverty in this part of the world. The United States cannot do it all. Small children with bloated bellies caused by malnutrition should be the concern of the entire human race.

Lurking always in the shadows of poverty-stricken nations are the Soviet Communists with their enticing message "All you have to lose are your chains." A married Singhalese couple—both medical doctors—we came to know in Galle received their training in Moscow, as did other educated people with whom we became acquainted. The Soviet presence throughout the Indian Ocean area is overwhelming and ominous.

To avail ourselves of the northeast monsoon, we had to leave Sri Lanka soon. We provisioned, and drums of fuel were brought to us in a bullock-drawn wooden cart.

In Galle Harbor with us was the circumnavigating Danish yacht *Kraka*, crewed by three rugged young Scandinavians. Lars, her skipper, had helped me replank *Morning Star* in Port Vila, New Hebrides. We had been good friends since first meeting in Tahiti in 1975. *Kraka* was also going to go through the Red Sea to the Mediterranean.

Lars dropped over to say good-bye to us as we prepared to leave Galle. He told us that he was going to stop in Aden, South Yemen. As Americans, we had been warned by consular officers not to stop in South Yemen. But *Kraka*, flying Danish colors, had no such concern. Lars was the only Dane sailing around the world, and his newspaper accounts of his circumnavigation had made him a national hero with the seagoing people of Denmark.

He seemed depressed, and I asked him if he wanted to talk about it. He said, "We have always had a crew of three men on *Kraka*, and now with the Red Sea ahead of us, our third man just quit and is flying home." He said, "It is just Jan and me now." Jan was a red-bearded, powerfully built Swedish diesel mechanic, who had been with Lars from the beginning of his circumnavigation.

Lars said that he drew encouragement from having observed how we—twenty-five years older than Lars—had managed to sail the *Morning Star* without other crew members. *Kraka* and *Morning Star* had been together in Tahiti, Fiji, New Zealand, Bali, Singapore, and now Sri Lanka. He said, "If you and Shirley can do it with a heavy ketch, we should make it with our fast sloop." Having built *Kraka*, a mahogany forty-five-foot work of art, Lars was very proud of his yacht. We shook hands and said good-bye without realizing that in a few weeks, disaster awaited *Kraka* in the Red Sea.

On the third day out of Galle, we suddenly had an infestation of bugs of several varieties. At dawn, using Polaris, Rigel Kent, and Vega, I determined my position to be 350 miles from Galle and 90 miles from Minicoy Island in the Laccadive group. These squadrons of bugs had flown great distances from the nearest land.

The northeast monsoon (an Arabic word meaning "season") winds were blowing at fifteen to twenty knots, and we were reaching along in moderate seas at five knots. Flawless sailing conditions! I decided to try to catch a fish. We have 400 feet of stainless wire on a large reel that we use when we want to visit

the fresh fish market all around. We call it the "meat hook."
Within minutes, the meat-hook alarm—a tin can tied to the
reel—began to clatter. As I began to reel in, I realized that
whatever was hooked was *big*, so I yelled below for Shirl to
bring up my .22 caliber Colt pistol. As I cranked on the reel, the
fish came into view. It was a six-foot-long shark. He was well
hooked, so I cranked him close to the stern of the boat. Hanging over the transom with the pistol in hand, I triggered eight
shots into the brain of the flopping fish.

Once assured that he was dead, I got a gaff hook into his jaw
and dragged and winched the ugly creature into the cockpit.
We filleted out about thirty pounds of steaks and dumped the
rest of the carcass into the sea, where the blood attracted the
waiting mouths of his brother sharks now milling around the
Morning Star. So we had shark meat for breakfast. The balance was wrapped and put into our deep freezer. Fresh shark
meat is tasty, but we tire of it rapidly.

On the sixth day out, in the Arabian Sea, February 14, Valentine's Day, we celebrated our thirty-sixth wedding anniversary. The weather was perfect. Our first few days of seasickness had vanished, and we felt zestfully alive, keenly aware of
how very much we still meant to each other. The logbook
shows entries of appropriate anniversary–Valentine's Day
greetings to one another as we each, on our four-hour watch
under the stars, had time to dwell on all of the events—good
times and bad times—that had filled our lives since 1942.

The big event of the day was sighting a U.S. Navy supertanker that changed course and slowed down to come over to
speak ship. Captain Dan Haff of the American tanker USNS *Susquehanna* told us on the VHF radio that they were curious
when they spotted our white sails. He said he and his crew
couldn't believe seeing a small sailboat out here in the middle
of the Indian Ocean.

We talked for two hours, first on the VHF, then on the ham
rig. He asked many questions. "Do you need anything?"
Answer: "No thanks, we are doing great!" When told that it
was our wedding anniversary, he said, "I hope I didn't inter-
rupt anything." A great, jovial guy whom we never saw, but

who was filled with curiosity. "How do you navigate? Where are you bound?" We were gratified to compare the coordinates of our position and find that the satellite, computerized navigational system on the *Susquehanna* put her one-half mile from our position, as advanced from my morning sights. As *Susquehanna* disappeared hull down over the horizon bound for the Persian Gulf, we felt a momentary sense of loneliness descend upon us. We may never meet Dan and the other officers to whom we had talked during our brief interlude on this immense desert of water.

Log entries on the Indian Ocean crossing ran:

Towering cumulo nimbus ahead. Looks like a long rough night. Charging through night on broad reach at 6 knots. Exhilarating but apprehensive sailing. She will not self steer. Struck mizzen and spent two hours trying to balance her to vane steer. 12–15 feet beam seas. Winds NW 20–25. Reefed main, jib and staysail. Fatigue is getting to both of us. Vane line snapped with a pistol shot crack. Too dangerous to try to fix tonight. Hand steering a workout in these conditions. Daylight—heave to and string new vane line while hanging over stern. Things starting to come apart. First 10 days too good to be true. Too rough to cook, so hard-boiled egg routine. Polaris, Vega, Antares, Rigel Kent fix Latitude 12° 34′ North, Longitude 58° 08′ East. Hove to, everything fixed and working again. Weather moderating. 142 mile run—life looks good again.
1730 Sunday, February 19: Killer whales all around us. Started motor to frighten them away. Beautiful night. Full moon. Porpoises frolicking around the boat. How we love these animals.

These are sample log entries of what we now have learned to accept as normal for a long distance, high seas passage. There was a time when gear failures would disturb me and make me angry. But now, as with everything in life, *acceptance* of the inevitability of the bad along with the good seems to have given me a calmer approach to the solution of these problems.

Since sailing out the Golden Gate in 1973, our westerly course had been taking us farther and farther away from America and home. Now, after having passed the halfway mark as we sailed west, we were sailing *toward* the United States of America. Our sometimes flagging motivation was psychologically boosted by this daily consideration.

Socotra Island, off the Horn of Africa, for centuries has been notorious among seamen as a nest of hostile pirates. The understated British *Africa Pilot* says, ". . . situated near the track of vessels bound to and from the East, Socotra is generally sighted by vessels entering or leaving the Gulf of Aden, but being exposed to both monsoons and having no harbours—*coupled with the unfavourable character the natives have hitherto borne*, it is but little visited."

In 1975, a Swedish friend of ours, Gus Ericksen, in his forty-one-foot ketch *Sisang* was captured by pirates when he anchored at Socotra. He was robbed and manhandled. But, thinking that Gus had transmitted his plight by radio, they released him.

Our course would take us sixty miles north of Socotra, and well off the South Yemen coast. On the sixteenth day out, the arid, barren coast of Arabia was barely visible off our starboard bow. We were 220 miles from Aden—335 miles from Djibouti—320 miles from Perim Island—460 miles from Al Hudaida, and 1,100 miles from Port Sudan.

Heeding the warnings of the American consul in Singapore, we timed our sailing past Aden in the "People's Democratic Republic of South Yemen" to be in the middle of the night. A former British base, which I had visited during World War II, Aden is near the mouth of the Red Sea. Controlled by the Soviets, it is a staging area for the Ethiopia-Somalia War as well as a training center for "Liberation Front" terrorists throughout the Middle East and Africa. The United States has not had diplomatic relations with South Yemen since 1969.

After ghosting by Aden at midnight, a murky dawn revealed five destroyers strung out in a picket line right in our path. We were flying twin headsails, so to change course I had to get the twin booms down and head south. As we saw that the destroyers were dead in the water, we jibed back on course, ran up the South Yemen flag, and sailed close by past the stern of one of them. A clutch of Russian officers and sailors was examining us through binoculars as we studied them in the same way. We waved, but the Russians didn't wave back.

Entering the Red Sea through the Strait of Bab el Mandeb late that night, we rounded Perim Island with twenty-five-knot following winds and large seas sweeping us past this hostile place.

Mixed with a sense of triumph over having sailed across the Indian Ocean in twenty-five days' sailing time from Penang, Malaysia, was some concern for what the dreaded Red Sea held in store for us.

ATLANTIC OCEAN

45°

ITALY

SPAIN

Balearics   Menorca   SARDINIA

Formentera

Overboard   Carloforte

Gibraltar   *Costa del Sol*   SICIL

Tangier   TUNISIA   Malta

Rabat   M

Casablanca

MOROCCO

30°

*Canary
Islands*   ALGERIA

WESTERN
SAHARA

S A H A R A

MAURITANIA

MALI   NIGER

Cape Verde

Dakar

SENEGAL

THE GAMBIA   **Around the Top of Africa**

Banjul

GUINEA

CHAPTER TWENTY-TWO

RED SEA ORDEAL

Now in the Red Sea, we were fatigued by the days of sail handling and avoiding ships. We were low on diesel fuel and had to stop someplace to rest and refuel. Amidst heavy shipping, we laid off a course for Jabal Zuquar Island in the uninhabited Hanish Island group situated in the middle of the Red Sea off North Yemen.

The next day, as we neared the Hanish Islands, we warily probed among them, looking for a protected anchorage where there would be no sign of man's presence. Any encounter with the Arabian pirates of the Red Sea must be avoided, no matter how tired we were.

On a clear, sunny day, with strong southerly winds, we rounded the tip of Jabal Zuquar, and taking cross bearings on mountain peaks and an ancient Arab tomb, we cautiously approached the north side of the island. We snuck into a cove, and the anchor plunged down twenty-five feet to a clearly visible white sand bottom. The *Morning Star* was motionless in the lee afforded by this island. The winds were blowing thirty-five and gusting to forty knots, but we found a blissfully peaceful anchorage after eighteen days of constant, sometimes violent motion. The silence and utter moonscapelike appearance of this desolate spot were awe-inspiring. Full of exultation, we stripped and plunged into the clear, blue green water. I dove to check the anchor. It was firmly imbedded in the hard sand. The fatigue vanished as we toweled ourselves dry and listened with our hearts to the solemn silence.

At anchor here for two days, we enjoyed the blissful, uninterrupted deep sleep of the dead. Pure ecstatic luxury! Simple earthy pleasures—swimming, sleeping, eating, laughing, and loving. Although we felt that we could have lingered here for weeks, we didn't want to push our luck too far. We hadn't seen a vessel of any kind nor any sign of life, but we couldn't be sure that we hadn't been spotted, lying vulnerably at anchor in this remote cove.

The unearthly silence of the first light of dawn was shattered by our windlass rumbling and clattering our chain and anchor up and into place. We headed northeast for Al Hudaida, North Yemen. Late that afternoon, the ancient minarets and block-houses of Al Hudaida came into view. Without detailed charts of this area, we made our way into the port of Al Ahmedi, North Yemen. As the sun sank over Ethiopia in the west, we anchored 100 yards off the deep-water channel.

At the nearby wharf, a Soviet freighter was discharging a cargo of bombs, tank tracks, mortars, and other crated military hardware. Within minutes, an LST-type craft bore down on us and rammed into our taffrail section, damaging us slightly. Surly-looking, uniformed, submachine-gun-bearing Arabs were attempting to step aboard. I could either be submissive or come on with British-style indignation about the clumsy bashing of our boat. Trying to keep my cool, I yelled for them to back off, pointing to the damaged taffrail. As they hesitated a moment, an authoritative, handsome civilian-dressed Arab stepped out of the wheelhouse and said in fluent English, "I apologize, sir, for this fool of a helmsman. What are you doing here? Where did you come from?"

I said, "We came nonstop from Sri Lanka to see your beautiful country."

"Just the two of you?"

"Yes."

"Okay, we will not board you, but please remain anchored here and come ashore tomorrow with your passports and ship's papers." As the LST propellers churned in reverse, he added, "Please accept a friendly warning. Do not take pictures here."

The next morning I rowed our dinghy in and was helped by a young Adenese Arab who told me in good English how he wished that the British had stayed in Aden, how much he hated the Russians and the Communists, and how good it was to see the American flag. Not knowing who he was, I smiled, shook hands, and asked for directions with no comment about his blurted statements.

Picking my way through tons of war matériel lying all over the dock as the Soviet freighter continued to unloaded her lethal cargo, I tried to locate the office for passport control. Uniformed Arabs bearing submachine guns were everywhere, glaring at this American, clad in shorts, from the sailing vessel anchored off the wharf.

Sitting forlornly on a crate was a white man. I walked up to him and said, "Do you speak English?"

He grunted in a heavy Russian accent, "A little."

I stuck out my hand and said, "My name is Ray. I have the American sailboat anchored out in the harbor."

With no reciprocal smile, he held out a flaccid hand and said, "I am assistant legation officer from Soviet embassy in Sanaa."

I sat down on the crate alongside him and asked him, "Where do I go with my passports?"

He tersely answered, "I don't know."

While he stared straight ahead unsmilingly, I told him how I had spent over a month in Russia in 1960—right after the U-2 was shot down (a remark I could have left unsaid). I rambled on and told him how I had been in Moscow twice; how much I liked Leningrad and Odessa.

Just then, three more civilian-clad Caucasians came striding up. My partner on the crate jumped up and, without a word, walked away from me. With his thumb jerked over his shoulder in my direction, I heard him say "Americanski." All four stalked off without a word.

After a chaotic morning trying to convince Arab interrogators, who repeatedly asked the same questions, I apparently persuaded them that we had just sailed in to get fuel and provisions and see their country. Then they were all smiles, but insisted on confiscating and holding our passports.

On the way back to the dinghy to get Shirl, I talked to the captain of a Seychelles tanker anchored near us. He was trying to wade through the red tape to clear out. I told him, "We want to get out of here. My wife and I just sailed nonstop from Sri Lanka and we need fuel. Would you sell to me three drums of diesel fuel?"

"No," he replied, "but I will *give* you whatever you need. So come over to my ship tonight and we will try to figure out how to get the fuel aboard your yacht." He went on to say that if we brought the yacht alongside his tanker, he would be arrested. He added, "I think that you should get out of here as soon as possible. These Marxists and Soviets have been talking about your antenna. They think you might be a CIA spy." Our ham radio antenna is called a "cat's whisker," and it juts up at an angle in an array of four dipole rods from the masthead. This antenna is conspicuous and so unusual that it always arouses questions. He warned us that their paranoia and hostility had caused the jailing and intense interrogation of a French yachtsman in South Yemen. Months later, in Cyprus, we met the Frenchman to whom the tanker captain was referring, and he told us the details of his ordeal.

Late that afternoon, I was ushered into the captain's suite. He had his officers there and, over drinks, they plied me with questions about our sailing voyage around the world. His boatswain was summoned and in the dark they loaded their gig with three drums of "gasoil," transported it alongside the *Morning Star*, and pumped it into our tanks.

The next day, while Shirl and I were looking for a place to land, we drove our small orange dinghy with its Seagull motor under the sterns of a group of gray unmarked corvettes, all manned by Russians. We waved and smiled, and one of them flicked a limp wrist our way in response.

We landed and toured ancient Hudaida. It was unchanged

from the Arabia I remembered from World War II days. One vast city dump, covered with flies, dirt, rubbish, and camel dung. It is a feudal, primitive place with veiled women and burnoosed Arabs strutting around with ornate daggers protruding from their sashes. Even the teenage boys wear daggers in this manner. Stray camels wandered about the outskirts of the town. Nothing had changed much here for centuries.

We provisioned in the open-air market—bought a lot of fresh stuff including California oranges and Washington apples. With their oil riches, the Arabs can import anything they want. We sell them fruit. The Japanese, as everywhere, are selling heavy equipment, automobiles, electronics, and other profitable merchandise. The Russians are selling war matériel.

We again ran into the tanker captain, and he told me that the Soviet freighter had left during the night with its cargo only partially discharged, and its captain had not even bothered to collect his crew's passports—an unheard-of thing for a ship's captain to do. He said, "I think that the last thing that they expected was for an American-flag vessel to find them unloading war equipment in North Yemen—supposedly America's friend. A few weeks later we heard on the news how the Soviets had sent an envoy to Sanaa to see the president of Yemen. When the envoy opened his briefcase, a concealed bomb exploded, killing both the Russian and the president of Yemen. One week later, the president of South Yemen, who had extended an invitation to receive a delegation from the United States of America, was assassinated—allegedly by the KGB.

The political power struggles in the Middle East and Africa are very real and very grim. Yet, it seemed to us that our media paid scant attention to the advance of Soviet imperialism in Angola, Mozambique, Ethiopia, and the Arab states. Quite the contrary, it appeared that the U.S. reporters presented to the American people consistent criticism of American foreign policy wherever it attempted to thwart Soviet self-declared designs for world domination.

The tanker captain very seriously said, in parting, "You

Balinese wood carvers

Pirate vessel at dusk

Pirates

Egyptian military base

blundered into something you weren't supposed to see, and you had better get out of North Yemen immediately."

We rowed back to the *Morning Star*, stowed the dinghy, hoisted the anchor, and with few regrets, left this politically explosive country.

With heavy beam seas, under only jib and mizzen, we slammed across and then up the Red Sea, staying well clear of Ethiopia and Eritrea, which countries were brutally engaged in an endless civil war. With reefs extending 90 miles out from both the Arabian and African coasts, we headed up the middle of the Red Sea in the shipping lanes, 430 miles to Port Sudan, arriving there before dawn on March the sixth. It was a fast passage with strong southerly winds until 100 miles south of Port Sudan, where the winds then spun 180 degrees and headed us as we beat the remaining distance into head seas.

The Sudan is pro-American and anti-Communist. It is the largest country in Africa, with borders on Egypt, Libya, Chad, Central African Empire, Zaire, Uganda, Kenya, and Ethiopia. It is where the Nile rivers—the White Nile and the Blue Nile— have their source, ancient Nubia.

We visited the last slave-exporting port, Suakin, just south of Port Sudan. As recently as 1948, when the port was closed, the Arabs were buying black African slaves from the Sudanese. Port Sudan is peopled with huge black Nubians. The coal black Nubian Sudanese in flowing white robes and white turbans are impressive human beings. Working the ships in Port Sudan are the ragged, filthy Fuzzy-Wuzzy tribes, which have their own unique culture.

Living on the outskirts of Port Sudan in makeshift shacks are over thirty-thousand refugees from the Ethiopian-Eritrean War, raging just a few miles south of Port Sudan. These people live in subhuman, filthy conditions out in the desert in a dry riverbed with the constant wind swirling clouds of dust around them whenever they emerge from their cardboard shacks.

The Sudan is also a Muslim country. Anchored right off a minaret, we could hear the plaintive cry of the muzzein calling the devout Muslims to worship five times a day. The men

Fuzzy Wuzzy tribesmen, Sudan

stop what they are doing. They wash their face and hands
from bottles of water that they carry with them, unroll their
prayer rugs, kneel and face east to Mecca, and commence to
pray and bow their foreheads to the ground.

We met two American engineers from Louisiana—Ken Wil-
lis and Dale Agee. They had spotted our U.S. flag and rowed
out to see us. They were stationed here building a $700 million
sugar-refining plant. Dale and Ken were enormously helpful

and obtained diesel fuel for us, preliminary to the arduous last six-hundred miles of head winds and head seas that stretched before us. Sudan is the breadbasket of Africa, and we provisioned with fresh produce and prepared to leave.

We talked with several native captains about our voyage to Suez. They all seemed dubious about the ability of just two people to beat against the constant northerly winds blowing with a venturilike effect down the Red Sea at this time of the year.

We had two choices—go up the middle, tacking among the shipping between the reefs extending from the Saudi Arabian side on the east and the Sudanese-Egyptian side on the west; or try to pick our way up the reef-littered coasts of Sudan and Egypt, anchoring every night.

The native captains told us ominously about how many vessels are lost on the reefs each year. They also told us that the Egyptian coast was heavily littered with mines left over from the recent Israeli-Arab War. But we decided that we would at least *begin* our journey north among the reefs. So, on March 13, we began what was to become the most grueling and dangerous passage of our lives.

The weather was clear with strong winds on our nose as we headed into them to go north. Within three hours, the wind came up to forty knots, blowing a filthy, choking red dust off the desert, covering the boat—mast, sails, everything—with a sticky residue. The sun shining through the dust storm was barely visible at midmorning. With me aloft in the mizzen ratlines and Shirl steering with a bandana over her face and plastic goggles protecting her eyes, we had gone only twenty-three miles when I decided that we had to find shelter.

At 1100 we probed into a niche in the reef called Marsa Fijab, following a chart tracing and sketches obtained from a fisherman in Port Sudan. Through the dust, I thought I had seen every coral head around us, but as the wind stretched the anchor chain, the *Morning Star* hit a submerged reef that neither of us had seen.

Again, the *Morning Star* was grounded fast, so I dove and found that just the deadwood and rudder shoe were jammed on the coral. If we could get any kind of push or tow, we could get her off. As Shirl and I surveyed the desolation of the place, the dust-storm-swept desert and heavy seas outside the tiny lagoon, we realized that other than a few wild camels we saw on shore through the dust, there probably wasn't a sign of life within miles. We briefly entertained the idea of hiking through the desert to Port Sudan twenty-three miles south, but abandoned that idea—too dangerous for us, too risky for the boat.

Sitting at the table below, I drew diagrams of coral, keel, angle of kedge-anchor placement, and determined that we would spend the rest of the day at least trying to haul her twenty tons off the reef. Over the side went the dinghy. First, I tried to row against the wind, as Shirl paid out 300 feet of chain and rope. But it was hopeless. The strength of the wind, the chop and the drag of the chain and rope in the water all made it impossible for me to get to the spot where I had pre-decided to imbed a forty-five-pound plough anchor.

"Maybe I can do it with the motor."

Back to the *Morning Star*, where I mounted our Seagull motor on the dinghy and tried again. With the antics of Key-stone Cops, I managed to get the swerving, broaching dinghy out at the desired angle, dropped the kedge anchor, dove twenty-five feet, and embedded it into the sandy bottom. This effort alone consumed another hour.

Now for the grand experiment! We set the mizzen sail to permit the wind to blow her stern off one way, and while Shirl used our own power, I windlassed the bow around and we pivoted her off the reef. (Later we learned from our French friends in Cyprus that they had been on this same reef, and had to get a tug out of Port Sudan to tow their steel yacht free.) The teak deadwood and shoe were mangled, but no damage affecting her seaworthiness was involved. Thank God.

The next day, after some difficulty getting both anchors up, we made another forty-eight miles to uninhabited Mukawwar Island. Log entries: "25 knot head winds. Steep seas 8–10 feet stop us dead in our tracks. Dust obscures everything. We can't make it here in this dust storm. Rat aboard from Port Sudan."

We decided on the following day that it might be less dangerous to head for the middle and tack our way up the Red Sea. This turned out to be an almost fatal decision.

For three days, we crossed and recrossed the Red Sea

between Sudan and Jiddah, Saudi Arabia. We sailed three-hundred miles over the bottom and made sixty miles northing. Tacking back and forth across the shipping lanes at night was too hazardous in these conditions for two people. On the radio we learned that four boats had turned back to Port Sudan. A fifth was lost on a reef, and another Frenchman had decided that it was "impossible" and headed south to sail six-thousand miles to go around South Africa rather than endure the six-hundred miles of the northern Red Sea passage.

Heavy seas continued to break over the boat. One tore loose our last remaining man-overboard pole (the first one had been lost in a storm in the Coral Sea) and shattered our beautiful taffrail, the worst damage we had experienced at sea in years. The heavy tool cabinet broke loose below our table and pinned my shin and calf against the salon seat. In one twenty-four-hour period, we made eleven miles north.

Things were really coming apart, and we were both sick from a bronchial infection contracted in dust-ridden Port Sudan. Also, we were full of insect bites from this dreadful place. We just could no longer take the fatigue of continuing beating in these conditions back and forth across the Red Sea. After a tanker narrowly missed us one night, I decided that I preferred the anxiety of the passage through the reefs.

It was so rough as we tacked toward the Sudan coast that I had to heave to in order to take sights! It was providential that I did stop because at dawn, Arcturus, Antares, and Altair put me ahead of my dead reckoning *eleven miles.* We had hove to and stopped that night just *four miles* from offshore submerged reefs!

(Weeks later, in Tel Aviv, we learned that our Danish friend, Lars, to whom we had said good-bye in Sri Lanka, and his crew on *Kraka* had struck a reef trying to do what we were doing. *Kraka* sank in a few minutes, giving Lars and Jan just enough time to get into their rubber life raft. They were picked up by a Greek freighter.)

At dawn, with the sun rising over Arabia at our backs, we picked our way through a maze of uncharted and mischarted reefs back to the Sudan coast to another slot in the reef, called Marsa Gwilaib. With the heavy northerly seas creating whitecaps all around us, it was impossible to see the reefs until we were close to them. Sometimes they were discernible by breaking water, sometimes by a leeward slick, but most of the time, from my perch aloft, I would shout over the wind to Shirl to maneuver right or left quickly to avoid reefs close by—within twenty-five to fifty feet—a boat length away!

We lingered at anchor in the lagoon and after twelve hours of solid sleep and a good breakfast, we started north again. We tried to time each day's passage so that we would have the sun at our backs and be anchored no later than 1600 before the sun setting over Sudan and Egypt would cause a glare on the water obscuring the coral. Powering into head seas in a sailboat is not a pleasant experience. Seas break over the entire boat with spray up to the spreaders, laying a thick coating of salt crystals on top of the gluelike dust. The Red Sea has an exceptionally high saline content because of the evaporation rate that this narrow body of water experiences, as it lies between two hot, arid deserts.

We anchored that night off the northernmost Sudanese village—Marsa Halaib. This is a primitive, feudal town of huts and minarets. Camels and goats were everywhere. Veiled women furtively peeked out of their doorways at us as we came ashore. At first, the people were so astonished to see an American sailing vessel anchor off their village that they were very reserved. But after I began to take color Polaroid pictures of children who went screaming and laughing with delight to exhibit their photos to the other villagers, the goodwill and friendship extended to us was overwhelming.

Soldiers fetched precious water for us, wading out into the surf to help us load it onto one of their dhows for transport to the *Morning Star.* I shot up three rolls of Polaroid film, taking pictures of men quickly decked out in their best burnooses and flowing turbans. As I snapped pictures of one group after another, Shirl remained in the background filming the scene swirling around me. These hospitable Arabs gave us eighteen scarce and precious fresh eggs. They were insulted when I tried to pay for the gifts that they thrust upon us.

We rested here for two days, recovering from fatigue, bronchitis, and insect bites. On Monday, the beginning of Holy

Week, we said sad farewells to the throngs of Arabs lining the shores. We resumed our northward reef dodging to our next arbitrarily chosen anchorage, Sha'b Abu Fendera—a reef twenty miles off Foul Bay.

We had heard on BBC shortwave news of the Palestinian Liberation Organization terrorist attack on Israel—the slaughter of thirty-six innocent people. That night we heard of the Israeli invasion of Lebanon. So there we were in quasi-hostile Arab lands, heading for Israel in the center of still another Middle East crisis. Our 1978 Red Sea transit was before the Camp David accords. Israel and Egypt were still in a technical state of war.

Easter Sunday, we anchored at noon in a small lagoon surrounded by reefs. It was called Marsa Toronbi. Military tents and beautiful white camels sprinkled the rise above the beach. Egyptian soldiers lined the beach staring at us, utterly flabbergasted to see us come sailing into their base.

As they helped us land our dinghy, we kept smiling and shaking hands. Within a few minutes, their initial suspicions melted, and we were laughing and trying to communicate in English and French with this contingent of camel cavalry stationed at their lonely outpost in the desert.

As the Polaroid camera came out, the officer in charge said, "No pictures." But by now, we had developed a technique. "You don't understand. These are pictures of *you* to keep right now." Once having taken their photographs and watched the pure glee light up their faces, it was a simple matter to say, "Now with this other camera, we can take pictures of *you* for us to keep." That always seems to be fair enough. So out comes the Leicaflex, and we are in business. Everyone is happy. The no-picture rule in these military bases is silly anyway because the Israelis, through photo reconnaissance, know every grain of sand in the Sahara.

The soldiers saddled up two white camels and took pictures of Shirl and me astride them with the *Morning Star* anchored behind us in the glittering blue green lagoon. The contrast was stark—the bleak Sahara and the white camels in the foreground, with an American sailing yacht anchored in the lagoon forming the backdrop.

The Egyptians were extremely kind to us. We had our Easter dinner in a tent, eating tough, chewy Arab bread, beans, and canned meat, washed down with strong Arab tea. The lonely soldiers insisted that we accept rare seashells and other personal treasures from them. They each and every one had to show us tattered photos of their girl friends, wives, and children back in Cairo, Alexandria, and other cities and villages in Egypt.

At predawn the next morning, we were again picking our way north to Quesir, Egypt. Here we were met by a boatload of officers and tommy-gun-bearing soldiers. They were quite friendly, but told us we would not be allowed to go ashore because it was a military base. They referred to the Carter-Sadat meeting in Aswan and Washington and said, "Americans good. Russians no good."

During our two-day stay in Quesir, we provisioned through a crooked ship's chandler who charged us exorbitant prices and ripped us off on the rate of exchange. But we had no way of doing anything about it because we were not permitted outside the immediate wharf area. Guards bearing machine pistols were posted to watch us around the clock.

But on the bright side, we made friends with their chief of guards and had him and his family aboard for coffee and what they really wanted—Polaroid pictures of each of their dark-eyed, beautiful children. Again, the picture-swapping technique worked, and we ended up posing with the guard, arms around one another's shoulders and me holding *his* machine gun.

As we proceeded north, we had to analyze each potential anchorage to make certain that we would have the sun at our backs and be able to leave the next morning with the coral heads and reefs around us plotted by bearings taken from the anchorage the prior afternoon. We discovered that predawn was the ideal time to see the shadowy submerged reefs, so would leave each of the eighteen anchorages we were in on our tortuous passage to Suez in this manner.

Out of Quesir, we had an offshore fifteen-knot breeze, and we made sixty miles farther north to Sharm el Arab, Egypt. This sixty miles northing in ten hours would have taken us thirty hours of tacking in the middle of the Red Sea. So, if one can stomach the anxiety of sailing amidst submerged coral reefs, this coast crawling was proving to be the best way for us to proceed to Suez.

Finally, we had finished with the Red Sea, and cutting between a complex of reefs in the southern end of the Gulf of Suez, we anchored at Marsa Zeitiya. We had heard all kinds of rumors that the whole Egyptian coast was heavily mined, but we simply didn't believe that any military purpose could be served by mining these waters against Israeli vessels, so we ignored the rumor and never saw any mine fields.

As we approached a cannon-studded military station south of our anchorage, however, an underwater explosion sent a geyser of water high in the air about five-hundred yards ahead of our bow. Someone was trying to tell us something, so we altered course fast and anchored well north of the military camp. We later learned from the Israeli naval intelligence, as they interrogated me, that the Egyptians on the one side and the Israelis on the other side routinely set off underwater detonations to discourage and kill any enemy frogmen in the area. These two countries, facing each other across the narrow Gulf of Suez, were still in a state of war, despite the cease-fire negotiated by Kissinger after the October, 1973 (Yom Kippur) war.

As a birthday present to Shirl on March 31, we were free of the clawing reefs and sailed in beautiful weather to our last anchorage in the gulf—Ras Abu Bakr—named after Muhammad's successor. On April 1, we had our first flat calm on the Red Sea passage—glassy smooth. With the Sinai Peninsula and Mount Sinai on our right and Egypt on our left, we headed for Suez.

At 1000 in perfect visibility, a freighter coming up behind us, suddenly changed course, heading directly for us. Shirl was below and I was forward. As I dashed for the autopilot control, the ship was almost on top of us. I changed course thirty degrees, heading directly for the Egyptian coast, narrowly avoiding being hit in broad daylight by the Russian freighter *Suvrovo*. As the hammer and sickle on his stack went by, I gave my customary salute to the officers laughing at us from the bridge. As we rolled in her wake, there was no doubt that she had deliberately tried to run us down. Whether they had been told of this American vessel with the curious antenna in Aden or in North Yemen, or whether it was an isolated act of a hostile mate or captain, we shall never know.

The Russians are fomenting all kinds of trouble in Africa and the Middle East. We had seen them in Arabia, and they are directly involved with the Cubans in the Ethiopia-Somalia War.

I filed a report with the Egyptian Suez Canal authorities. The Egyptians, who despise the Russians, told me that they had had complaints like this before, and that there was just nothing that they could do, except try to "hold up with red tape" *Suvrovo's* passage through the Suez Canal. Later in Tel Aviv, I was interviewed by American naval and CIA personnel in their fortresslike consul offices, where they and the ambassador are ensconced behind marine-guarded bulletproof glass entrances. They said that they would file a complaint through Washington and told me that these near-miss incidents were not uncommon.

As we entered Suez Bay at dusk, an anchored pilot boat blinked at us. I tried to ignore him, but he bellowed on his loud-hailer for us to come alongside. So I turned to approach, but refused to tie up to him as he instructed. It developed that this was the beginning of officialdom in Egypt wanting baksheesh. He wanted cold beer, cigarettes, and Coca-Cola. When I told him we didn't have anything, he told me to anchor eighteen-hundred feet astern of him. It was now too dark to make the inner, breakwater-protected harbor, so we reluctantly anchored with the ships awaiting canal transit out in the open Gulf of Suez.

That night a forty-knot southwesterly—the first southerly winds we had experienced since leaving Port Sudan—came roaring up the gulf, making the anchorage ghastly and dangerous. I had 350 feet of chain out and later discovered that our stainless steel bobstay had almost sawed through the chain during the night. Had we had that wind from Port Sudan, we would have made the trip to Suez in four days instead of the eighteen it took us.

But we had been very lucky. We later learned that one French yacht, as well as the Danish yacht *Kraka*, had been lost on reefs. Another French yacht was fired upon and they showed us the bullet hole through their windshield. Four yachts had come up on the deck of a freighter from Port Sudan, and one fifty-foot Force 50 Garden ketch, manned by a husky, all-man Dutch crew from Brunei, was towed from Port Sudan by a freighter. As the results came in, we learned that out of eleven yachts attempting this passage in March and April, we, along with two French craft, were the only ones that had made it to Suez under our own power. Each of the two French boats had been on reefs, but had gotten off. One had been arrested and detained by the Saudis, and the other had been bullet riddled. We were the only yacht that had tried the passage through the reefs—eighteen anchorages from Port Sudan to Suez. But the strategy had paid off, and we had been extremely fortunate.

While in war-ravaged Suez, we visited Cairo, and I showed Shirl some of my World War II haunts. We visited the pyramids, the Sphinx, the Cairo Museum, and had lunch on the Nile at Shepheard's Hotel. Just as in 1943, Suez was filthy. The ruins of bombed-out buildings, left over from the Israeli wars, were everywhere. It looked as it did when I was there in 1943, only then it was being bombed by the Germans.

On April 5, we were assigned a pilot (compulsory) and began our transit of the Suez Canal. Another adventure awaited us.

The pilot's name was Ali, and he came aboard looking a little queer—as though he was high on booze or something. We immediately cast off from our tie-up alongside an Egyptian tugboat named *Omar* (extremely cordial captain who entertained us for lunch aboard his craft) and got under way, entering the Suez Canal. The khamsin was still blowing hard, and visibility was less than a mile.

I allowed Ali to steer while I analyzed the chart. He was yawing wildly with the boat, steering ten degrees on either side of the designated channel in the canal. As he fumbled with the wheel, he said, "Never mind, captain. I know what I am doing. I have been a pilot for thirty years."

Ali was sprawled out at the wheel. When you are seated at the helm, there is no visibility forward because of our cockpit dodger and the upswept sheer of the *Morning Star*. The helmsman must stand and steer with his feet in close quarters. I was

leery of Ali's self-professed expertise, so I came up to the cockpit to find us heading straight for a large bell buoy. I yelled at
him, but his reflexes were nil, so I rudely elbowed him aside
as I grabbed the wheel. We missed the buoy by inches. He was
shaken, so I sent him below for a cup of coffee and continuation of his chain-smoking. I steered from there on, passing
ships—a southbound convoy within a few feet in the narrow
ditch through the desert.

Ali stayed below, moaning to Allah, and muttering about
"hobbly gobbly." I asked him "What is 'hobbly gobbly'?" He
said, "Hashish. Don't you have some?" I told him that if I
caught him smoking hashish, I would pitch him over the side,

Suez Canal transit

and he would have to swim the few feet to the canal bank on the Israeli side. After that, he was very subdued and contrite. On the VHF radio, we then learned that the canal was closed to all traffic because of the khamsin sandstorm.

At each station along the way, the stationmaster tried to get us to come in alongside. Knowing that what they wanted was baksheesh, I kept going. Yachts are prohibited from transiting the canal at night, so I was heading for an anchorage in Great Bitter Lake.

As I looked ahead, with visibility down to about one-half mile, I saw coming out from the Egyptian side what first appeared to be a barge. But the "barge" had no end. It was a pontoon bridge being dragged by a contingent of Egyptian troops across to the Sinai side directly in our path. Ali barked, "A bridge! We must anchor." We quickly did a 180 degree turn, and as Shirl headed the boat back south, the current swept us within a boat length of the bridge. I was forward, preparing to anchor. With the hook down, we began to drag toward the bridge in the strong northbound current and the forty-knot southerly winds. As Shirl headed the boat against the current, I flaked the anchor chain onto the deck, with Ali watching helplessly, and headed one-half mile south.

We reanchored and held—sitting there for two hours while the Egyptians drove trucks and half-tracks across the bridge as Ali fell asleep. The Israeli forces were twelve kilometers east of the canal as a result of the Kissinger cease-fire line, so the military activity along the canal was intense.

As soon as the bridge was withdrawn to the Egyptian side, we raised anchor and proceeded north. I made a mistake and allowed Ali to use the VHF radio. Chattering in Arabic with El Kabrit station ahead of us, he told me that they were commanding us to come in and pull alongside to "sleep there" that night. I shut the radio off and told Ali that I wouldn't do it.

In the Suez Canal transit, the pilot is only advisory, and all final decisions rest with the captain of any vessel—decisions and responsibility. So we passed El Kabrit with more shouting and waving between the stationmaster and Ali. At dusk, we entered Great Bitter Lake. The ships in the canal were allowed to proceed to Great Bitter Lake to anchor while the canal was closed, and I chose this option.

As night fell, we were square in the channel passing ships, one after another, when Shirl smelled smoke below. With her relieving me at the wheel, I flung open the engine hatch and a cloud of smoke poured out. The gearbox was overheating, and the pressure was down to 40 pounds from 150. We had lost most of our hydraulic fluid.

I told Ali we must stop the engine and anchor out of the canal instantly. He understood the smoke and was terrified. But he complied, and from the foredeck, with Shirl relaying to me, he waved his arms in all directions, conning me east out of the ship traffic. Still not trusting him, I was watching the fathometer drop as we shoaled. Suddenly, from forty feet, we went *aground*.

Ali came tearing back, stared at the *gearbox pressure gauge* (thinking it was the fathometer), and as we rose and fell on the ground, he asked, "How much water we have?" I said, "None, you idiot. You piloted us squarely aground." Shirl finally got the idea across to him when she yelled "zero water, zero water!"

Ali then said profoundly, "We can't stay here. Go back to Kabrit." I said, "The motor is broken. We don't go anywhere." But with the gearbox pressure gauge now diving to zero, I risked burning up the whole transmission by going full astern and backing off the bottom into forty-five feet of water right next to the ship channel.

After anchoring, Shirl and I tore apart the gearbox housing to analyze the problem. Ali held a flashlight while continuing to mutter to himself—praying to Allah. Having determined to my satisfaction that we were just clear of the parade of ships, I told Ali, "We stay here all night." My options were to scream on the radio for a tow to Kabrit, where there was a mechanic, or sweat out trying to analyze and repair the gearbox, if at all possible.

In the meantime, to prevent panic and depression from setting in, I asked Shirl to fix dinner to give us a chance to calm down. There we were—pitch dark—no moon—with ships passing us a few hundred feet away—pitching and tossing in the seas kicked up in the large, shallow Great Bitter Lake.

After dinner, I found the source of the leak in the hydraulic line—a cracked plug, which houses an alarm system. Then began the frantic search for a plug that could withstand heat and 150 psi of pressure. We had none—we physically cannot carry duplicates of every part of this complex machine.

Soon I had figured out how to bypass the alarm and plug the leak with a metal-to-metal two-part epoxy, which I had been carrying for five years. The repair took two hours, but to test whether it was going to hold would take another twelve hours of drying time to allow the epoxy to harden.

I told Ali, "Now we sleep."

He cried, "I will be sacked if you don't go to Kabrit. Let me call a tug on the radio. This anchorage dangerous because of seas."

I told him that the anchorage was safe with 300 feet of chain out, that a tug would wreck my boat in the towing and landing process at Kabrit in this seaway, and that I was going to bed.

Then the pitching *Morning Star* was illuminated by high-powered searchlights, and there was a 100-foot tug bumping into us alongside. The skipper could speak English and asked me what I was doing there. I described the problem. He said, "No problem. We will tow you to Kabrit, where maybe we can fix gearbox."

I told him, "No, we are staying put until I see if my jury repair will work at daylight."

He said, "Impossible! You cannot stay here because of ship traffic."

I knew that I was out of the ship traffic, and that with my lights and the slow speed of transiting ships, we should be comparatively safe—much safer than if we submitted to the inept seamanship I had seen on the part of some of these tug-boat operators. Angry words flew back and forth, and the tug left with the admonition that he would radio the "big captain" in Suez and would be back to take us in tow by force. It was then 2000—nine hours before predawn.

I figured that the "big captain" would be hard to find and that before definite orders could come back from Suez to Kabrit, after going through the maze of red tape, I would have a chance to test my jury rig. With Ali moaning and groaning and prepared to sit up all night, I took a couple of aspirin and went to bed.

At 0500, Ali said, "Captain, it's daylight." No further sign of the tug had been seen all night long. Now came the moment of truth. As Shirl started the engine, I had my eyes glued on the jury-rigged joint in the hydraulic line. It worked! Better than ever—150 pounds steady. We were underway for Ismailia, where we would get rid of Ali in exchange for another "pilot" to Port Said.

The khamsin had subsided. It was a *beautiful* day! We had coped with another emergency, and there is just no feeling like it in the world—the feeling of gratitude and satisfaction that comes with victory over obstacles that, at one time in my life, could have caused me to throw up my hands in impatience and frustration. Shirl, as usual, was a cool head, but quite firm—for her—with our goofy pilot.

At Ismailia, we had two sailors come alongside while we waited for our new pilot. They were carrying a submachine gun, and, as usual, wanted baksheesh—cigarettes, anything. They were sent out to "guard us" while we waited for the pilot. The pilot had been promised in thirty minutes, so two hours later Mahmoud showed up. After our experience with Ali, Mahmoud was easy to handle. I just told him to relax and enjoy the ride, gave him a pack of cigarettes, some lunch, and he was no problem.

It is against the rules to sail in the canal, but I told Mahmoud that the only way I could make it to Port Said before dark was to set sail as well as motor. Mahmoud said "Okay." Up went the sails, and as we progressed north through the ditch in the desert, we had a twenty-knot west-northwest wind that put us into Port Said just before dark.

Each stationmaster screamed at us to get the sails down, but Mahmoud made obscene gestures and yelled offensive words to them in Arabic. We took many pictures of sailing through the narrow canal with southbound ships of all nationalities meeting us.

In Port Said, we anchored and tied up stern to a wharf in a small "yacht club." The people were very nice to us, and we stayed there resting and repairing the Red Sea damage for the next five days. From South Yemen to Suez, we had discovered that the American flag may be less than an asset. During our stay in Port Said, machine-gun bearing soldiers were posted to guard us twenty-four hours a day.

Although the Red Sea passage among the reefs was fraught with hazard compounded by the volatile and uncertain political situation, it had the effect of bringing Shirl and me closer together than ever before. This sustained period of danger made us more vibrantly alive somehow. I teased Shirl, "At the end of every day, you were so darned glad to be alive that it made you super nice to me. You figured that I was the only game in town to get you through this ordeal, that there was no room for argument about anything that I decided to do." But, as I watched her, with her face swathed in a bandana and her eyes protected by goggles, I thought, "How lucky I am to have this incomparably brave woman as not only a shipmate, but a mate for life."

During the years of our voyage, I had watched Shirl shopping in primitive native open markets in malaria-infested Malaita or washing clothing in a plastic garbage bucket with a rubber "plumber's helper" plunger and thought of how she could be home with other American women, surrounded by luxury and free from danger and hardship.

In summarizing our feelings, we thought about Christy Tews of the heroic American women's Himalayan expedition when she said, "This is the only thing we have ever done that requires all that we have—all the spiritual strength, the mental strength, the physical strength. We are so involved that it requires everything that we have. It is a journey into our souls—a process of knowing ourselves and our capacities. If we die, we die happy. We owe ourselves our lives, and being this deeply involved is being alive—that is what it is really all about."

CHAPTER TWENTY-THREE

IN THE WAKE OF ULYSSES

⚓ When you cleared from Egypt or any of the Arab countries, you did not say that you were going to Israel. The hostility was so intense that some way would be devised to harass or detain you if the Egyptians thought that you were heading for Israel. So we cleared for Greece.

At the outer buoy north of Port Said, we "changed our minds" and laid off a course at 0600 for Tel Aviv. The seas were calm, and we were elated to have the Red Sea and the Indian Ocean behind us. We were in the cobalt blue Mediterranean Sea at last!

At dusk a Phantom jet roared over us at masthead height. Then he circled us repeatedly. I told Shirl that this was a prelude to an encounter with an Israeli gunboat. So "not to worry." Then at 1915—pitch dark—the *Morning Star* lit up with strong searchlights on our sails, antenna, and right in our eyes. There, out of nowhere, had come a gunboat maneuvering about fifteen feet abeam of us, with guns manned and trained on us.

They yelled, "Where are you going?"

I yelled back, "Identify yourselves. Who are you?"

They called over the loud-hailer, "Israeli navy."

Both the Egyptian and Israeli flags were furled on the flag halyard. As their machine guns and searchlights swung to bear on me, I walked up to the mast and hoisted the Israeli flag. Our American flag was snapping from its proper place astern. Back in the cockpit, shielding my eyes from their blinding quartz lights, I yelled, "We are heading for Tel Aviv."

We were forty-five miles off the Egyptian-Gaza Strip/Israeli border in international waters. But the Israelis were in a state of war and had been particularly jittery since terrorists had landed in rubber boats launched from a mother ship off their shores. The marina at Tel Aviv, which is surrounded by large hotels such as the Hilton, had been a target for the P.L.O. Their idea had been to hold a hotel and all of its guests as hostages for the release of P.L.O. terrorists imprisoned in Israel and Germany.

A storm had blown the rubber boats north of Tel Aviv, and two or three terrorists had drowned. But the survivors had landed and killed thirty-six innocent people on a bus—men, women, and children. This caused the Israelis to attack southern Lebanon to rout out the P.L.O. All of this happened just before our arrival, so we were sailing into a country mobilized for war.

We could hear them shouting on the radio in Hebrew to their superiors in Haifa. Fifty-caliber machine guns and 20-mm. cannons were trained on us. As they wallowed alongside, the guns pointed at us made us increasingly apprehensive. One accidental squeeze of a trigger by a nervous sailor and we would be blown to bits.

One of their searchlights continued to play up and down the mast, focusing on our antenna array. They questioned, "What is that on the top of your mast?"

"It is my amateur radio antenna." I asked them to get on the VHF radio to me, so I could talk to them free of their blinding lights. But the officer in charge ordered me not to go below. Coming up the Red Sea, I had several contacts with an Israeli ham operator—Sam Kruglak—but while sailing off or in the Arab countries I didn't dare use my American call sign or name my vessel. As it was, our contacts were frequently jammed by hostile signals emanating from Saudi Arabia. But

Sam read between the lines, and once cleared of Egypt, on our last contact, he told me that he would alert the Israeli Defense Forces concerning our arrival.

Finally, the searchlights flicked off, and a pleasant voice floated out of the black night, "Welcome to Israel, *Morning Star*. You are right on course to Tel Aviv. If you have any trouble or the weather gets bad, you have permission to come into Ashdod. Bon voyage."

With a roar of their high-powered engines, their unlit craft sped off into the darkness.

We arrived off Tel Aviv before dawn, after having been scrutinized by still another patrol boat. At 0700 Miki, the marina manager, came out and piloted us through the narrow entrance to the marina—three inches under our keel through a silt-filled pass twenty feet wide. The Israeli police, navy, and customs searched the boat more thoroughly than we have ever been searched anywhere. They said that they were looking for anything a terrorist may have planted on the boat in Egypt.

The Indian Ocean crossing and the Red Sea ordeal had trimmed every surplus ounce off both of us. We were exhausted and were looking forward to recuperating from the thousands of miles we had sailed in the past four months since leaving Singapore at the beginning of the year.

We left the boat and went to Jerusalem, where we ensconced ourselves in the King David Hotel. We could not cope with the invitations and the hospitality extended to us through the bank and other connections. Sam Kruglak, the amateur radio operator, entertained us in his home. The banker, Israel Herman, and his wife, Miriam took us all over the country. We had dinner in their home and attended their family Seder—the feast preceding Passover (*Pesach* in Hebrew). This was a great honor extended to two Christians. The sense of family, their love for one another, the singing and laughter of these indomitable people deeply impressed us.

On our own, and with the help of a Franciscan priest based out of Jerusalem, we visited the Holy Sepulcher, Way of the Cross (Via Dolorosa), Last Supper Room, Gethsemane, Courtyard of the Flagellation (where Jesus was flogged), Bethlehem,

Bethany, Hebron, Jericho, Qumran (Dead Sea Scrolls), Dead Sea, Nazareth, Sea of Galilee, Tiberias, Capernaum, Cana, and Caesarea.

Our visits to the sacred places in the Holy Land brought our religion into an enormously enlarged perspective. We stood in awe at the places where Christ was born, lived, suffered, and died. In this war-ridden land, surrounded by deep-seated centuries-old hatreds, feuds, and grievances, we speculated that the golden rule—Love Your Neighbor as Yourself—hasn't failed. It simply has never been tried.

We went to the Golan Heights, and Israel and Miriam Herman took us to the Lebanon border. Israel is a very small country—about 265 miles long, and including the West Bank of the Jordan (now occupied since the 1967 war) was only 40 miles or so wide. It is one vast archeological museum with Crusader castles, temples, mosques, aqueducts, and ancient ruins everywhere.

The P.L.O. terrorists are a real problem. At every tourist attraction and marketplace, scattered prominently throughout the country, are machine-gun-armed guards—young men and women carrying their submachine guns with them wherever they go—home after duty—everyplace. They are prepared to assemble with guns and ammunition within five minutes of an alert.

While we were there, a tourist bus was pipe-bombed in Nablus, killing five West German visitors. Tourist buses are stoned by the Arabs. They are trying to disrupt tourism—Israel's principal source of income. An apartment house was rocketed by Russian Katusha rockets in Jerusalem just a few blocks from where we were staying. The newspapers were full of warnings to be alert to terrorist attacks over the Jewish holidays and on May 11—the thirtieth anniversary of the founding of the state of Israel.

The marina where we berthed the *Morning Star* was heavily guarded; searchlights played on the pass, and jeeps armed with machine guns patrolled everywhere. Living aboard the *Morning Star* in the Tel Aviv Marina, we were probably the safest people on earth.

We were objects of curiosity to the Israeli people in that we had sailed from California across the Pacific and Indian oceans, up the Red Sea, through Arab countries. At one time or another, we had aboard as our guests an admiral of the Israeli navy and his wife, a general of their defense forces, and numerous other prominent Israelis who congregated at the marina on weekends.

We had been invited to remain and attend many functions marking the thirtieth-year Independence Day celebration, but with the radio and newspapers full of terrorist warnings, we felt that, especially as Americans, without whose aid Israel could not exist, we could be particularly vulnerable to an act of terrorism.

On May 10, we had a party on board with the Hermans and other Israelis who had lavished so much kindness on us. After clearing with the navy, we probed our way out of the Tel Aviv Marina, escorted by a police boat, and laid off a course for Larnaca, Cyprus. It was a beautiful clear spring day, and we were happy to be at sea again.

At 1145 a destroyer came up over the horizon proceeding at forced draft from the direction of Haifa. We maintained our course and speed. The destroyer slewed up to us with siren blaring and shouted commands to "heave to—stop!" As I broke out my camera, they shouted, "No pictures!" We were on the high seas in international waters. As we hove to, the destroyer wallowed in the seaway alongside us, with crew in full battle dress—helmets, flak jackets, all training 20-mm. cannons and machine guns on our tiny craft stopped alongside them. As they rolled, the guns would swing to remain aimed straight at us. Planes were circling us just above our masthead.

We wondered, what with all of the security surrounding our leaving, why they should come on with such an overwhelming array of force. We were clearly out of Israeli waters and heading away toward Cyprus. Yet they detained us for almost an hour in this position. Again, our concern was that any itchy trigger finger could accidentally touch off a few rounds, blowing us right out of the water. As time wore on, I could hear them transmitting in Hebrew to the naval base in Haifa. We became increasingly upset with the treatment we were now getting. After having so thoroughly established ourselves with

Israel warship through porthole

the Israelis during our stay in Tel Aviv, we figured that their plot boards in Haifa would know of every ship in their waters, and that this harassment was a display of force for no apparent purpose.

Finally, a particularly surly officer who had been questioning us said, "You are free to proceed." But until nightfall we had one after another Israeli plane buzz us and continue to maintain their surveillance. We could only speculate that this extraordinarily hostile conduct was brought about by the general nervous tension that pervaded the country the day before their Independence Day celebration. That night it was clear and cold, and we were fifty-nine miles off the Lebanon coast and seventy-two miles from Cyprus.

The next morning we entered the harbor in lovely Larnaca, Cyprus. The Greek Cypriot officials were kind to us, and with words and deeds made us feel welcome! We had expected strong anti-American feelings because of the resentment toward the Turks, armed with U.S. weaponry, who had invaded and occupied 40 percent of Cyprus in 1974. One official gave us a "political-orientation" talk, and asked me not to take personally any display of resentment toward the United States of America that we might encounter among the Cypriots. At that time, the U.S. arms embargo was still in force against the Turks.

Larnaca was full of refugees from Turkish-occupied Cyprus. People who, in terror, fled the Turks with what they had on their backs, in taxis, buses, on foot—any possible way to escape. The slaughter and atrocities described to us during that war, which had taken place just four years earlier, must have been terrible. U.N. troops were everywhere. But again, on a one-on-one basis, Shirley and I were invited into the homes of prominent citizens of Cyprus—Armenians and Greeks. We made friends with one very special Armenian couple who drove us all over Greek Cyprus. Dinner in their home, a picnic in the mountains, dinner on the boat, a visit to Nicosia—they couldn't do enough for us.

While we were working on the boat one day, a group of British schoolchildren trooped up, armed with note pads and pencils. They had been assigned by their teacher to write an essay about the American couple who were sailing around the world. With punctilious British courtesy, they solemnly asked me all sorts of questions about the boat, how it was built, our voyage, and the many adventures that we had. I stopped my work and gave these attractive youngsters—so serious about their essays—my total attention.

After the class of boys and girls had left, one particularly bright ten-year old boy clad in shorts remained, standing on the dock. I resumed my work as he silently watched me for the next few minutes. Then, with a pensive look, he said, "Sailing around the world, eh? You know, sir, I have been thinking that what you are doing is much easier said than done." Startled at his concise summation, I said, "Son, you go home and tell your mummy and dad that the American said that they have a very precocious and profound young man as their son."

From Larnaca, we went to Paphos. Here again we were intrigued with the idea of following in the footsteps of the apostle Paul. Again, in Paphos, everyone was exceptionally kind to us. We spent days wandering through ancient Roman and Turkish ruins.

Even though Cyprus is another political tinderbox of seething, centuries-old hatreds—Greeks versus Turks—we loved the place and reluctantly sailed from Paphos on a clear Sunday morning with friends on shore waving as we sailed out of the channel. Our course was 308 degrees, heading for Finike, Turkey, on the southern Anatolian coast of Asia Minor.

In characteristic Mediterranean weather behavior, the barometer began to plunge at 1600, and we knew we were in for a nasty storm, which the Mediterranean can dish out with very little warning. That night we had a Force 8 gale out of the west-northwest.

The "Med" develops a short, steep, ugly sea condition. I shortened sail to a storm jib and reefed mizzen. It was too rough for Shirl to steer, so I stayed up all night during the storm, bashing into some of the roughest sea conditions we had ever encountered. One sea crashed against the port bow with such velocity, causing *Morning Star* to reel and shudder so violently, I thought she surely would come apart. It was as though we had struck something solid and unyielding. We did not want to heave to for fear of being blown too close to the hostile Syrian coast, far to the east of us.

At dawn, we came into the lee of Asia Minor and made our landfall on southern Turkey. The clean smell from heavily wooded mountains and the distant snow-capped peaks made us think of the Sierras at home.

Alongside the wharf at Finike, Turkey, we were boarded by extremely courteous officials. Bearing in mind that the United States had an arms embargo on Turkey, which the Turks intensely resented as NATO partners, bordering on the Soviet Union, we didn't know what to expect from the Turks. Despite an almost total language barrier in this tiny-out-of-the-way port where tourists never come, we got along famously with our Turkish/English dictionary.

The Turks didn't search us, but they asked about scuba gear. There are so many (as we were soon to discover) still-unexplored underwater remains of ancient civilizations that the

Turks do not want precious artifacts hauled away by divers with boats taking them to otherwise inaccessible spots. The penalty for being caught with an ancient artifact is confiscation of the yacht. But as we lacked a compressor for our three scuba tanks, they did not seal them.

In Turkey, we reestablished radio contact with home through our friend Rich Feldman, who relayed from Ohio our messages to Bud and Jeff in California.

From Finike, we slowly cruised and anchored in remote places under ancient Lycian tombs set into steep cliffs and in coves overlooked by centuries-old, abandoned Crusader castles. By probing between rock formations, we came upon one place that obviously had been an ancient seaport. It was not marked on the chart or referred to in any of our books. As we free-dove beneath the boat, we found tons of ancient calcified vases and pottery remnants buried in the sand. We stayed in this isolated place for several days. Shirl called it our "Lost City Anchorage." The water was quite cold but invigorating, and we swam, snorkeled, and explored in peace-filled, tranquil days. With its wooded mountain smells and blue green transparently clear water, it was easily one of the most strikingly attractive anchorages of all time.

We spent days on the Turkish coast, with a stop at Kastellórizon, the easternmost Greek Dodecanese island, lying just a few miles off Kas in Turkey. We have heard many yachtsmen criticize the Mediterranean, but we love it. Especially Turkey. Lazily, we cruised along the coast, into deep fjords with names of anchorages unfolding in the log like Ilbiz Burno, Tersani, Adasi, Fethiye Korfezi, Skopea Limani. Entering one of these breathtakingly beautiful fjords, Shirl shouted at the top of her lungs in sheer exhilaration, "I love cruising!" I stared at her, somewhat amazed at this uncharacteristic outburst.

More remote uninhabited anchorages were explored by the *Morning Star:* Dalyan Island, 4 Fathom Cove, Domuz Adasi, Koycegiz Limani, and finally to Marmaris, just north of Rhodes, Greece.

While in Tel Aviv, we had received a letter from our daughter Teri imploring us to make it possible for her to spend her summer vacation from her registered-nurse studies, cruising

Greece with us for forty-five days. How could we refuse such a request? Teri received a cable, "Meet us in Rhodes, Greece, June 13."

We sailed from Marmaris to Rhodes to keep this rendezvous. Teri's radiant, sparkling personality as a passenger aboard the *Morning Star* brought back happy memories of the shakedown cruise in the faraway South Pacific so long ago. With Teri aboard, we experienced the heightened pleasure that accompanies sharing adventure with an enthusiastic, youthful companion.

After Teri's arrival, we cruised around Rhodes to Lindos, back to Turkey, exploring archeological ruins at Knidos, Kusadasi, and Ephesus—the largest ancient city in Asia Minor during the time of Saint Paul's travels over the same route. Then through the Aegean Sea and the Cyclades Islands while we related to Ulysses and ancient Greek voyagers of centuries before Christ.

One island after another was visited and explored by *Morning Star* and her temporary passenger, days filled with adventure, laughter and close companionship.

Ports of call in the logbook: Nisos Ikaria, Ormos, Mykonos, Tenos, Thera (Santorini)—the legendary Atlantis—the sunken city covering the ancient Minoan civilization with thirty feet of pumice from an enormous volcanic eruption.

At Santorini, we anchored over the volcano, and the sulphurous bubbling sea cleaned the marine growth from the *Morning Star's* bottom. Then to Heraklion, Crete, where we explored the Minoan ruins at Knossos.

With the Meltemi winds blowing down the Aegean, we sailed to Folegandros, Milos Portokheli, Idra, Akra Sounion, anchoring under the ancient temple of Poseidon—the Greek mythological god of the sea. A tour of Athens and on to Salamis—then to Laurakian through the Corinth Canal to Galaxidi.

We explored the ruins of Corinth, where Saint Paul spoke to the Corinthians. More exploration of ancient Delphi. The passage through the Corinth Canal—conceived by the Caesars—put us in the Ionian Sea.

As we cruised around the late Aristotle Onassis's exquisitely

Through the Corinth Canal

beautiful island of Skorpios, I said to Teri, "Up there on that hilltop is buried one of the wealthiest men of our times—a billionaire. He seemingly had everything. Money, beautiful women, homes all around the world. Alongside him is buried his only son, who had been killed in a plane crash. No matter how much money or power he had, he ended up right where we are all going to end up. Judging from what I have read about his troubled life, his millions didn't bring him happiness. His yacht *Christine*, formerly moored over there in his private harbor on his private island, could only take him through these same waters, under the same sky, to the same beautiful places in the Mediterranean as our humble little wooden *Morning Star* has taken us. Yet, although he had the money, he didn't have the time to cruise *Christine* very much. And when he did, he had to have a retinue of servants to run the yacht for him. He couldn't even have the enjoyment of being the captain of his own ship. Now he has no more time, and someone else has his money. Possibly, he didn't realize that time, not money, is the real currency of life. How to use each hour—each day—to live life—to be—not just to accumulate.

"It doesn't seem to make much sense does it, Teri? Now, maybe you can better understand why mom and I are trying to live this kind of universe-connected life—while we still have the time."

On the island of Levkas, we met Andrew Hadzopoulos, a former Greek contestant in the Olympic sailing matches and one of the most charming, generous, and intelligent human beings we have ever met anywhere. Andrew is a Greek tycoon and a man of the world. We were drawn to him by his gracious personality and towering intellect. He was fluent in seven languages. Andrew couldn't do enough for us.

The remainder of Teri's days with us were spent anchored near Andrew's yacht *Manahiki*, on beautiful Corfu Island. Teri water-skied and we enviously watched Andrew surf-sail. Teri's time aboard the *Morning Star* ended all too soon, and with leaden hearts Shirl, Andrew, and I said good-bye to her as we put her aboard the plane in Corfu.

In one of the most heart-wrenching farewells for us in our entire voyage, we said good-bye to our kind, Greek friend Andrew and sailed across the Ionian and Adriatic seas to Leuca on the heel of Italy's boot. Then across the Gulf of Taranto to Cape Colonne and Cape Bruzzano, Italy, to Calabernardo, Sicily, and finally to historic Malta.

After obtaining independence from Britain, Malta had been taken over by a leftist government closely allied with America-hating Islamic Libya, 180 miles to the south. The Libyan dictator Khadafy had promised the Communist-oriented Maltese government financial support, gained from its oil riches expropriated from the Americans. Part of the quid pro quo for this arrangement was the denial of the use of Maltese harbors to the American Sixth Fleet or to any NATO warships. Libyan warships are free to come and go. Another suggestion advanced to the Maltese is that they abandon Christianity and become Muslims. The apostle Paul was shipwrecked on Malta, and his experience converting the people of the island to Christianity is described in the New Testament. It is the oldest Christian country in the world.

Malta has had a brave and glorious past. Had not the vastly outnumbered Knights of Malta successfully defeated the Turks during the Great Siege of Malta in 1565, all of southern and western Europe would have fallen under the sword of Islam. Were it not for this historic battle, we could all, quite possibly, be Muslims today.

Malta was one of the most heavily bombed Allied targets of World War II. Day and night, wave after wave of German and Italian bombers, flying out of Sicily and North Africa, saturated Malta with thousands of tons of high explosives. But the courageous Maltese people held out. It was one of the staging areas for the invasion of Sicily. General Eisenhower used Malta as his headquarters. The Americans built a large boatyard to provide service and marine railways for invasion craft.

The vast majority of the Maltese people are Catholic, and they despised the rejection of their Western sympathies in exchange for the Communist-oriented government inflicted upon them by questionable elections. But now they found themselves under the repressive control of a puppet government manipulated by Marxist Libyan Arabs.

Our Red Sea–battered *Morning Star* was in need of a dry-docking and yard work. While in Turkey, I had been on the ham radio with a Maltese amateur radio operator—Tony. Tony checked into the facilities and reported back to me that arrangements had been made to haul us out at Manoel Island—the American-built shipyard.

During our stay in Malta, Tony helped me in many ways, and Shirl and I became very attracted to him, his wife, Rosemarie, and their two small children. Tony was a twenty-eight-year-old RAF-trained electrician.

One day, Tony emotionally pleaded with me, "Ray, I would be forever in your debt if you would help me immigrate to America. I've got to get Rosemarie and the kids out of here before my country goes completely Communist. I voted the wrong way in the last election, and now I am being discriminated against in my work. Like most of the Maltese people, I am pro-British, and pro-American, and there will never be an opportunity for me or my kids under Communism."

I said, "Tony, America has plenty of problems. The streets

are not paved with gold. You may not like the rapid pace of life. The kids may be exposed to all kinds of things you don't see in Malta. Rose may get very lonely."

Tony replied, "Ray, what you don't understand is that freedom is more valuable to me than all of the problems we are certain to face."

Struck with the simplicity of his reply, I said, "Okay, Tony, let's go down and talk to the American consul." Tony replied, "I've already done that, and they told me that if I don't have any relatives or anyone to sponsor me for work in America, I cannot have a work visa."

I said, "Let's go anyway." We saw the top consular officer (who later was transferred to Iran and was held hostage for over a year). He pretty much confirmed what Tony had told me. But I told him that I would find a sponsor for Tony and that I would help him immigrate to America. With the cooperation of a close friend at home, two years later, Tony and his family legally immigrated to the United States, and he has a fine job with IBM in San Jose, California.

The *Morning Star* wintered in Malta and weathered several "gregale storms," the Maltese name for the northeasterly storms that wrecked Saint Paul centuries ago. The British formally were withdrawing from Malta in March, 1979, and we found ourselves in an increasingly uncomfortable position with the Stars and Stripes fluttering from our stern as overtly hostile Libyan warships maneuvered and berthed near us at Manoel Island. We decided to get out of Malta as soon as possible.

This resolve was strengthened after I was struck in a head-on automobile collision between my rented Mini and a Czechoslovakian diplomat's Fiat, who, although he struck me while I was at a standstill, enjoyed diplomatic immunity and was not subject to prosecution. I ended up in a government hospital, attended to by dubiously qualified Pakistani and east bloc doctors. When the leftist takeover occurred, 180 of the U.K.-trained physicians fled Malta en masse. Despite multiple cuts, abrasions, bruises, and a slight concussion, I got up and walked out of the hospital, making straight toward the police station. The Maltese police confided in me that I was clearly blameless; yet the government attempted to detain us and impound the *Morning Star*. First, we sought help from the American embassy, but found them reluctant to "get involved."

So, in desperation, we went to a prominent Maltese family who had befriended us during our months there. Their law-yers obtained clearance for us, and we slipped our moorings one black night, sadly relieved to depart this historic country whose people we had grown to love so much. At dawn, we were clear of Maltese waters, bound for Sicily. But we often reflected how depressing it was that the brave, fiercely inde-pendent, devoutly religious Maltese people had been deceived and taken over by the same type of leftist governments—clearly in the minority—as we had witnessed so often in other countries.

We lingered a month in Syracuse and Taormina and cruised Sicily past snow-capped volcanic Mount Aetna—through the fabled Strait of Messina—into the Tyrrhenian Sea. We leisurely explored the Lipari or Aeolian islands, including Stromboli and Vulcano. The Sicilian people, from the fishermen we rafted up to in crowded harbors to the people—peasants, shopkeepers, intellectuals, officials—we encountered ashore were warm and friendly toward us as human beings and as the two Amer-ican grandparents who had sailed their own sailing vessel around the world to visit them.

Then, ever westward, we sailed to southern Sardinia, where we learned in Cagliari of inland "bandidos" kidnaping tourists for ransom. An American family was still being held for ran-som as we sailed from Sardinia. It seemed strange that, having come from unbelievably Stone Age, primitive places in the Sol-omon Islands and the New Hebrides, through pirate-infested waters in the Java Sea, South China Sea, and Malacca Strait off Sumatra and Indonesia, as well as the politically fragile Islamic countries in the Red Sea such as North Yemen and Turkey in the Mediterranean, we were now becoming aware of a new type of criminality in the historical heartland of Western civilization.

While cruising the Mediterranean, we were disheartened to find among "friends," "allies," as well as overt enemies of

Communism in Sicily

America, an increasing contempt for our country and its *appearance* of weakness, lack of resolve, and lack of leadership. In countless discussions with people in all walks of life— common fishermen, peasants, intellectuals, doctors, and highly educated, articulate citizens of Western alliance countries, the central lament was uniformly the same, "If we can't rely on America, to whom can we turn?" With the Swiss, West German, Italian, Dutch, Greek, French, and British people we came to know in our eighteen months in the Mediterranean basin, international politics were in the forefront of their thinking.

Consistently, the opinions volunteered to us were that our friends and allies had been traumatized by our abandonment of anti-Communist Vietnam, the deterioration of our relationship with Taiwan, and the sensational reporting of the events of the Watergate incident.

These situations, combined with our seeming impotence in dealing with Soviet adventurism via their Cuban and East German surrogates in Africa—Angola, Mozambique, Ethiopia—

and elsewhere in the world, have, from all of the inputs we received, shattered much of the respect for and confidence in America and its reliability as an ally.

From the lovely island of Carloforte, Italy, we sailed across the Ligurian Sea to Menorca and the fascinating Spanish Balearic Islands of Majorca, Cabrera, Ibiza, and Formentera. We were enchanted by the Balearics and Spain and enjoyed our cruising of this area more than any place in the Mediterranean with the exception of the Anatolian coast of Turkey.

"Lost City" anchorage, Turkey

Aegean anchorage

"Almost too much to ask
of a lady"

Sandstorm

CHAPTER TWENTY-FOUR

OVERBOARD

⚓ Probably the principal fear that haunts a couple sailing the high seas is falling overboard from the vessel under sail out in the open sea. Over our years of ocean sailing, Shirley and I have rehearsed and planned for this dreadful contingency more than for any other accident that could befall us.

The *Morning Star* was on a broad reach with all sails set. Northeast twenty-to-twenty-five-knot winds—called levanters in this part of the world—were driving us at six knots across the sixty-mile span of open sea between Formentera in the Balearics and mainland Spain. The winds came unbroken from the Gulf of Lions in France, and the seas were eight to ten feet high. The Mediterranean in this area is 1,000 meters (3,280 feet) deep. It was the best sail we had had in our entire eighteen-month Mediterranean cruise. We were energized, and all was well despite an ominous overcast sky. We were looking forward to crossing the zero degree meridian; reentering the Western Hemisphere.

The steering vane hadn't been used for months. Preliminary to the Atlantic crossing lying ahead of us, I wanted to activate Jonathan from his long period of hibernation. The servopendulum rudder projecting out from the stern of the boat was corroded in a cocked-up position. Shirl was below preparing lunch, but for some—possibly intuition-directed—reason, came up into the cockpit to watch me struggling with a boat hook over the stern, pushing against the jammed servorudder. With the foolish complacency born of doing something which I had done many times before, I did not don a safety harness or life jacket.

Suddenly, with no warning, the boat hook skidded off the servorudder. The boat lurched—I lost my balance—and with Shirl's scream and the shattering of wood echoing in my ears, I pitched headlong over the stern into the heaving sea. In the plunge, my right shoulder had splintered the plywood wind vane, jaggedly breaking it off at its base.

As I surfaced, still clinging to the boat hook, and (Shirl said later) "spouting orders," I beheld the awesome sight of the *Morning Star* with all sails set, sailing away, leaving me thrashing in her wake.

As we quickly drew out of earshot of one another, I shouted, "Come up into the wind! Turn to starboard! Heave to!"

Then as the boat drew farther away—50 yards—100 yards—200 yards—I saw Shirl begin turning the *Morning Star* into the wind.

To conserve my energy, I slowly treaded water, using the drown-proofing system. Curled into a balled-up tuck, I would breathe slowly, sink a little, surface, breathe again, and keep repeating to myself, "Keep cool, Ray. Don't panic. Oh, God, don't let Shirl panic."

Flashing thoughts flickered on the screen of my mind. I had a fleeting vision of sharks. But we hadn't seen sharks in the Mediterranean since southern Turkey. My shoulder was slashed and bleeding from its encounter with the shattered vane, but I didn't think it was enough to attract any sharks coming in from the Atlantic through the Strait of Gibraltar. "Why did I ever abandon the practice of towing a 300-foot floating safety line?" I thought of three men I had known who had been lost overboard during the past five years. I thought of the training which I had received during the war regarding hypothermia (the loss of body heat inducing a state of shock and death). I thought of how my thirty-seven-year-old father had drowned in forty-two-degree water in northern Minnesota. "Is this the way my life is going to end?"

As these transient, kaleidoscopic thoughts paraded through my brain, my concentration was on the *Morning Star*, now hove to on a port tack, forereaching under the still-drawing mainsail. I had swallowed a lot of seawater in the initial surprise plunge, and I knew that there was no way to swim against the breaking, white-capped seas to the distant craft; so I decided to stay put in my curled-up position, hoping that Shirl could spot me bobbing in the troughs.

Then I saw smoke spurt out of the exhaust as the yacht rose and fell in the beam seas. Shirl had started the motor! Over the years, I had instructed her in such a contingency to steer on a reciprocal course toward where she had last seen me, and to try not to lose sight of me as she aimed the boat directly at my head. Now, her mind returned these instructions to her, and I watched the bow swing toward me. Shirl was standing up, steering with her feet, scanning the area where she had last seen me. Although I shouted "Turn more to starboard. I am to leeward from you," she couldn't hear my cries against the wind. Then, her wildly waving arms indicated that she saw me! She turned south to where the seas had swept me and headed the boat directly toward me. If she could keep this course, I could grab the bobstay as the yacht swept by me.

As the boat's bow—looking like the *Queen Mary* from my perspective—bore down on me, she put the motor in neutral to avoid the risk of the whirling propeller cutting me to pieces in the water. Struggling to reach the wire bobstay as the boat bounded off a following sea, my clutching fingertips missed it by inches, and the forty-six foot *Morning Star* began to sweep past.

Shirl then threw the balance of the bitter end of the mainsheet in the water off the port quarter, but as she did so, she again secured it on its cleat and the boat took off like a startled gazelle. With the yacht again drawing away from me, I managed to get one hand wrapped around the trailing end of the mainsheet line—the other hand still clinging to the twelve-foot-long boat hook that had been in my grasp as I pitched over the side. I clung to the line with the desperation borne out of the realization that this might be my last chance.

Gradually, I inched forward, wrapping the trailing line around my waist as the boat continued to gain speed. I was

being dragged like a hooked fish with the breaking seas causing me to swallow still more seawater.

I yelled to Shirl to luff the boat back into the wind, which
she immediately tried to do without engaging the propeller.
Slowly the boat slowed and hove to, pitching into the curling,
snapping seas.

Then I began to make progress ever so slowly—dragging
myself along the line wrapped around me—toward the port
quarter of the *Morning Star.* As I inched myself toward the
pitching yacht, Shirl mounted our boarding ladder amidships
on the port side. But I couldn't make it in the seas breaking
around the bow of the yacht, so she threw over an emergency
rope boarding ladder, which we have carried on several boats
for the past eighteen years.

Man overboard

As the emergency ladder streamed astern, I entangled my legs in its plastic rungs and rested, trying to overcome the nausea caused by the swallowed seawater. The *Morning Star* continued to forereach at three knots as its bow fell off the wind.

Rung by rung, I drew myself under the lee of the curving turn of the bilge section and thrust the boat hook toward Shirl, instructing her to hook it into a shroud. Instead, she bravely tried to pull me closer against the force of the sea; so, in mortal fear that I would pull *her* over the side, I released my hold on the boat hook, and Shirl reeled back into the cockpit. With both of us overboard in these rough seas, the episode could have, in seconds, turned into a major disaster.

Recovering a man out of the sea, up and over the pitching stern quarter of a yacht, requires much more strength than a 110-pound woman can muster, so with the aid of more lines secured across my chest, I managed to place one foot at a time carefully on each successive rung of the streaming ladder, and finally, with every surge of adrenaline I could muster, dragged myself up free from the clutching tentacles of the breaking seas, over the taffrail, and into the safety of the cockpit.

I was cold, trembling, and nauseated, but as I sprawled on the cockpit cushions, we both profusely thanked God for this deliverance from a watery grave for, quite possibly, both of us. The whole episode had lasted only forty-five minutes.

Had Shirl lost me out there, she could have proceeded to Spain, forty miles to the west, and attempted to get help. But this would have taken her eight to ten hours—night would have fallen, and we shall never know whether or not I could have withstood the hypothermia for what would have been a minimum of eighteen hours before dawn of the next day. After a sun sight, we resumed course, and at 1900 we were safely anchored at Ensa de Benidorm, Spain.

Then began the postmortem—the debriefing. What we did right and what we did wrong.

First, I had made the grave error of not securing myself to the yacht with a safety harness. There is no excuse for this. One gets so accustomed to living in and on the deep that complacency sets in and the potentially lethal nature of the open sea is pushed way into the background of the conscious mind.

We carry on each side of the cockpit a man-overboard horse-shoe-shaped life ring with electronic flare, sea anchor, twenty-foot weighted floating fiberglass pole with a flag on its tip, yellow dye marker, shark repellent, and whistle, all attached. This should have been dropped into the water immediately, to enable me to stay afloat and to enable Shirl to see the flag, marking my position. For some reason, in the turmoil of the moment, Shirl had not done this. I teased her about this. "You had to first think about whether you *wanted* to come back and get me. Here was the perfect chance to collect on my life insurance."

I should not have initially exerted any energy trying to swim into the seas, but rather immediately curled up with my back toward them. The temptation to watch the yacht maneuvering in the distance overwhelmed my good judgment, and the breaking seas forced more water down my throat than was necessary.

Shirl should have cast off the halyard of the mainsail, allowing it to tumble on the deck, once she was assured that the motor was going to start.

It is quite easy to "Monday-morning-quarterback" your own mistakes or the human error of others. The fact that we both survived this incident indicates that we conquered the chief killer—panic. Panic is the number one enemy, and fortunately, through the grace of God, we have yet to see its devastating effect arise in either of us at any time in our many years of high seas voyaging. This does not mean that we are immune to panic in any way. What it does mean is that as panic inevitably surges within us, we, through conscious, determined *effort*, repeat aloud to ourselves, "Keep calm," "Panic kills," "Slow down," "*Think* it through." I call this technique "self-talk." It works for us and could save lives for others.

For the next month, we cruised the Costa del Sol of southern Spain—Torrevieja, Cartagena, Almería, Roquetas, Motril, Torremolinas, José Banus, Marbella, Malaga, Estepona, and finally, there ahead of us, reared the Rock of Gibraltar! In a leisurely eighteen-month cruise, we had sailed the length of the Mediterranean from Port Said, Egypt, to the Atlantic Ocean.

As we lingered in Spanish ports enroute to Gibraltar, the papers were full of reports of bombings by Basque terrorists. In an effort to disrupt Spain's $5 billion tourist industry and to destabilize this staunch friend of America, the Communists were assassinating generals on the streets of Madrid, bombing the Madrid airport, and succeeded in reducing the tourist influx from northern Europe 30 percent during the months we were in Spain.

It seemed that the anti-American noose was being tightened everywhere in our wake. In Izmir and Istanbul, Turkey, tourists were being wantonly murdered by "terrorists." Just a few months earlier, we had spent weeks in Turkey, most particularly, Ephesus near Izmir. During this time, the Muslim Turks we had met were generally open, helpful, and friendly toward us.

But now, we were genuinely looking forward to the Atlantic crossing awaiting us. Out in the open sea, we are safe and self-contained, independent, and, for a time at least, totally liberated and free from the man-created problems besetting our planet.

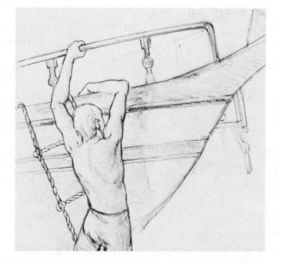

Climbing aboard

CHAPTER TWENTY-FIVE

TO THE ROOT OF ROOTS

The overland border between Gibraltar and Spain is closed. Spanish and British soldiers stand guard on either side within a few yards of one another. Spain no longer recognizes Britain's right to occupy this fortresslike bastion, standing sentinel over the strategic entrance to the Mediterranean. But the people of Gibraltar do not want the British to vacate Gibraltar—their last Mediterranean base. So the stalemate continues.

After final preparations for the Atlantic crossing, we sailed out into the Strait of Gibraltar, crossing the densely trafficked shipping lanes to Tangier, Morocco. Then, with twenty-knot northeast levanter winds, we swept around Cape Spartel on the northwestern tip of the African continent, bound for Casablanca, Morocco. Casablanca! The Casbah—Humphrey Bogart—"As Time Goes By"—World War II North African Allied Headquarters—Casablanca has a romantic connotation for many Americans.

American embassy people in Rabat, the capital city, were dubious about our going to Casablanca in a yacht. While it could be a tourist attraction, it has attained an ugly reputation for rip-offs, muggings, and theft. Our days in the large commercial harbor of Casablanca were spent tied up in a tightly guarded small-craft facility, enclosed in a barbed-wire fence.

Casablanca is a city of 1 million. The new part of the city is French in layout and architecture. Walking tours were fascinating. The language barrier is total, so our limited French again enabled us to get by.

King Hassan of Morocco is pro-American, but he has a million-dollar-a-day war on his hands with the left-wing Soviet-sponsored Polisario guerrillas in southern Morocco—formerly Spanish Sahara.

Casablanca is indeed no place for a yacht. On two successive nights, three Moroccans tried to board us at 0300 in the night. Each time some sixth sense awakened me, and I stormed on deck with a powerful light and many strong words. The water-borne thieves fled, but these episodes were beginning to make us feel uncomfortable.

Cruising the world in one's own yacht has many advantages. We are in our own floating home, complete with our own clothing and cooking and sleeping facilities. We aren't herded around in tourist buses, nor are we on a tightly regulated schedule. But, it also has its disadvantages—especially when anchored in a large commercial seaport. The waterfront areas of big cities are usually located in the most disreputable part of the city. Whenever leaving the boat in this part of the world, we not only have to arrange for its guardianship, but we must come and go through unsavory sections of the city.

To climax this discomfort, we were walking down a side street in broad daylight in Casablanca when a tall, skinny Arab in his twenties veered toward me on the sidewalk and attempted to throw me to the ground as his hands clawed at my wallet. Shirl was about twenty paces ahead, window-shopping, when she saw me tussling with this hoodlum. So she started running back, shouting "Your wallet, your wallet." My wallet was the last thing I cared to think about at that point.

The thug was rough and mean, but I used his own momentum to get my foot behind his heel, spun him around, and gave him a vicious jab in the kidney with my bony elbow. With that, he let out a shriek, and as he tried to run down the deserted street, he met Shirl running back toward me. This further disconcerted him, and he gave her a rude shove and disappeared around the corner.

We emerged from this unscathed; remembering that worse things happen on the streets of America, we overcame the human tendency to generalize. A few years ago, a business acquaintance of mine was shot dead in broad daylight in a plush residential section of San Francisco while out for a Sunday walk with his wife. So we didn't allow this to become a "big deal" in our minds.

The next day, we hired a Moroccan—Muhamed—and spent the entire day in the Casbah with him. Arabs selling water from goatskin bags—veiled women—the finest fruit and vegetable market we had ever seen—throngs of colorfully dressed Muslims—no Europeans or white men in sight—a vastly different culture, which we found completely fascinating.

On September 1, we sailed from Casablanca, bound for the Canary Islands, 430 miles southwest. We sharply headed well away from the coastline of Southern Morocco and the Western Sahara because of Polisario guerrilla patrol boats off the African coast, which had reportedly attacked unarmed small craft in these waters in recent months.

We had a fast passage with twenty-five-knot northwest winds, and on the third overcast day we were uncertain of our position, so I hove to at 0430 to await a possible celestial observation at dawn. While we were hove to, our faithful Aries self-steering vane broke before we could clear it from the pitching action of the vessel.

At daylight, we could dimly see the unlighted Allegranza Rock through the rain and made our way into the beautiful, deserted anchorage in Estrecho el Rio, between Graciosa Island and Lanzarote. We rested, swam, and were treated very kindly by the Canary Island fishermen, who gave us fish and a moray eel, which we boiled and had for dinner. Then we cruised the islands of Lanzarote, Fuerteventura, and ended up in Las Palmas, the capital city. After a month cruising among the Canary Islands, where we had Jonathan repaired, we sailed from Puerto Rico, Grand Canary Island, bound for

Dakar, Senegal, where we had French friends—a doctor and his family.

Staying well off the Western Sahara and Mauritania coasts, we had a fast six-day passage to Dakar. We sailed amid a concentration of ships more dense than any we had experienced since the Red Sea. We got a concept of the magnitude of the oil business as we observed the parade of supertankers coming and going up and down the coast of West Africa, bound from and to the Persian Gulf, around the Cape of Good Hope, heading to and from the European and Mediterranean ports with their hundreds of thousands of tons of crude oil.

Sailing a small craft at night amidst a concentration of shipping such as this is always an unnerving proposition. These mammoth supertankers simply do not see our running lights down in the troughs of the sea until they are very close to us. So the burden of avoidance, while legally resting on them, is really on us. They are simply bigger than we are and could run us down without any awareness on the part of the crew that they had struck anything. It takes a modern supertanker five miles to stop, and this is about the distance from our deck—four feet above the water—when we first see its lights. We must then calculate its speed, course, and distance from us. Our radar is of great value in these encounters.

Numerous times we had five or more ships speeding at twenty-plus knots all around us. While their lights are bright, we have to compute our course in relation to the simultaneous courses of these goliaths. The process kept us frantically busy and required all our concentrated abilities as we changed course to avoid them.

At 0400 on October 14, my fifty-eighth birthday, we had the Cape Vert Light in sight and began to close with the reef-strewn coast to round Cape Vert at dawn, then pick our way into the crowded harbor of Dakar. The steaming heat with 89 percent humidity rolled out toward us from the African continent as we sailed into an anchorage near a collection of local boats. We sat there with our yellow quarantine flag flying, awaiting boarding from Senegal authorities. Nothing happened—no one appeared.

At midmorning, a Frenchman came out to us and told us in French, "No problem. Just go ashore. We will guard your boat, and don't bother with officialdom."

I found a telephone and called Dr. Paul Duval, our French doctor friend, who had invited these American circumnavigators to Senegal. He immediately canceled his day's appointments and arranged to meet us and take us to his lovely home, where we met his beautiful wife, Nicole. They had their servants prepare an elaborate French cuisine meal for us.

Inevitably, Paul drew me into a political discussion—volunteering in the "Western-ally" style all of the things that were wrong with America and its foreign policy. I try to avoid these discussions, but we, as an American couple who had spent the last six years sailing alone around the world, found ourselves to be curiosities and quasi celebrities in many of these remote parts of the world seldom visited by yachts. We couldn't ignore the demanding line of questioning of our hosts.

Unlike in America, geopolitical considerations in this part of the world are in the forefront of every educated man's thinking. Our essential mentality at home still to some degree turns on our "two-ocean" isolation. Also, the hectic pace of our daily lives leaves scant space for intense preoccupation with global affairs. Yet, our open society is under a constant microscopic analysis by the rest of the world. Our friends and enemies alike examine America's daily domestic and foreign attitudes, as expressed by our media, with magnified scrutiny.

In the Arab countries, we were criticized for our "special relationship" with Israel. In Israel, our flag would attract challenging statements directed toward us regarding supplying Saudi Arabia with F-15 fighter planes. In Cyprus, the Greeks say, "Why didn't the American Sixth Fleet stop the Turkish invasion?" In Turkey, "Why does America continue this foolish arms embargo against us?" In Greece, our unfortunate siding with the military junta (the colonels, as the Greeks call them) brought down on Americans the wrath of the Greeks. My standard response to these undisguised criticisms is, "Don't complain to me. I am just an American taxpayer who keeps financing all of this. There is a limit to our horn of plenty, and there is a limit to our ability to control world events. Also there is a limit to our patience. At the end of the war, your protestors said, 'Yankee go home! You are not the gendarmes of the world'."

Despite what often struck us as a basic belligerence toward America—we seemed to detect a love-hate ambivalence toward our country, expressed by the educated people with whom we came in contact. One thing is certain—the dreams of hundreds of people we encountered from the South Pacific, Southeast Asia, the Middle East, Africa, and the Mediterranean basin involved immigrating to America someday.

However, Shirl and I, on a one-on-one human basis, somehow got along with people of all countries, despite their institutionalized attitudes created by the unrelenting Soviet anti-American propaganda war waged without cessation against us since the very inception of the Bolshevik Revolution.

It was a source of continued frustration to us, as mere private citizens, to observe that as Soviet expansionism continues to swallow into its gaping maw state after state around the world, we seem to have no effective apparatus to counter this staggering mass of falsehoods pouring daily out of our short-wave receiver from Radio Moscow.

Sitting in the cool breeze wafting over the veranda of Paul's luxurious home in Senegal, I continued to listen to his critical comments about America (which, as a French colonial officer, he had, typically, never visited). Despite the fact that we were guests in his home, my patience began to wear a bit thin.

I said, "Paul, *mon ami*, we are mere citizens of America, but we love our country, so I am going to try to tell you a bit about our perspectives."

I began, "Paul, I think that you would agree that both the French and the Americans are an intensely liberty-loving people. We are both the products of revolution. In the French Revolution, your people threw off the yoke of monarchy dictating and regulating every aspect of the lives of the citizenry. In the American Revolution, we successfully, with the help of the French, established independence from the control of a foreign tyranny. The Americans have not forgotten Lafayette.

"Then, during the twentieth century, France was decimated by World War I to a point where it couldn't withstand the ruthless onslaught of Hitler and his Nazi panzer divisions only twenty-two years later.

"In each instance, the Americans responded to the desperate aspirations of our French and British friends across the sea and liberated France from the barbaric Nazi forces occupying your country. And, Paul, you may agree, if this weren't enough, the people of America made enormous sacrifices with their historically unprecedented act in rebuilding France and Western Europe in the form of the Marshall Plan.

"Similarly, we rebuilt and revitalized the society and economy of our archenemies, the Japanese.

"Where in the history of mankind can you point to this kind of conduct of a victor in dealing with the vanquished?

"Yet, Paul, we are a very young and sometimes naive nation. We make mistakes and may appear inept in our sometimes thankless and uncomfortable role as leaders of the free world.

"When, as private citizens, we encounter intense criticism from our allies and friends, we are puzzled and have a tendency to retreat into isolationism—a 'fortress America' mentality. Many Americans are frustrated to the point where they become prone to accept the counsel of our founding fathers and avoid all entangling foreign alliances." I asked, "Did you ever stop to consider, Paul, what kind of world would this be today if there were no United States of America?"

Sitting across from me, Paul flushed a deep carmine. After regaining his composure, he said, "Ramon, possibly you have a point or two there." From a Frenchman this is a major capitulation. He sprang up from the table and went into his library and emerged with a huge leather-bound, elaborately illustrated French dictionary. With a big smile, he extended the heavy volume to me with the words, "S'il vous plaît, Ramon, accept this book as a gift from me. It will make your heated, grotesque French more intelligible." It must have been a very precious possession of his.

Then Paul showed me an elementary school textbook—of course, written in French. He pointed to a section wherein the children were being taught about America. It said that "the American people through the American Legion, Ku Klux Klan, and the John Bird [*sic*] Society suppress the black people, deprive them of opportunity, and are very cruel to them."

At this, I exploded and said, "Paul, *mon ami*, this is an outrageous lie! Don't you realize that this is pure Marxist propaganda? Is this what you Frenchmen are teaching these black African children?" Paul looked me in the eye and said, "No, Ramon, this is a primary school primer from France. This is what our government is teaching *French* children about America. What we are teaching the Senegalese is much worse."

As he probed and questioned, I felt that he was genuinely puzzled and really was trying to learn from us what we perceived to be the truth.

Paul had seen our TV during the fifties and sixties emphasizing police dogs attacking blacks in Birmingham, and all of the seamy demonstrations of the sixties. The power of the electronic media creates and leaves a lasting detrimental impression on most foreigners.

I told Paul that today, Birmingham, along with many other southern and northern cities, had a black mayor. He was flabbergasted. Our Voice of America, and especially our commercial TV, apparently never seeks to show the rest of the world what is right, good, and decent about our country and our people. They see only the vivid portrayal of crime, violence, and a seeming guilt about our power and position in the world. What with the incessant drumbeat of masochistic self-denigration of America by our media, which the entire world watches intensely, why should Americans be surprised when everyone in the world wants to join in the game?

After this interchange, Paul and I had many other discussions about Soviet intentions and the threat of Soviet expansionism to engulf not only freedom-loving French people, but to consume all of the non-Communist states of the world.

After several days of touring Senegal with Paul and Nicole, we had to leave. We enjoyed and appreciated the warm friendship that all four of us had developed. They were worried about our sailing across the Atlantic, and we, quite frankly, would have liked to remain with them a little longer. Ahead of us, we were looking forward to sailing to The Gambia—the root of the book *Roots.*

Since reading and rereading the book *Roots*, we wanted to sail in the path of the sailing slave ships of old and to some extent learn for ourselves more about this barbaric chapter in American history—the West African slave trade.

At dawn, we left Dakar and sailed the ninety miles to the entrance of the mighty Gambia River. During the day, we dodged and darted among eight Russian purse-seining trawlers illegally poaching fish in Senegal waters. As one "trawler" cut across our bow, dragging his steel cable nets, I called him on the VHF radio in English and asked him, "How close can we safely cut across your stern? How deep are your nets?" Our American flag was proudly fluttering from our stern, and we were literally surrounded by the crisscrossing trawlers. To our surprise, a voice came back in fluent English, with a heavy Slavic accent, asking who we were, and where we were bound.

I told him we were out of Dakar, bound for The Gambia. There were a few moments of silence, and then he came back and asked us if we would like an accurate position. Although it was overcast and the African coast was flat, undistinguished, and obscured by haze, I knew exactly where I was. So I thanked him, but told him that this was not necessary.

But he came back and, more or less imploringly said, "Let us give you an *exact* position." He added, "We have *exact* satellite navigation equipment and can do so in seconds."

As long as he was swerving out of our way, I had nothing to lose, so I said, "Okay, we would appreciate a position report."

In about thirty seconds, he came back, "*Morning Star*, you are now at latitude fourteen degrees, twelve minutes, thirty seconds north, longitude seventeen degrees, six minutes, eight seconds west." A minute of arc is one nautical mile, so the *seconds* given were literally in feet. I was impressed, and told him so.

But he made his point—whatever it was—nationalistic pride, friendly display of helpfulness, or an attempted put-down of this American pleasure yacht in this remote corner of the world. It is difficult for the Western mind to fathom the inscrutable Russians.

The Gambia,* a former British colony, became "independent" in 1965 and a republic in 1970. As typical with the emerging nations, when the seemingly desirable independence is obtained, and the European technicians leave, things mechanical begin to deteriorate rapidly.

My chart of the entrance to Banjul (formerly Bathurst) showed the existence of range lights. When we arrived into an area of shifting mud banks on a black moonless night, we found that there were no range lights. So, in the style of the square-rigged sailing slave vessels, we slowly sounded our way into a place off the mouth of the river in thirty feet of water and let go the anchor.

An uncanny silence, broken only by the animal and bird noises coming from the African bush, descended on the boat as the anchor dug firmly into heavy mud. We were anchored in a place called Cutter Roads, where the slave vessels had anchored to await the turn of the tide and the formidable current sweeping out of the river.

The boat was immediately infested with huge beetlelike bugs attracted by our lights below. We had never seen insects like this elsewhere in the world, so we turned off all the lights, fired up mosquito coils, and munched a late-night snack before going to bed.

At predawn, as the oppressive African heat and humidity descended on us, we inched our way into the mouth of the mighty Gambia. We had paved the way with a British ham radio operator connected with a medical research project, and he had strongly urged us to come to The Gambia. A remark that he made didn't sit well with Shirl. It was "This is a white man's graveyard."

*Following an attempted Communist takeover, The Gambia recently merged as a political entity with Senegal and is now called Senegambia.

While the British contingent live in a self-contained compound, with sentry and Doberman guard dogs, in really raja-like conditions, the rest of the nation is in abject poverty. The average male life expectancy is thirty-two years. Disease—malaria, leprosy, elephantiasis, blindness, yaws—is everywhere in the squalor of the streets of Banjul.

We were royally entertained by the British and by the American contingent of foreign aid people and embassy personnel, but we didn't come to The Gambia to fraternize with other *tubobs*, as they call the white men. As always, we felt the powder-keg atmosphere of the contrast brought about by a few select American, British, French, and other foreigners who are government employees (civil servants) living in these colonial outposts in the style of pashas while the aid given somehow doesn't seem to filter down completely to the people.

We made friends with a young Mandinke Muslim—Osman Yallow—who crewed on the president's yacht. The president was in Mecca on his annual pilgrimage, so I retained as interpreters Osman and another young Gambian named Francis, who was fluent in English as well as the tribal languages of Mandinke and Wolof.

Francis had been assigned to us by the government to give us the official version of the slave trade and the history of the tribes' people; so accompanied by these two young Gambians, we set sail up the river into the African bush, bound for Juffure, the supposed ancestral home of Alex Haley's Kunta Kinte.

To our dismay, many of the educated Gambians we talked to told us that Haley's version of the *Roots* story was substantially fictional. They explained that in all of The Gambia, you could not find anyone who could recount his or her oral history (there is no written language) beyond a generation or two.

Francis, the educated government-assigned interpreter, with ambitions to attend law school in the United Kingdom, told us that slaving had been going on for centuries among the tribes. Slaves were procured by intertribal warfare, and in some cases, when famine struck, whole villages would offer themselves as slaves to their new, more affluent masters, who would feed them and care for them.

Then, as Francis explained, in the late eighteenth and early nineteenth centuries, the *tubob* ("white men") began to appear with their large canoes (sailing ships) and would buy slaves from the tribal chieftains in exchange for rifles, gunpowder, and whiskey. While the British abolished this barbaric practice in 1807, the American slavers continued to come to West Africa to buy slaves until shortly before the American Civil War.

The Mandinke tribespeople are essentially gentle, intelligent, kind, fun-loving, and tractable, and our hearts went out to them as we saw malnutrition-bloated bellies of children, flies crawling on babies, and the general lassitude induced by perpetual illness as we wandered through the village of Juffure. The Mandinkes were kind to us, and told us how they detested the Arabs and the "other *tubobs*," who they said treated them like dogs.

The Gambia River is the principal resource of this small country bisecting Senegal. It stretches hundreds of miles into the African interior and is inhabited by crocodiles and hippopotamuses. We were warned not to dip a hand in the water from our dinghy because crocodiles swim toward game in these muddy waters almost unnoticed and very fast. Remembering the stories of Australian friends in Papua New Guinea who had a friend devoured by a crocodile, Shirl and I did not swim while sailing into the African interior.

Along with apes, baboons, and assorted African creatures, Shirl and I were most attracted by a small, dainty, gazellelike creature called a duiker. We were particularly impressed with the proliferation of bird life. These birds were in size, habits, coloration, and music like no birds we had ever encountered anywhere. The Gambia must be an ornithologist's paradise.

While on the Gambia River expedition, we would watch Osman—approximately twenty-four years old—go to the foredeck, wash his face, hands, and feet, spread his prayer rug, face east (toward Mecca), and bend face down in prayer to Allah. Osman and I became fast friends, and many nights in the cockpit, anchored in the Gambia River, we would talk about the religious philosophy of Islam. One night I pointed at the crescent of the new moon and told Osman how Americans had walked on the moon. I was astounded when Osman said, "Ray, I have heard this, but I don't believe it. The moon is sacred to Islam. No man could ever walk on it."

Since leaving Morocco, I had been chronically sick with an intermittent intestinal obstruction. I was deeply touched when Osman assured me with tears in his eyes that Allah would not allow me to become sick or to die in The Gambia or crossing the Atlantic Ocean. This devout young man said, "Allah sees all. He sees that you are kind to our Mandinke people. He will reward your love for our people. You will not be sick or die here."

As events later unfolded, while crossing the Atlantic, I had many opportunities to think and wonder about Osman's prophecy.

An important Muslim religious feast was due to fall on November 1. At this time, a Muslim must repay all debts and buy and kill a sheep to offer to Allah. Cash is required to fulfill these obligations. Sometimes, paradoxically, stealing from "infidels" is the only way available to raise this necessary money.

After returning to Banjul from our up-river expedition, two attempts to steal our dinghy and motor were made during the night. I lock the dinghy with a steel cable to the yacht, and the motor is similarly locked, but each morning I would find that the dinghy rope painter had been untied as nocturnal thieves had silently slipped out from shore in their dugout canoes. The expensive Zodiac dinghy suspended from the davits of the president's unoccupied yacht right next to us was stolen at the same time.

When I told the chief of police about this, I was shocked to hear him say, "If this happens again, shoot them!" I couldn't believe my ears! He went on, "I mean it—shoot them—they are not Gambians. Gambian people don't steal. They are Guinea-Bissau tribesmen who are thieves. You will save us the trouble if you shoot them."

I told the chief that there was no way I was going to shoot anyone unless he attacked Shirley or me. His retort, "Then it is your problem. There is nothing we can do."

It was two days before the religious feast when we began to feel somewhat vulnerable lying at anchor in the waterfront section of Banjul. So, at dusk, we left Banjul and anchored in Cutter Roads, preliminary to our starting our Atlantic crossing the next day.

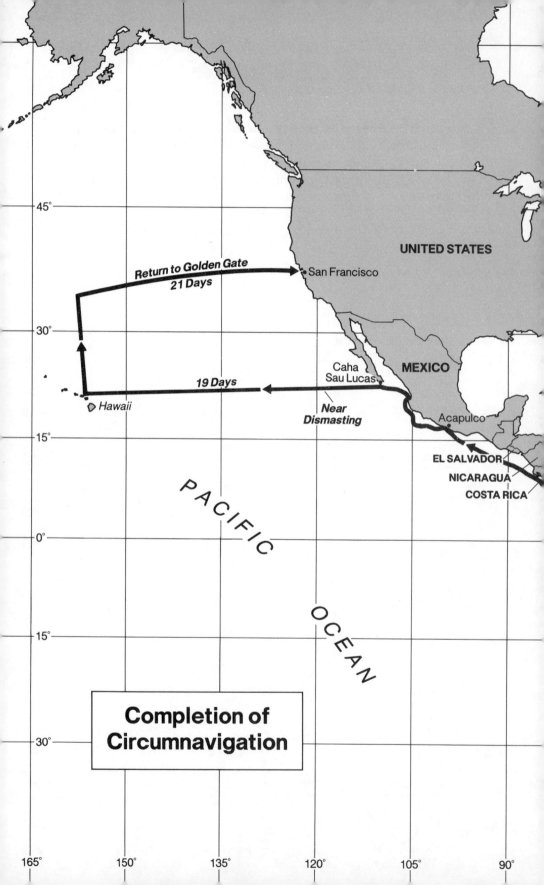

Completion of
Circumnavigation

45°

30°

Return to Golden Gate
21 Days
San Francisco

UNITED STATES

Caha
Sau Lucas

MEXICO

19 Days

Near
Dismasting

Hawaii

Acapulco

15°

EL SALVADOR
NICARAGUA
COSTA RICA

PACIFIC

0°

OCEAN

15°

30°

165°   150°   135°   120°   105°   90°

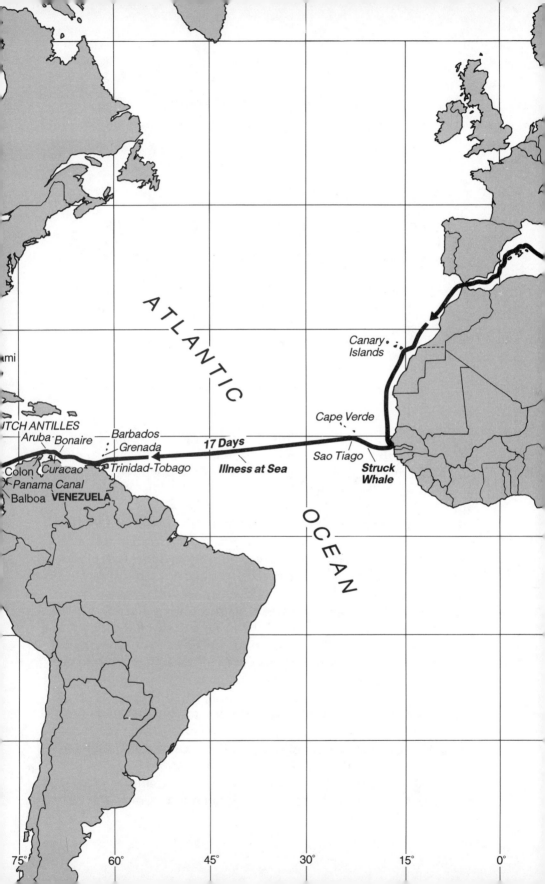

CHAPTER TWENTY-SIX

THE ATLANTIC CROSSING AND THE "WHAT IFS"

With a fair tide and fifteen-knot winds, we sailed from Africa the next morning. As the land disappeared in our wake, we were again escorted by a school of porpoises, which we deemed to be a good omen for what might be ahead of us in the Atlantic Ocean.

In the middle of a black moonless night, three hundred miles off the West African coast, the *Morning Star*, under full sail, struck a surfaced whale. Shirl was on watch, and I was sleeping. As the boat heeled sharply to starboard, I came hurtling out of my bunk into the cockpit. Twenty feet off our starboard beam there was a gigantic threshing and blowing as the phosphorescent sea was churned by the leviathan of the deep. I started the motor in the hopes that the noise would frighten him away from us. With a mighty flap of his enormous tail, he submerged, and we never saw him again.

Coming from the Canaries, Shirl and I had seen whales at least the size of our yacht and had talked about the problems of encountering them. We know of three craft sunk by whales in the last four years. One was a steel yacht owned by a Belgian friend, Patrick, off the Brazilian coast. Patrick and his pregnant wife, Wendy, sailed seven hundred miles in a rubber dinghy to Brazil. Another was attacked by killer whales near the Galapagos, and the captain, Dougal Robertson, wrote a book entitled *Survive the Savage Sea* about their thirty-seven days in a survival raft after their craft had sunk.

And still another yacht was sent to the bottom by a wounded whale (from nearby Japanese whale-killing operations), again near the Galapagos Islands, causing its crew to spend 145 days in their life raft before they were rescued.

We began to take water at the rate of twenty gallons an hour, then thirty, and finally forty gallons an hour. We were pumping every five minutes during our watches. I dismantled all of the cabin floorboards, checked all through-hull fittings, and ascertained that the water was coming in through a sprung plank inaccessible from the interior of the boat, midway up the forward starboard side.

Then, in what turned out to be a totally unrelated series of bizarre events, while I was crouched over the open bilge, still pondering what our best strategy would be, all hell broke loose! Large volumes of water began to flood the boat. Thinking that we might have to abandon the *Morning Star* in our emergency six-man life raft, I hastily got on the radio and raised a ham in faraway Atlanta, Georgia.

I emphasized that this was *not* a Mayday Situation *yet*, but I asked him to record our coordinates. He, then, on his own volition, contacted the U.S. Coast Guard, twenty-five hundred miles from our position, and they, along with five other hams, including Bud Alvernaz in San Jose, California, stood by on frequency while Shirl and I busied ourselves with this new crisis.

We have aboard one permanently installed electric pump, one heavy-duty portable electric pump, one portable whale-gusher manual pump, one navy manual pump, and a high-powered, motor-driven clutch pump. The two of us could only man two manual pumps at a time. With these plus the two electric and the motor-driven clutch pumps going, the water still continued to climb up into the boat to where we were now ankle deep. The pumps were just holding their own. Then Shirl yelled, "We are on fire!" Smoke was pouring out of the engine compartment as the water mounted up over the base of the motor.

Then, in seconds, as bilge-flooding alarm bells went off to add to the chaos, I thought I had the diagnosis, and a plan of action developed. The engine had been running since just after colliding with the whale. When I tore open the diesel engine compartment, I saw that it was boiling hot; thus accounting for the smoke and steam.

So after shutting the engine off, I zeroed in on the engine intake sea cock—everything okay there. Following the route of the seawater intake through the gearbox cooling, through the freezer condenser on the opposite side of the boat, I found the problem!

The New Zealand–made copper condenser had failed just out of Tel Aviv. So refrigeration mechanics in Tel Aviv had secured, via a dielectric union, a copper pipe to a new stainless steel condenser. When I asked them about the dissimilar-metal problem, they had assured me that with the dielectric union, "the condenser would last longer than I would." I made the mistake of believing them. Water was being pumped into the boat faster than we could pump it out.

But, after we shut off the engine and closed the intake sea cock, the inrushing water, other than our plank leak—which was controllable—terminated. We pumped the boat dry as it continued to sail ahead under vane-steering control. I then profusely thanked all of the great ham radio operators who had stood by for over an hour and secured the radio.

During my watch that night, Shirl awoke to find me boiling a two-inch plastic hose in a pan on the stove. I had figured out a way to jury-rig the condenser cooling system with plastic hose, rubber hose, and scrap copper pipe so that the engine would work as well as ever while the refrigeration system would be temporarily repaired.

Because of the sprung plank leak, I decided that we had better make for the nearest land, which was Praia, São Tiago, Cape Verde Islands—two hundred miles west-northwest of our position.

During the next morning's radio contact with our friend Bill in the U.S. embassy in Rabat, Morocco, I reported to him what had happened. He told me that the United States had just opened an embassy in the newly independent Cape Verde Islands. We were also told that when Angola fell to the Cuban-Russian-led "Liberation Front," the formerly Portuguese Cape Verdes had been infiltrated by the Soviets and the Cubans. But Bill seemed to think that if we sailed in there as a port-of-refuge with "need-assistance" and "disabled-vessel" signal flags flying, we should be all right. In all events, we had little choice. This was the only land for the next two thousand miles.

On November 3 at 0700, I got a perfect star fix, using Canopus, Jupiter, and Sirius, and altered course to 318 degrees. The barren island of São Tiago came in sight over the horizon exactly on schedule. We were heading directly for the white-topped buildings of Praia and anchored at 1015 among a flotilla of primitive lateen-sail-rigged fishing vessels.

A group of armed, ragtag-looking "officials" came out in a sailing vessel—no motor—clumsily pulled alongside, and clumped aboard with their heavy boots and dangling sidearms. After they asked us for whiskey, beer, and cigarettes for themselves, they mellowed a little, but when they left, they confiscated our passports and United States ship's federal document—an illegal act.

For four days, we remained aboard, while I dove repeatedly with scuba gear to recaulk the butt blocks and leaking plank on the starboard side. I discovered caulking cotton hanging out of the seams along the length of a plank and at a butt block, so I recaulked it and lined it with underwater epoxy putty.

The generator, which also runs the emergency bilge pump, had been damaged during the flooding episode, and despite every effort for two twelve-hour-a-day sessions, there was no way I could get it to work again. It would have to be completely rewound. We had been told by the officials that the nearest slipway was 180 miles northwest of us at the Island of São Vicente—one of the Cape Verdes Islands—and that there was a three-month waiting list to use it.

The people of Cape Verde are pathetically poor and, we were warned, would steal anything stealable. But as fishermen came alongside with fish and beggars rowed out, we gave them clothing and canned foods. We correctly felt that as we made friends enough on this level, the word would spread; no effort was made to board us such as in Casablanca.

On November 6, I went ashore and made a beeline for the American embassy, where the chargé d'affaires took over to solve our problem. He dispatched a Portuguese-speaking embassy employee with me in a chauffeur-driven embassy car, and we recovered our passports and ship's documents from the officials who had illegally confiscated them. This was two days after the hostage seizure in Iran, and our embassy personnel were quite concerned, as were we all, about that situation, particularly with Cubans and Russians crawling all over São Tiago.

As we recovered our papers and cleared to leave, the attitude of the officials of this latest Third World poverty-stricken country was one of cold contempt. It seemed to relay to me that they felt a sense of satisfaction in hearing of a group of militants challenging a superpower in another Third World country of far off Islamic Iran.

As soon as I returned to the *Morning Star*, we set sail with the Atlantic Ocean crossing now lying before us and no intervening land for the next two thousand miles.

Wherever we go, home or abroad, we are asked by well-meaning friends and relatives "What if you get sick at sea? What if you need medical attention? What if you have a heart attack? What if Shirl has appendicitis?" The litany of the "what ifs" can be expanded into infinity.

There is no real, cut-and-dried answer to any of the myriad "what-if" questions. We are prepared for many contingencies, but no one can prepare for every one. So, our only answer to the "what ifs" is that with the grace of God, we shall *somehow cope*. If we succeed in coping, we live. If we fail to cope, we die. Some survive. Some do not survive. Those are the stakes of the game.

We don't think that there is much difference between that philosophy and the philosophy of everyday life—whether you are sailing across oceans in small boats or whether you are living a more sedate, conventional life-style at home.

But to set out to sail a small craft around the world, one must have a survivor mentality. If one dwells on the "what ifs" and painstakingly prepares and prepares, and then thinks of another "what if," we have observed that this would-be adventurer never overcomes the inertia to leave port to drop over a distant horizon into the relatively unknown. If fragile man had cowered in fear of the "what ifs," there would have been no Columbus, Cook, Magellan, Wright brothers, covered wagons, or outer space adventures.

As we sailed from the Cape Verdes, bound west across the Atlantic Ocean, we had a momentary attack of "what-if" disease. Since leaving the Canary Islands, I had been feeling lousy—nausea, lassitude, severe abdominal cramping—nothing working right.

When I was a young man, I spent two months in a hospital undergoing extensive abdominal surgery, aggravated with gangrene, rotted holes in the abdomen, and other complications. The result of all of this produced multiple band adhesions along with adhesions of the intestines to the abdominal wall.

Following the war, I went to the Mayo Clinic, and their verdict was that there was nothing that medical science could do—that unless it was a lifesaving necessity, no additional surgery should be permitted. The top gastroenterologist in his field at Mayo's told me "You will have to live with the pain and problems the rest of your life." So I accepted this, and during the past thirty-nine years have gotten by pretty well with only one hospitalization required. Shirl and I weighed all of this through the years and decided that included among the fears that prevented life from being lived to the fullest was the fear of getting into remote places (such as the middle of an ocean) where no medical help is available.

In Dakar, I brought the matter up with our French doctor friend, but when he showed us his hospital, I decided that "it will go away." Then in The Gambia with the British Medical Research Project, I found that their X-ray equipment was broken down, so decided to take the calculated risk of crossing the Atlantic to the West Indies to get Shirl and the *Morning Star* out of Africa, as well as to enable me to get to an American hospital.

In reviewing the log of this seventeen-day passage from São Tiago to Trinidad-Tobago, it seems like a blurred nightmare.

Sample log entries from November 8 ran:

Running before trade winds. Auto pilot broke. Impossible to repair without replacement part. Must hand steer during calms. Carried 3 oz. spinnaker 8 days and nights. Fastest day 152 miles. Slowest 98 miles.

Severe abdominal cramping. Spinnaker halyard broke. Shirl fished sail out of sea. A brave but dangerous thing to do without my help. Vane line breaks. Must repair or hand steer. Hanging headfirst over stern *with harness on*—restrung new vane line. All well. Navigating with dawn sights of Sirius, Jupiter and Capella.

Avoiding heat of sun during day. Maybe sun exposure contributing to continued illness. Saw one ship. Intestinal swelling comes and goes.

Seventh day out:

1,200 miles to Barbados. 1,350 miles to Trinidad—1,280 miles out of The Gambia, 860 miles out of the Cape Verdes. The middle of nowhere. We are sailing the track of Columbus' third voyage to the New World. From Cape Verdes to Trinidad, which Columbus named. Heavy seas. Shipped sea over port side into cockpit. Force of water lifted out horseshoe ring and fractured plastic rain guard on port hole.

Ninth day out:

Caulking in Cape Verdes stopped leaking. Now pumping every watch change less water than pumping every 5 minutes before caulking. If only my guts hold out. ESE winds, 15 knots, spinnaker and twin dampens roll. Georgous trade wind sailing.

Eleventh day out:

Set clocks back again—only 720 miles to Tobago, 658 miles to Barbados. Thinking about calling AMVER.

AMVER means "automated merchant vessel emergency rescue." It is a computerized system, located in Long Island, that can determine in an instant the location, track, speed, medical facilities of every participating merchant vessel in the world.

The Blue Mediterranean

Gambian women, Juffure village

"Dangling like a toy sailboat"

Victory celebration

As I sat out in the cockpit at night, trying to reason out my options for getting medical aid if total intestinal strangulation occurred, I analyzed AMVER, then eliminated it for now. AMVER could probably have a ship get to us in two or three days. An attempt to remove a stricken crewman from a small craft at sea can be fraught with hazard in heavy seas. Then how long would it take a ship to get to a port with good medical facilities?

During the Fastnet Yacht Race off England that August of 1979, numerous sailors lost their lives, several during an attempted rescue by merchant ships. Helicopters and sailboats don't mix because of the sailboat's tall mast. Rescue is accomplished by jumping into the sea and being picked up in a basket and winched up to the hovering chopper with the help of a crewman lowered from the helicopter. The seas were consistently too rough to allow the landing of a seaplane.

As these options were analyzed in the quietude of my night watch—the pros and cons of each—even written down, they were dismissed one by one;—God would somehow enable me to get Shirl to the safety of Trinidad.

I printed up specific instructions to enable her to operate our new Drake radio, elaborately prepared for us by our close friend Rich Feldman, so that if things got to where I couldn't even operate the radio, she could then shout a Mayday. I maintained running-fix determinations in the log so that Shirl could instantly read off our position.

Thirteenth day out:
Heavy squalls and lightning activity. Thanksgiving Day! Only 390 miles to Tobago! White bosun birds at the masthead, porpoises around us—all good omens. We are going to make it! ETA Tobago north tip 79 hours. Venus speed line. Should sight land at 0700 tomorrow!

On the seventeenth day out from Cape Verde at 0700, through the murk twenty-five miles ahead of us, was the hazy north tip of Tobago. God had enabled us to cross the Atlantic despite our problems and despite the ominous presence all the way of a major "what if"—critical illness at sea.

Trinidad-Tobago, formerly a British colony, is a newly independent, oil-rich country, standing just off the northeast tip of Venezuela on the South American continent. Trinidad is the southernmost West Indies Island.

We dropped our anchor in an exquisitely beautiful cove in Man of War Bay, Tobago. Deserted white-sand beach, leaning coconut palms—we were back in the Americas after six and a half years around the world from San Francisco! We had been in this cove only two hours when the blaring siren of a marine police boat awakened us and we were boarded by uniformed police.

They asked why we hadn't come to Scarborough on the windward coast of Tobago, their official port of entry. I showed them that the most recent *British Pilot* listed no port of entry for Tobago. Moreover, the east coast of Tobago that day was too dangerous in our fatigued condition and with an inoperative mainsail. I showed them how the main halyard had jumped off the masthead sheave that morning, and the sail wouldn't go up or down. Then I showed them on the chart the four-knot currents setting into the rocks on the windward side of Tobago, and legitimately claimed Man of War Bay as a port of refuge for emergency repairs.

They are very up-tight about the enormous drug traffic in the Caribbean, and naturally view everything that floats with suspicion. They were reasonable, polite, and quite impressed with our circumnavigation, so they gave us permission to stay there the remainder of the night, providing that we would come to Scarborough the next day. At dawn the next day, Shirl hoisted me aloft with our electric windlass, and I fixed the mainsail halyard.

We spent the day sailing around the lee side of Tobago past Buccoo Reef to Scarborough, where we were again boarded by police, C.I.D., customs, and immigration. By December 5, I had the boat safely moored in front of the Trinidad-Tobago Yacht Club near Port of Spain, and had arranged for an Indian custodian.

The intermittent intestinal obstruction was getting worse, so I radioed a doctor friend in New York. When I told him of the situation, he advised that I get to New York immediately.

He arranged hospital admission there and, alternatively, in Miami. With the aid of the American consul in Port of Spain, I was on a Pan American flight to Miami the next morning. Shirl was perfectly safe on the boat with friends and marine police watching over her twenty-four hours a day.

One of the best friends in need a man could ever have is Marshall Wolper in Miami. As I came off the plane, there he was. When he heard the story, he concluded that it might be too risky to go to New York, with weather conditions there possibly forcing a diversionary landing in Philadelphia or some place other than Kennedy or La Guardia.

So Marshall got on the telephone in the airport terminal and within minutes had used his influence with doctor friends to admit me immediately to the Miami Heart Institute near Marshall's home. There I spent eight days undergoing tests by extremely competent physicians in various specialties.

Their conclusions: "No more crossing oceans. Experimental medication. Stay under observation for three months." But I rationalized that any prudent doctor would tell even an Olympic athlete not to remove himself from the availability of emergency medical care.

Shirl flew to Miami as soon as she could work things out with the Trinidad officials concerning the leaving of the *Morning Star* with no owner aboard. We flew home to be with our family at Christmas and returned to Trinidad in January.

CHAPTER TWENTY-SEVEN

ALONG THE SPANISH MAIN TO PANAMA, CENTRAL AMERICA, AND MEXICO

The stars were beginning to fade in the gray predawn tropical sky. The eery silence of jungle-encircled Scotland Bay, Trinidad, was shattered by the crashing clatter of the anchor-chain windlass as *Morning Star* maneuvered to get under way. The racket set off a deafening clamor of protesting growler monkeys in the trees rimming the small bay.

After almost three months in Trinidad and Tobago, interspersed with a month in Miami and California, Shirley and I were ready to head the *Morning Star* west on the final leg of our circumnavigation of the world. There remained twelve hundred miles across the Caribbean Sea to Panama. Then forty-seven hundred miles out into the Pacific to Hawaii—the point from whence we had started out alone in 1975.

While in Miami, we became acutely aware of the magnitude of the drug traffic running between Venezuela and Colombia to the United States. During our stay in Trinidad, a large yacht got into a shootout with the marine police, who captured them very near our anchorage. The boat was loaded with large plastic garbage bags bulging with marijuana.

Even while at anchor in Trinidad, we had endured numerous surprise visits and searches from the marine police. There is so much money involved in this traffic that everyone is suspect. The U.S. Coast Guard had issued multiple warnings to yachtsmen concerning the dangers of shorthanded, private yachts being accosted by professional drug smugglers.

The smugglers' technique, as we later learned, is to overrun the slow-moving sailboat, or find it in a secluded anchorage, murder the people aboard, steal the yacht, and head for an inlet or river on the Colombian coast. Here professional crews take over, repaint the yacht, rerig her if necessary to alter her appearance substantially—all within twenty four hours. The boat is then loaded with marijuana and/or cocaine and embarked for the Everglades area of Florida.

An inspector of police in Panama who visited us (on a social basis) explained that sailing vessels are preferred because they don't have to stop en route for fuel. He told us that our boat would hold over $1 million street value in marijuana and millions more in cocaine.

As he described the multibillion-dollar operation to us, he said that once the hijacked yacht was in the southern Florida area, she would rendezvous with another vessel lying off the coast—anything from a small freighter to a flat-bottomed LST or "cigarette"-type speedboat. At the secret rendezvous point, the contraband drugs would be transferred from the yacht to the waiting drug runner.

Explosive devices would then be placed in the keel of the yacht, whereupon she would be cast off with sails set. In a few minutes, as the explosive charges detonated, she would be plunging to the bottom of the sea in 2,000 fathoms (12,000 feet) of water. The perfect crime!

The newspapers in Miami were full of this information, and one article stated that 95 percent of the contraband was getting through—worth about $5 *billion.*

On April 15, 1982, the Knight-Ridder newspaper chain carried the following article headed "Retired Pilot, 62, Kills Would-be Pirates."

NASSAU, Bahamas—A 62-year old retired Miami pilot, on an island cruise with his wife, killed three would-be pirates Tues-

day, shooting the Bahamians after he said they boarded his
boat, demanded money and attacked him.

Lawrence and Audrey Holloway, who own a home in Miami,
had anchored their 37-foot motor cruiser at Joulter Cays, three
small islands clustered off the northern tip of Andros Island.
They were alone on the boat, the *Whip Ray*, on a cruise through
the Bahamas' Berry Islands.

About 2 P.M., according to Bahamian police, a middle-aged
man and two teenaged boys boarded the Holloways' boat. One
brandished a knife.

The Holloways were armed with a pistol. Police said the
Bahamians tried to seize the gun, but Holloway fought them off
and shot all three.

The Holloways, after reporting the shooting Tuesday evening, were flown from Chub Cay, a fishing resort north of Joulter Cays, to Nassau, where they were questioned. They were
released Wednesday evening. Police said the couple faces no
criminal charges.

The Holloways said they radioed ahead and pulled into Chub
Cay, a fishing resort, later that afternoon. The police found the
body of the 45-year-old man and one of the teenaged boys on
the Holloways' boat. The body of the third was found washed
up on an island later that day.

For the first time since sailing through the pirate-infested
waters of the Java, South China, and Red seas, we had guns
loaded and at the ready.

After sailing through the Dragon's Mouth, separating Trinidad from Venezuela, we decided to set a straight course for Isla
Margarita, off the coast of Venezuela. The winds and currents
were in our favor, and while we were close to the Venezuelan
coastline, we thought that we were still east of the main north-
south drug routes.

We would have liked to sail to Grenada, where in the 1960s
we had spent many enjoyable cruising days. But, as in many
places in the Caribbean during the last several years, the
Cuban Communists are firmly installed in Grenada, and the
American flag and white faces are not assets any longer.

Reeling off the miles under the northeast trade winds along
the Venezuelan coast, we were impressed by the beauty of this
coastline, along with the abundance of sea life around us—

majestic frigate birds wheeling on high, pelicans, boobys, flying fish, and porpoise. We even saw a large whale off our port beam.

Our port of entry in Venezuela was Pampatar, Margarita Island. We were the only foreign yacht there, and as we floundered around trying to determine entry procedures, we were picked up by a young man who spent the entire day with us, escorting us all over the island—from one bureaucracy to another. He and his parents were Portuguese and had fled Angola in Africa when the Russians, via their Cuban surrogates, had taken over this mineral-rich country.

Venezuela is oil rich (member of OPEC), and we bought diesel fuel for fourteen cents a gallon. Gasoline was sixteen cents a gallon, so the rich Venezuelans crowd the streets with large gas-guzzling American cars. Margarita Island is a tourist center for mainland Venezuelans who come over from Caracas (population 5 million plus) in a constant flow of ferryboats.

After visiting the ancient Spanish forts, we had had enough of this congested island and headed west for Tortuga, then northwest past the penal colony of Orchilla to the Islas de Roques, a cluster of numerous islands and reefs surrounding an enormous lagoon. Here the fishermen and local inhabitants were very kind to us, and we could have cruised among these islands for months. With pristine white beaches, rustling coconut palms, clear water, an abundance of fish and lobsters; Islas de Roques are a cruising paradise. We were running late so far as the weather patterns were concerned, so had to abbreviate our stay in the Roques group in order to spend more time in the Islas de Aves, an uninhabited group of reef-fringed atolls ninety miles north of the Venezuelan coast.

In the late afternoon of February 29, we eyeballed our way among the reefs to find a windswept deserted anchorage near a seabird rookery. We swam ashore, and I dove for huge lobsters for our dinner.

The leak which had persisted ever since striking the whale in the Atlantic was still bedeviling us, so we wanted to get to Curaçao in the Netherlands Antilles. There we reasoned that with the Dutch still running things, we could be dry-docked— something that we weren't able to do in Trinidad after weeks of waiting for the availability of a marine railway.

From Islas de Aves, we sailed for Bonaire and then to Curaçao. Despite the Dutch influence, the Antillians were very much in charge. These islands, lying off the coast of Venezuela, have always been a haven for smugglers. The black Antillians are descendants of slaves. The original natives were Carib Indians, who are now virtually extinct. There is racial unrest here, as elsewhere in the Caribbean, and while the Dutch were most cordial—even effusive in their welcome—the Antillians were surly and rude.

We had, with permission, entered Spanish Water, a sheltered bay on the southwest side of the island. The Dutch navy gave us all of the privileges of their private club, and a Curaçao businessman, Herbert Haltmayer, dropped everything to drive us around Willemstad and try to facilitate our entry into Curaçao. But the arrogant Antillians had to flex their newly gained "independence" by conducting a harassment-type search of the *Morning Star*, using a Doberman dog.

The Dutch maintain the largest dry dock and oil refinery in this part of the world. The dry dock didn't want to be bothered with a small yacht, but the Dutch agreed to crane-hoist us out of the water so that I could recaulk the hull. They were very good about it and warned us not to use their workmen, who were unskilled in wooden-boat construction. So a sixty-ton crane lifted us out of the water, and we dangled on its cables like a tiny toy sailboat.

After they set us up on chocks on the ground, I proceeded for ten days to recaulk the entire hull with the help of a group of Colombian fishermen whom I recruited, along with a Dutch navy sailor who had some experience with wooden navy minesweepers.

With the help of a young Dutch electronics engineer, we got our autopilot repaired sufficiently to get us to Panama. We had been hand-steering in calms since leaving Africa, and the enormous relief of having the autopilot semioperational alleviated the tyranny and fatigue of manual steering.

On March 23, we cleared Spanish Water and gained express permission to anchor on the northwest corner of the island at Sint Kruis Baai, en route to Aruba. From Spanish Water, past the pontoon bridge at the entrance to Willemstad Harbor, we proceeded up the west coast of Curacao to Sint Kruis Baai, anchoring there about four hundred feet off the white-sand beach at 1500 hours.

At 2230, we were awakened by a blaring bull horn and flood-lights from the shore, bathing the boat in their stark white light. Because of the distance, we could barely hear them shouting at us, and they couldn't seem to hear us against the prevailing offshore wind.

As I sleepily stumbled to the foredeck, I was dismayed to hear "This is the police. This is your last warning. Proceed to Willemstad at once, or we will open fire on you."

I shouted through our electronic loud-hailer that we had properly cleared, and asked them to check with their immigration department. They ordered me to put a boat over the side and come ashore immediately.

I didn't really know who they were, so I refused to unstow the dinghy packed for a sea voyage, and the shouted argument raged on.

Finally, I said, "Okay, we will return to Willemstad."

As we got the anchor up, I told Shirl to stay below if they started shooting. She said, "What are you going to do?"

I said, "I am going to stay up here and steer south to Willemstad to get out of their rifle range, then head out to sea."

She said, "Well, if you are going to be shot, I might as well be shot also," and she refused to leave the cockpit.

Once the anchor had broken loose, I shouted, "See you in Willemstad," then headed southeast until out of their range as they continued to yell and shine their spotlight on us. Well clear, I turned off all lights and altered course to head north-west to Aruba. Then I called Willemstad Harbor Control on the VHF radio. I couldn't do so earlier because VHF is line-of-sight transmission, and land obscured our location at Sint Kruis Baai from Willemstad. I explained to them what happened with their trigger-happy cops, and they profusely apologized.

Because of the surliness of Antillian officialdom, we were utterly turned off by the Dutch Antilles and sailed right past Aruba, bound nonstop for Panama. The winds were howling with what are described in this part of the world, as "augmented trades," so we streaked through the overcast night and rounded the southern point of Aruba at 0430. Second only to the oil refinery, tourism is the largest source of revenue of the

Dutch Antilles. Cruise ships regularly come to Willemstad. But with the growing antiwhite attitude of these Antillian officials, some cruise captains are now threatening to refuse to spend the expensive fuel to bring their passengers this far south in the Caribbean.

With the Soviet-Cuban Communist disease spreading throughout the Caribbean, it is becoming a less attractive place for tourists to spend their dollars, and the drug-piracy problems, coupled with racial hostility, make it an increasingly difficult part of the world in which to sail a private yacht.

Heading WNW from Aruba, we wanted to give the Colombian coast a wide berth—a minimum of sixty miles—so with the "augmented northeast trades" pushing us past the Gulf of Venezuela, Barranquilla, and Cartagena, we ran through the nights with no lights under a pale half moon, scudding in and out of the clouds in the broken, overcast sky. With strong winds and large seas, at times we were surfing at eight or nine knots with reefed down sails.

In five days, we had sailed the 690 miles from Curaçao to Panama and at predawn were approaching the San Blas Islands, a group of low reefs and sand atolls. Coming from the east, the San Blas Archipelago of reef-strewn atolls presents one of the most dangerous lee shores in the world.

It was possibly this fact that enabled the tiny tribe of Cuna Indians to maintain their culture, dress, and political autonomy throughout centuries of occupation in the area by the conquistadores and other European exploiters who used the Isthmus of Panama to transship the Inca and Aztec gold overland to the waiting treasure ships in Portobelo.

We were fascinated by the "civilization" of the San Blas Cuna Indians. Some of the outstanding elements of the conduct of their affairs deeply impressed me. One is that every night their appointed chiefs meet with the people. At these meetings, all grievances are ventilated and resolved. There is no lapse of time for real or fancied wrongs to fester and create lasting enmities and hatreds.

Another interestingly unique aspect of the Cuna culture that made a lot of sense to me was that after hearing both sides of a dispute, the chiefs will make a decision on the fundamental premise that the desired result is *harmony* of the community above all. In other words, even if you are right, you may be adjudicated to be wrong if the net result of your righteousness causes friction and disharmony in the tribal society.

In many other ways, the Cuna civilization is quite different from any others we have seen anyplace in the world. The Cunas have successfully resisted all efforts to colonize or control them. Actually, they have little that anyone would want—fish, coconuts, and whatever they can grow in the jungle on disease- and poisonous-snake-infested mainland Panama. A few years ago, the Panamanian government tried to bring the Cunas under more direct control, but after a few crushed skulls and stabbings in the middle of the night, they decided to leave these Indians alone.

As we entered the breakwater on the Caribbean side of the canal at Colón/Cristobal, we were assigned to a particular

Trading with Cuna Indian

anchorage area where, first, U.S. customs came alongside. How refreshing it was to hear Americans after so many years. But their visit was just pro forma. Since the previous October, the Canal Zone had ceased to exist. The American flag was hauled down, and the Panamanian flag hoisted up in its place. In short order, the Panamanian officials boarded to ask us a host of useless questions and to fill out interminable forms. The transition and giveaway had become effective in October, so now in March-April, the Panamanians were undergoing job training under their reluctant American mentors.

The next day, we moved to the Panama Yacht Club, where, standing on the dock was a couple we had met in Curaçao— Susan and Fred. After securing our mooring lines, Susan burst into tears and told us how their boat, with all their life's savings tied up in it, had been stolen while they were checking into the southern San Blas only a few miles north of the Colombian border.

Our first few days in Cristobal were spent trying to help these people, with radioed telephone patches to Texas and in other ways. The Colón police inspector who had taken a special interest in their case was aboard our boat several times, and told me a lot about yacht hijacking, the crime rate in Colón, and what the Panamanian people thought about the Americans leaving the Panama Canal. The cities of Colón and Cristobal have a 70 percent unemployment rate. A German boat owner and his wife were mugged at knife point right outside the gates of the Yacht Club.

After a few days, the Panamanian police discovered the stolen yacht in Turbo, Colombia, with its motor burned out. In Curaçao, Fred and Susan had been extolling to us the virtues of the crewman they had picked up in Grenada. He had told them that he wanted to escape from the Cuban Communists now occupying his island, so they took him along. Apparently, he had stolen the boat and headed for Colombia when its owners failed to return from checking into Panama. The Panamanians recovered the boat and arrested the thief. They told us he would be shot.

Approaching Panama, we had formed a friendship on the ham radio with a Special Forces (Green Beret) master sergeant, so when we got to Colón, we were met by our new friends, Dave and Jane, who extended every hospitality to us. We didn't leave the compound unless we were in a taxi or in Dave's jeep.

Since the canal "treaties," the Cubans were pouring in by the planeload. The hammer-and-sickle posters were stuck on buildings everywhere. We had been told by the American media that unless we gave the canal to General Torrijos, a military dictator, there would be insurrection, riots, terrorism, and sabotage of the canal by the "Panamanian terrorists."

After several weeks in Panama, mingling with the Panamanian people—grocers, taxi drivers, businessmen, pharmacists, entrepreneurs—we discovered an astonishing fact. The *people* of the Republic of Panama—not the American Zonians—but the ordinary people, lamented to us, "Why, oh why, did America give the canal to Torrijos? Doesn't your government know that now the Russians, via the Cubans, will take over? They are beginning now. We don't want the Americans to leave us. Look what is happening in Nicaragua, Guatemala, and El Salvador. What utter fools you Americans are." One embittered Panamanian told us that if the American people do not elect effective and strong leaders, then, he said, our country will deserve everything it gets from Iran and Africa to Central America and Mexico.

To another third-generation Panamanian, I said one day, "Wait a minute. As I understand it, the polls showed that eighty percent of the American people opposed the giveaway, but the Carter administration, the Congress, and the media rammed it down their throats. What about all of the rioting we saw on television, described as the citizens of the Republic of Panama demanding the canal 'treaties'?"

This man told Shirley and me, "Here is how that was done. The Communists hire buses, go to the university, and fill them with students, gather up for hire a sprinkling of street people, beggars, idle peasants, et cetera, descend on the American embassy, and stage a shouting, fist-shaking 'demonstration.' Torrijos' soldiers stand by while the American TV emphasizes with their camera angles and blowups the magnitude of the demonstrations."

I asked, "If you feel this way, and most of your compatriots feel this way, where were you when all of this was happening?"

He said, that "Most of us lack the organization, and even where spontaneous counterdemonstrations would break out against the Communists, Torrijos' soldiers would break them up. Moreover, your American TV wouldn't cover them to the degree they covered the Communist-led riots."

I said that the American people were told that making a gift of this strategic waterway would endear the United States to the other Latin American countries and serve to dispel the notion of "Yankee imperialism," whatever that is supposed to mean.

He said, "Nonsense! Venezuela and Colombia, along with Brazil and other South American countries, regard you as fools in your dealings with the Communists. In your eagerness to be loved, you Americans have lost the respect of the world. It is better to be respected than loved." We heard this story and variations thereof throughout the country during the weeks we were in Panama.

The political entity called the Republic of Panama was literally created by the United States of America out of what was once Colombia. At a cost of billions of dollars and countless lives, the Americans built the canal after the French and others had declared the undertaking impossible.

Panama is one of the most interesting places we ever visited at length during our circumnavigation. We transited the canal with Dave and Jane and two of their Green Beret friends acting as line handlers. It was an exciting experience. Now we were back in the Pacific, after having left this great ocean three years earlier when we entered the Indian Ocean through Torres Strait, Australia.

In Panama, we heard numerous stories about Nicaraguan gunboats arresting American yachts found in what they considered to be their waters. Also, the reports from El Salvador and Guatemala were not good. Communist agitators have all of Central America, with the exception of pro-U.S. Costa Rica, in a state of turmoil and chaos. The so-called people's liberation fronts are, with the direct aid of the Soviets, using their Cuban puppets, subverting this entire area, literally at our back door.

Later in the year, we learned that the Sandinista guerrillas

Panama Canal transit

in Nicaragua had been subsidized with $75 million of American taxpayers' money. At the first annual celebration of the Sandinista victory, attended by Yasir Arafat, Fidel Castro, and other heads of terrorist and Marxist states, Castro complimented the United States for having made the $75 million "gift" to the new Marxist regime. This astonishing piece of news was treated only superficially by the American news media.

Foreign observers, watching the foreign policy of the United States of America, not only shake their heads in disgust and wonderment at what appears to be, at best, incredible naiveté and stupidity, but are beginning to look with fear at their own situation, if, in the past, they have been dependent upon the United States to protect them against Communist expansionism.

We have a book, *Ocean Passages of the World*, that depicts the best sailing-ship routes from Panama to Hawaii and/or to San Francisco. For the month of May, the ideal route would have been to head south from Panama, passing between the

Galapagos Islands and Ecuador. We would have encountered the southeast trade winds, and could have either run three thousand miles west to the Marquesas Islands or reached in a long loop up across the equator to either Hawaii or San Francisco.

The Gulf of Panama is notoriously calm; many sailing ships of old would find themselves becalmed for weeks, only to return eventually to Balboa low on provisions and with their bottoms encrusted with barnacles.

In Panama, we had tried to obtain permission to visit the Galapagos Islands (of Darwin fame), but the Ecuadoreans flatly refuse to allow private yachts to stop in these islands for more than seventy-two hours, and then only in a demonstrable emergency. So we decided to visit the primitive Chiriqui Indian country along the coast of Panama. With any kind of wind, we would have enough fuel to reach Golfito, Costa Rica.

Before leaving the Gulf of Panama, we lingered in the Islas Perlas and Contadora, where the Shah of Iran was ensconced after leaving the United States of America. The Gulf of Panama is a marine zoo. We saw numerous basking marlins, sea turtles, porpoises, manta rays, and fish life of all description. It was now late April and the hurricane season off the Gulf of Tehuantepec in Mexico starts in late May and June. The route we had taken was carefully weighed against the alternate southerly route, where *Ocean Passages* said we would encounter "more salubrious" weather. But our desire to see the Chiriqui Indian country, as well as Costa Rica, outweighed the disadvantages of calms, early hurricanes, adverse currents, and the political volatility of Central American countries.

As we cruised along the southern coast of Panama, anchoring every night, it was swelteringly hot and humid. It was the first time in all of our years of sailing that we were extremely uncomfortable night and day at sea. The cabin temperature hovered around the 100-degree mark, and there wasn't a breath of breeze.

In a beautiful, remote anchorage, a group of Chiriqui Indians came around a bend in their dugout canoes, chattering excitedly as they surveyed the lines of the *Morning Star*. They gave us live lobsters, fish, and coconuts, and we heaped upon them clothing and canned food for which we would have no more use, as our voyage was drawing to its termination. With their tattooed faces and primitive dress, they were a savage-looking lot, but actually were most gentle and good-humored. We communicated adequately in sign language and fragmentary Spanish.

On April 23, we entered Golfito, Costa Rica, where Chiquita bananas come from. As we anchored at dusk, visibility dropped, and the heavens literally opened up with the most intense downpour and lightning storm we had ever encountered anyplace in the world.

Our freezer and refrigerator, despite the ministrations of self-styled refrigerator mechanics in Panama and all over the world, continued to give us problems. This New Zealand installation caused us infinitely more grief than any other piece of equipment aboard. We were much better off on the boat when we had no refrigeration other than possibly an icebox. One can quickly adapt to living without some amenities, and refrigeration is one of them.

When we arrived in Punta Arenas, we went to San José, Costa Rica, the beautiful capital city, and located a German engineer who had fled the Nazis in the 1930s. I spent a couple of hours with him as he tutored me with the aid of an engineering refrigeration manual I had sent from the States.

He taught me enough—how to purge a system without vacuum pumps as well as many other tricks of the trade—so that for the first time I felt I could diagnose and repair refrigeration defects more effectively than could some of the mechanics who had been aboard at various ports around the world.

From Costa Rica, bordering on Nicaragua, we headed due west to give Nicaragua, El Salvador, Guatemala, and the infamous Gulfs of Tehuantepec and Papagayo a two hundred-mile berth. By catching every whisper of a breeze and using favorable currents, we made an eight-day nonstop passage, to arrive in Acapulco at dusk on May 8.

Here we met another yacht that we had seen in Panama. I had tried to teach these people celestial navigation so that they could stay well out to sea, but they just weren't motivated enough to learn, feeling that they would rely on Loran C—a long-range electronic navigational device. Moreover, they felt confident that they could hug the coastline, never losing sight of land, just as they had made it this far from Florida.

What stories they had to tell! They had been apprehended by a Nicaraguan boat, full of armed men, near San Juan del Sur. They were shepherded into port with armed Sandinistas aboard, where they were removed from the boat and clapped into a filthy jail. They were repeatedly interrogated by Sandinistas and Cubans before finally being released and ordered out of the country. Upon returning to their boat, they found that the yacht had been searched and stripped of all valuables.

Then, as they motored along the coasts of Guatemala and Mexico, with the shoreline of the Gulf of Tehuantepec in sight, they were struck by the infamous "Tehuantepecer" northerly winds, which came roaring between the mountains at the 120-mile-wide isthmus separating the Pacific Ocean from the Gulf of Mexico. They said the winds reached a velocity of sixty knots. Desperately afraid to run out to sea, they motored into the heavy offshore breaking seas. They rode the storm out in this fashion, but sustained damage to their vessel and engine. We were two hundred miles offshore due south at the same time and felt the swell coming out of the north, but experienced no difficulty.

Ships usually get into trouble near land. To us, safety almost always lies at sea. During the course of sailing alone around the world, we encountered many storms. With ample sea room, we have ridden these storms out like a gull on the water—offering minimal resistance to the sea.

We spent a few days in Acapulco, where we had been in the past, at the most elaborate yacht club we have seen anyplace in the world. The Mexicans treated us very well, and we were delighted to refuel at eighteen cents a gallon. Seeking wind, we headed from Acapulco bound for Socorro Island, but in three days, we found no wind, so turned north again to Manzanillo and to Puerto Vallarta. Then on to Cabo San Lucas—only 780 miles south of San Diego.

CHAPTER TWENTY-EIGHT

AROUND THE WORLD— HAWAII TO HAWAII

It seems that often in life we see commitment die just when its fulfillment is at our very fingertips. People do so well—keep struggling toward their goals—then when about to attain them, they give up, fall back, and retreat in disarray.

The candle of our commitment almost flickered out in Cabo San Lucas. Shirl and I had vowed to one another to sail around the world *alone*—just the two of us—Hawaii to Hawaii. Now, at Cabo San Lucas, seven years from the date we had sailed out the Golden Gate, we were only a few days from the United States of America and home. Although we would have sailed around the world were we to head for San Francisco, coast-crawling the easy way, we, in fact, had not sailed around the world—Honolulu to Honolulu—alone and unaided by crew. Yawning between Cabo San Lucas and Hawaii lies twenty-seven hundred miles of open ocean.

Sitting in the secure cockpit of the anchored *Morning Star*, Shirl and I drew from our infinite repertoire of rationalization and excuse-making as we discussed this final challenge.

Ray: "What do you think we should do, honey?"

Shirl: "We made it this far."

Ray: "On the other hand, we've been pretty lucky."

Shirl: "Let's bite the bullet and head west for Hawaii."

Ray: "Let's not push our luck too far."

Shirl: "You're right. Maybe we should quit while we're ahead."

Ray: "But then, how are we going to feel about ourselves? Maybe we should complete the challenge we accepted seven years ago."

Shirl: "We're not trying to prove anything to anyone, so what's the difference?"

Ray: "In the final analysis, no one else is going to be impressed or really care whatever we decide to do."

Shirl: "Ray—let's cast off for Hawaii."

Again, with the help of a Higher Power available to all of us, the spirit of commitment prevailed. The die was cast—Hawaii it was! But we had no idea then of the near disaster which lay ahead of us. Had we but known what was in store for us, we might have settled for the victory at hand.

On a gray Sunday dawn, we rounded the cape and headed due west into the open sea, bound for the romantic islands from which our journey alone had begun. Born in the Gulf of Alaska, strong northwesterly winds came roaring down the Baja Peninsula. Tropical storms were forming south of us. Such storms have devastated the Baja Peninsula in past years.

Sample log entries during this passage:

Set all sail. Close reach with large rolling seas forward of the beam. First time since Panama, 2,200 miles in our wake, have we had strong winds and precious sea room. Liberated from calms at last! No more lee shores. Three or four days of windward torture. Then the Trades. It is cold! ¾ moon as we slam into seas on close reach. Boat hasn't been sailed this hard since the storm off Turkey.

This is supposed to be fun? We are out of condition and ache all over. Southerly tropical disturbances setting up counter swell to steepen northwesterly seas. Motion atrocious.

Moonset. Night black as a pit from pole to pole. Out of all shipping lanes now. Only sign of human habitation, tiny red glow from our binnacle light.

Seas gray. Skies overcast. Memorial Day—latitude 21° 31′ N, longitude 115° 03′ W—2,490 miles from Diamond Head. Could easily sail to San Francisco in 18 days. Wind keeps hauling into the north. Where are the Trades? Meteorologist on radio patch says another 500 miles to trade winds. Black dawn. Continued overcast. No sights.

May 29: Damp blankets. Cold chill in air from Gulf of Alaska northerly winds. 2,206 miles to Diamond Head. Clock back one hour. Friday, May 30: 700 miles out. Heavy seas. 25 knot winds—new crisis of the day.

At 2200 on my watch, the forestay eyebolt at the bowsprit literally exploded! The spruce mast is supported fore and aft by stainless steel wires and furling tubes. The mast is a strut under compression. Without this support, along with the athwartship support of stainless steel wires called shrouds, the mast would simply fall off the boat. This support envelops the ship. Each is a part of the whole. The weakest link destroys the continuity of support from the keel to the bowsprit, to the masthead, and returning to the stern. When the three-quarters-inch diameter stainless steel eyebolt erupted, it released the two-inch diameter stainless steel reefing spar supporting the mast. Not only was the forward support for the masthead gone, but the flogging, heavy, fifty-foot-long steel spar placed a strain on the masthead. We would have been dismasted immediately—within a split second—had I not anticipated this problem way back in Gibraltar.

One of the keys to survival that I have found to be effective is to try to anticipate not only where and how an accident could happen, but to construct vividly in my imagination what my step-by-step procedure would be in coping with the sudden danger, with the thought that preparation is the enemy of surprise.

Preliminary to crossing the Atlantic, while moored in Gibraltar, I examined the rigging from stem to stern. I usually sandpaper and clean with acetone every stainless swage fitting because I have had five failures of these fittings in my sailing career. But, unless hairline cracks are visible to the eye through a magnifying glass, there is no way—short of magnafluxing every stainless fitting—to tell if crystallization is taking place in the core of stainless steel.

Even though the eyebolt presented a clear, shiny surface, I thought at the time, "If this thing ever let go, the sudden release of the fifty-foot-long, heavy stainless tube would sweep the deck, probably knock one of us overboard, and inevitably break the spreaders and dismast the boat." After this speculation, I secured two large shackles to the tack fitting as a safety measure.

Now, on this black Pacific night, seven hundred miles from the nearest land, these shackles did their job. As the tension was released, the shackles held the base of the now slack furling spar, which, in the heavy seaway, was unmercifully flogging and snapping the masthead. I immediately turned the boat downwind and put the seas and wind astern. Then, harnessed to the boat, I crawled out to the end of the bowsprit and gradually turned the drum to furl the snapping genoa jib. By this time, Shirl had awakened and could help from the cockpit with snagged sheets and furling lines.

Once the sail was wound around the steel spar, it increased the weight, and the accelerated snapping of the sagging spar caused the entire rig to vibrate, threatening to break the masthead off at the top. With harness attaching me to the bow pulpit, I climbed up the spar as high as I could get, considering the pitching, rolling motion of the boat. At the highest point I could reach, I secured a tight band of lines, which I extended downward in a pyramid-shaped support system to the deck. There the guy ropes were tightened up around mooring bits, anchor windlass, and whatever could give me the widest angle to stabilize the flogging spar. In the dim glow of the spreader lights, we surveyed the job and felt it was the best that we could do that night. It was now after midnight and we were heading WSW—2,186 miles from Diamond Head.

As we analyzed our position, it boiled down to this:

1. We were out of fuel range of any land.
2. If the mast went over the side, we would have to cut it free. We carry large bolt cutters just for this purpose. With its maze of wire rigging and floating alongside, a fifty-foot mast, attached to the boat, could act as a battering ram in these heavy seas and in short order

punch a hole through the hull, causing the boat to promptly sink.

With a full crew of strong men aboard, dismasted boats have managed to get the heavy spar out of the sea and back aboard before it damaged the hull. But we couldn't rely on our ability to do this, so had to reckon with the worst—cut it free as soon as it went into the sea. With this segment of our strategy worked out, we laid out the bolt cutters and hacksaws, ready for instant employment.

3. If the mast went over, radio contact would be lost because two antennas—the "cat's whisker" on the masthead and the backstay—would go with the mast. Rather than get an alert off that night, we decided to wait until the next afternoon when I had a regular radio schedule with Bud Alvernaz in San Jose, California. I told Shirl that if we lost the mast that night, I could rig up a mobile whip antenna in a few hours and make contact with someone.

In the meantime, we didn't want to get a lot of people unduly concerned about our plight.

I trimmed the boat with the forestaysail, main, and mizzen and sailed her on a broad reach with the continued twenty-five-knot northwesterlies coming over the starboard quarter. On this point of sail, the twisting action at the masthead was reduced to a minimum, and the vane steered the boat quite well. I felt that this was safer than heaving to because in a hove-to configuration, the boat pitches, and the resultant pumping action of the unsupported masthead could snap it like a matchstick. There remained nothing else to do except for me to get some rest while Shirl spent the remainder of her watch apprehensively eyeing the swaying headstay spar.

At dawn, the skies were clear, enabling me to get a star fix. The cold northerly winds persisted. We were at latitude 21° 48′ north, longitude 124° 26′ west, but the weather reports indicated trade winds at 130° west—about 360 miles, or three days, ahead of us.

Once in the trades, I could set the twins, transferring most of the pressure to the backstays. I felt with a bit of luck and east-northeast trades, I could reach in the manner of the square-riggers, regain my northing, and run out to Hawaii with the winds and seas off the starboard quarter. Only nineteen hundred miles to go.

While going through my regular dawn rigging and chafe check, I noticed to my horror that the port mizzen upper shroud had snapped at the stainless terminal fitting. Whether this was a coincidence or whether it happened when the rig was so severely vibrating didn't matter. It had to be fixed, or the mizzen mast could go, pulling the main mast with it.

Again, this kind of contingency was thought out literally years ago, and a preestablished plan of action was tucked back into the recesses of my psyche. Using cable clamps, I doubled the upper shroud back onto itself, forming a loop. Then with a length of chain and a shackle, I secured this jury rig to the turnbuckle and restored the necessary support to the mizzen-mast. The whole operation took two hours, and Shirl wasn't made aware of the problem until we arrived in Hawaii. The swaying headstay was enough for her to think about without introducing more anxiety.

I examined all of the swage fittings, and almost every one had developed cracks and splits, which certainly must have been caused by the stress of the events of the last twenty-four hours. There was one thing that this chain reaction of rigging failure had done for us. It had foreclosed all options other than to try to get to Hawaii, running before the wind. There was no way that the rigging would have held had we attempted either to beat eight hundred miles back to Mexico or reach up to San Francisco in the prescribed path of the nineteenth-century sailing vessels. The most prudent course of action was just to keep cool and to keep the wind abaft the beam.

On the radio schedule that afternoon, I felt I had to tell Bud about what was happening. The problem with a radio communication like this is that it sets off not only a lot of anxiety with loved ones, but a tendency on the part of many super helpful ham radio operators to "do something," to "call the Coast Guard for help."

We most emphatically do not like to call for help unless it is a last-resort effort to save our lives. Too many times we have heard "cry-wolf" Maydays from sailors who are out of fuel, seasick, or just plain scared. One couple we know screamed Mayday when they became disoriented in a fog off San Francisco. All they would have had to do is sit there until the fog lifted. They were in no real, life-threatening danger; yet they mustered all possible rescue efforts to come out and find them. This sort of conduct gives a bad name to all amateur sailors and, moreover, often involves unnecessary risk on the part of the would-be rescuers.

But, in this situation, I told Bud that we were in danger of losing our mast and radio contact. I instructed him that no alarms were to be given out if we suddenly went off the air for a few days. I would need time to jury-rig a whip antenna—not that this job would have been all that time consuming. We carry a vertical deck-mounted antenna for just such a dismasting emergency.

If we were dismasted, however, my prime time was going to be spent either disentangling us from the wreckage or attempting to recover the mast. If, in some way, we could get it back aboard, I could possibly rig a sawed-off version of it on the stump of what was left. We carry a steel-strap banding kit, along with an assortment of other tools and gear, to cope with precisely this emergency. As long as we maintained the integrity of the hull, we would be safe enough. We had food and water to last us for months, so conceivably we could have, in the manner of the raft *Kon Tiki*, drifted with the currents and winds the two thousand miles to Hawaii.

Bud was most understanding, and he and his wife, Ann, who, I submit, has a direct pipeline to heaven, said that they would polish up their prayers again for us. We told Bud that we would be especially conscious of exact position reporting. We explained to him further that we had three emergency position locator beacons aboard, and that after a week of radio silence, it might be well to put out an alert to ships and aircraft in the vicinity.

The EPLB transmitters send out an ultrahigh frequency signal, and all commercial and military aircraft are compelled to monitor these frequencies and report these signals immediately. For example, if a Boeing 747 flying at 30,000 feet within fifty miles or so of us heard our EPLB signal, the pilot should alter course to home in on this beacon. Aircraft pilots are particularly responsive to these signals because it is always possible that they may be coming from "one of their own" down on the sea.

It was June, and as we continued west, the sun became directly overhead in its annual journey north to the Tropic of Cancer. Sailing with the wind, we crossed and recrossed the northward path of the sun. We were at latitude 23° 06′ north, and the Tropic of Cancer lies at 23° 30′. At this point, a meridian passage or noon sight is useless, so I just relied on running fixes with the sun, moon, and the stars.

On the ninth day out, the winds began to haul into the northeast, lightly at first. At last the trades!

Down came the mainsail, forestaysail, and mizzen, and up went 900 square feet of boomed-out twins, and I told Shirl that the next time the twins came down we would be off Waikiki Beach.

Log entries:

Pressure now on back stays. Twins pulling like mules. Averaging 6.5 knots over bottom. Seas 10 to 15 feet; winds 20 knots.
11th day out: Port twin down haul broke. Dropped, replaced and rehoisted in 20 minutes.
Day after day, vane steering, course 265°. Remains cold. Strange crash on starboard side like hitting whale in Atlantic. Just fell off freak sea, I guess.

Shirley's log entries during June 7:

The orange light from the rising moon astern is splendiferously spreading across the eastern horizon. An awe-inspiring sight in a pitch black night. Schools of flying fish all around us.
14th day out: Broken forestay swaying rhythmically as boat rolls downwind. I think that we will make it. Vega, Moon fixes our position 1,730 miles out of Mexico in 14 days. Not bad considering crippled condition of boat.
June 8: Crisis of the day. Evening chafe check showed D ring on clew of starboard twin split in half. Another stainless steel failure.

The twin is a 450-square-foot triangular sail that is secured at the bow, top of the mast, and at the end of a boom protruding eighteen feet from the center of the mast. The jaw at the end of the pole is secured at a stainless steel D-shaped ring sewn and heavily reinforced into the clew of the sail. Looking up during my inspection tour, I saw that the D ring had parted (after ten years' service) at the weld. One lurch of the pole would disengage it, causing the twin to fly forward free from its sheet.

Night was coming on fast. Shirl had to stop all dinner preparations. And there we sat on the foredeck with the downed twin on our laps, hurtling along under the port twin while I furiously sewed in an entire triangular section of a spare clew D-ring assembly from a blown-out twin that I had carried with us from New Zealand.

It took two hours to do this job right, punching holes in the eight layers of eight ounce Dacron reinforcement, pushing my needle with a sailmaker's palm through the hole until I was satisfied that this jury rig would last the remaining seven hundred miles to Honolulu.

As we sat cross-legged on the foredeck, sewing feverishly, the humor of the situation made both of us laugh. I said, "Wouldn't our friends think that we must be really crazy to be sitting out here in the middle of an ocean with huge white-capped seas sweeping past us above eye level, sewing away on a piece of cloth?"

With the jury-rigged twin rehoisted, the boat spurted forward, and the next morning, the glittering stars Vega, Fomalhaut, and Altair showed that we had a 154-mile run—only 540 miles to go!

On the seventeenth day out, Hurricane Agatha, which had developed six hundred miles southeast of us, began to move at twenty knots, distantly across our wake. It was developing winds of ninety knots, and we began to feel the southerly swell conflicting with the northeast trades. This made for an atrocious motion. My log entry on June 11 reads:

If I ever get sea fever again, I want to recall vividly this whip-sawing, snap-roll motion which permits no rest for the body.

We ache constantly, and there is no such thing as a restful sleep.
The motion now with only the squared-off twins is brutal, but
I don't dare set fore and aft sails.
Another 162 mile run. Shirley finding it extremely difficult to
cook with the violence of this snap-rolling motion.
18th day out: Honolulu broadcast stations coming in loud and
clear. Wow, what a thrill! Jet airplane contrails in the sky.

Five years ago, our friend, Louis Valier, had cast off our lines
as we sailed from Honolulu. On Friday, June 13, I talked to him
on the radio and told him that we would be abeam of Makapu
Light the next morning at 0300 and should enter Ala Wai Boat
Harbor at 0500. Louis said that he would meet us.

"Land—there—off to the southwest!" Almost imperceptibly
rearing its head above the clouds was eleven-thousand-foot
Haleakala on Maui, and off our port bow was the low, dark
streak of Molokai.

A perfect landfall nineteen days out of Mexico!

Louis had told us that small-craft warnings had been up for
several days, and the Molokai Channel was very rough. But
flying along with the seas and wind astern, we couldn't care
less. We were going to make it! As we passed Diamond Head,
by prearrangement, we turned on our strobe light, which
Louis saw clearly from his apartment lanai.

Coming out of a rain-filled squall, we dropped the twins and
just at predawn, crossed our outbound path and entered the
narrow channel at Ala Wai Boat Harbor. What an incredibly
welcome sight was the tall, lean, smiling figure of Louis Valier,
standing on the wharf in front of the Ilikai Hotel, his arm
draped with aloha leis! As I maneuvered the boat alongside,
Shirl cast our mooring lines to Louis.

The *Morning Star* was tied up and at rest—after an adventure-packed voyage around the world.

We were elated and felt a deep sense of personal achievement, coupled with mixed emotions of sadness that it was finished. We had fulfilled our dream, and the dream of many sailors—to circumnavigate the globe. Alone, we had sailed our
traditional little wooden ship *Morning Star* the full circle of the
earth. The *Morning Star* had safely carried us across most of

the oceans of the world and across and through dozens of the seas of the world.

Shirl and I had lived through so many adventures—grounding on coral reefs, rescue at sea, storms at sea, pirate encounters, sailing through the reefs and mine fields off Egypt. We had seen and experienced so much that we could never be the same two people again.

As we tried to adapt to the anticlimactic letdown, memories of faraway places with strange-sounding names kept flickering through our minds:

The Marquesas Islands, the Tuamotus, Ahe, Tepoto, Taenga, Katiu, Raroia, Makemo, Fakarava, Tahiti, Mooréa, Huahine, Raïatéa, Tahaa, Bora Bora, Niue, Tonga, Samoa, Uvea, Futuna, Fiji, New Zealand, New Hebrides, Solomons, Papua-New Guinea, Australia, Bali, Maduro, Borneo, Indonesia, the Java Sea, Sumatra, Singapore, Malaysia, Thailand, Sri Lanka, Arabia, Sudan, Egypt, Israel, Cyprus, Turkey, Greece, Italy, Sicily, Malta, the Balearics, Spain, Gibraltar, Morocco, the Canary Islands, Senegal, The Gambia, Trinidad-Tobago, Venezuela, San Blas, Panama, Costa Rica, Mexico—and now the full circle was completed.

Concluding our adventure, we were deeply grateful to the God of the Universe in whose palm we rest secure from minute to minute of our brief lives on this planet. We know that what we casually call "luck," is divine Providence.

We are convinced that no event is an accident. Everything has purpose. We know that without his mantle of ever-patient protection, interest, and love for us, we could never have accomplished the circumnavigation. Without his hourly guidance, it would have been impossible for us to have fulfilled our Voyage of Commitment.

CHAPTER TWENTY-NINE

RETURN TO THE GOLDEN GATE

On our one-year shakedown voyage—what seemed like an eternity ago—our then eighteen-year-old son Ray was a crew member. But we discovered that the situation of teenage boys confined with their parents on a small boat at sea does not produce a harmonious crew arrangement. Now Ray was twenty-six—a grown man about to be married.

When he graduated from college, he wrote a beautiful letter to us. One particularly poignant passage touched Shirl and me very deeply: "I don't see how I could have hassled you so much on our South Pacific voyage. I only wish that I had it to do over again."

When Ray phoned his congratulations to us in Honolulu, he asked, "How about me coming over there and sailing back with you? I would love one last high seas voyage."

I reminded him of what a rough, windward passage this was when in 1968 we sailed from Hawaii to San Francisco in our thirty-five-foot sloop *Voyageur.* Ray was only thirteen then, and we have a tendency to remember the good and to forget the bad.

Ray said, "Dad, it was wet, cold, and uncomfortable—I remember it well. But I would love it—and, dad, this time you can be sure, after what you and mom have just done, I will also remember that at sea there can be only one skipper. How about it, dad?"

My answer, "You're on, son. We would love to have you back on the *Morning Star.* As soon as she is rerigged, hop on a plane and aloha."

On August 6, 1981, Ray deplaned in Honolulu, and on August 8, we slipped our moorings and began the grueling slog against the northeast trades back to San Francisco.

Caught in a heavy North Pacific gale, my heart swelled with pride as I watched this courageous young man standing his lonely watch despite violent seasickness. He was all man now. No complaints. No negativism.

One cold, overcast day, the rudder and vane became sluggish, and the wheel became hard to turn. Hanging over the stern, Ray and I saw a heavy fishnet hopelessly entangled in the rudder, propeller, and vane. It had to be cut free.

We hove to, and as I tied a line around my waist, preliminary to jumping into the cold sea, Ray said, "Dad, let me do that." I replied, "No, Ray, I am used to the pitching action of the hove-to stern, so I'll dive down there and cut this thing free. If you get under that rudder, it could snap your spine like a toothpick."

Slashing away at the wirelike Japanese fishnet, I dove again and again. Finally, when I had cut the net free, I surfaced and climbed up the boarding ladder back on deck.

As I toweled off the chilly water, Ray, with a wide-eyed look, said, "Dad, you are one tough old hombré." I glowed with the compliment and said, "Thanks, son, but dammit, don't call me old."

Another day, watching his mother fighting to keep her balance as she cooked in our pitching galley, Ray declared, "Mom, you are something else! I just don't see how you two did what you did all alone! I hope that when I am fifty-nine years old, I have half the guts and stamina that you two have."

How different had become the perspective of this young man! He was seeing his parents through a new set of eyes.

Notwithstanding the mighty sea hurling what seemed to us

like one last reminder of her fickle, volatile nature, we had a happy, love-filled twenty-two-day passage.

Colorfully dressed, with all of the flags of the many countries visited fluttering from her rigging—with forty-five thousand miles under her keel—a little over eight years from the date of her departure—the *Morning Star* sailed with the tide under the Golden Gate Bridge.

Home were the sailors—home from the sea.

Return to Golden Gate

EPILOGUE

LESSONS LEARNED

People often ask us these questions:
"What did this change of life-style—this voyage around the world—do for you? What was the essential purpose of your voyage? In what way did these eight years change your life? What were your most significant learning experiences?"

We learned many valuable lessons, among which was the value of silence.

The mentor of Confucius, Lao-tzu, said, "Silence is the great revelation." To become acquainted with the revelation that is the reward of silence we found that we first had to achieve prolonged daily periods of silence, a quality of silence that can be listened to only with the heart.

Whether during our long, lonely night watches at sea, under the stars, with the silence only broken by the hissing, bubbling sea, accompanied by the soft, sighing of the trade winds, or anchored in the uninhabited glittering lagoon of a remote South Sea island, we found and luxuriated in the silence of the universe.

These interludes of silence gave us unmatched opportunity to turn within—to quell the turbulence of our inner being—to tune out the clamor and pace of everyday life in our ordinary milieu, in order to tune in to the essential purpose of our lives.

"Who are we? Where did we come from? What are we doing here? Where are we going? How are we going to get there?"

As we indulged in extended silence, we were confined to just observing rather than searching or striving. We simply absorbed everything that presented itself to our sensual consciousness—the vast, empty sea, its creatures, the vaulted heavens above. We discovered that as the essence and quality of our awareness improved, our inner silence became more profound and we began to experience subtle changes and heightened perceptions. With the spirit-cleansing effect of the sea, we became aware that the self-revelation attained was not mere knowledge but rather an all-transforming awesome power. As this awareness increased, we became more alive in the present than ever before. We were afforded the priceless opportunity to get into intimate touch with our feelings, to know and to love ourselves and others in an entirely different way.

As we developed a deep awareness of the perceptions of our *senses*, we learned that our lives had been lived *too much in our heads*. Our sense of aliveness had been obscured by the abstract thinking and fantasizing going on in our minds. This overemphasis on mental activity had heretofore diminished the perceptions of our physical senses.

Consequently, we had rarely lived in the exclusive present— the now—the circumstances of the moment. Our minds, for the most part, had been preoccupied with what was past or what lay in the future.

The past was saturated with regrets over mistakes made, guilt about past errors of omission or commission, wallowing over past triumphs, and seething in resentments for real or fancied past affronts inflicted upon us by others.

Dwelling on the future, our immediate sense of awareness was beclouded by apprehension of the "What Ifs" or the contemplation of future delights and daydreaming about future expectations.

Life at sea excludes the past, and coping with the present crowds out the anxieties of the future. The cares of what might happen tomorrow simply had to wait until the present day was done. We learned how to savor the daily gift of life.

Our life at sea taught us acceptance. How to accept every-thing that daily life throws at us. Not to become angry or impa-tient but to *accept*. In a storm at sea it would be an act of insan-ity for me to stand on the deck of the *Morning Star* shaking my fist in anger at the towering seas sweeping down on us. We couldn't fight the sea; we couldn't flee from the sea; so we learned to just flow with the sea—to bend in order not to break.

The voyage taught us how to cope. How to make do or die. Cut off from dependence on others, our dependence was trans-ferred from the unreliability of self and other human beings to the total reliability upon and surrender to the will of our Cre-ator. Brought into sharp focus was just how totally were our lives suspended—from breath to breath—from heartbeat to heartbeat—by a fragile thread clutched between the fingers of Almighty God.

In visiting dozens of underprivileged countries, we came to a sense of deep appreciation of and renewed love for America. We became humbly grateful to God that we were born in this great land of freedom and opportunity. As I saw the suffering, hunger, and disease of peoples all over the world, particularly in Asia and Africa, I, many times, thought, "There, but for the grace of God go I." I related to these people because I pondered this proposition: "God put me on this earth. He could just as well have put me into conditions of ongoing human suffering like this. It was none of my doing that I am here at this time. So how can I claim credit for anything?"

"I am not a self-made or self-guided man."

In carrying to successful conclusion the fulfillment of our voyage of commitment, we reflected on just how our commit-ment was formed—first with a dream; then an analysis of our ability to fulfill this dream realistically. Then a burning desire that, when kept constantly in our stream of consciousness, inevitably transformed our dream into reality and fulfillment. As the great poet Carl Sandburg said, "All we need to begin with is a dream. Nothing happens until first we have a dream."

Shirl and I subjected our dream to the scrutiny of assess-ment—commitment—trust—and noted that the first letters of these words spell *act*. We observed that every human being has his world to circumnavigate—his mountain to climb—his private dream. The dreams of all of us vary and are as unique to us as is our individuality.

We learned that along the way, in the fulfillment of our commitments, all of us inevitably encounter our personal Heartbreak Harbors, reefs, storms, and, yes, even pirates. We all are strongly tempted to stray off the path of commitment—to rationalize—to make excuses. But by drawing on the infinite resources of God we learned that every human being can fulfill his or her personal Voyage of Commitment. Taken in its entirety, the essential lesson learned and relearned daily taught us truly that only a fool can say in his heart of hearts "There is no God." We came to the obvious, stark conclusion that either God is *everything* or he is nothing.

Shirley and I really didn't sail around the world alone. There were three of us in the crew of the *Morning Star*—Shirl, me, and God.

> *"God begins at any point one thousand*
> *miles from the nearest land."*
>
> JOSEPH CONRAD

GLOSSARY OF NAUTICAL
AND FOREIGN TERMS

Aback   Backward against the mast—an unmanageable condition because of a sudden shift of wind to the opposite side of the sails

Abaft   At or toward the stern or rear of a ship

Abaft the beam   Behind the beam. See Beam

Abeam   Abreast of the middle of a ship's side

Ahull   Lying with no sails set in a storm

Aloft   Up above, up the mast or up the rigging

Amidships   In or toward the middle of a ship—midway between bow and stern, neither port nor starboard

Anemometer   A gauge for measuring the speed of the wind

Antifoul   To paint bottom with cuprous oxide paint, which poisons marine growth

Astern   Behind the ship

Athwartship   Across; from one side to the other—opposite of fore and aft

Autopilot   An electronic/mechanical steering device

Back   To reverse, to back sails against wind, wind backs when it shifts in a counterclockwise direction. Opposite: see *Veer*

Backed sail   Wind pushing sail backward

Backstay   A stainless steel wire support leading aft from the top of the mast to prevent it from bending forward

Barnacle   Saltwater shellfish that attaches itself to a ship's bottom

Batten down   Prepare all ship's openings for storm

Beam   A ship's breadth at its widest point, the side of a ship or the direction extending outward on either side at right angles to the fore-and-aft line of a ship

Beam reach   Sailing with wind striking sails from a direction off its beam

Beamy   Broad beam, broad, massive

Bearing   A direction relative to one's own position or to the compass

Beat   Sailing as close to the wind as possible in order to make progress to windward

Beaucoup   (French) Many, a lot

Becalmed   Motionless from lack of wind

Bedded   Caulked with puttylike material

Bilge   The rounded, lower part of a ship's hull. The space in a boat beneath the cabin floorboards

Binnacle   The case or stand enclosing a ship's compass

Bitt   A cleat or object around which a rope is wound

Bitter end   That end of a rope or cable that is wound around a bitt. The end of a rope or line

Boat hook   A pole with a hook on the end

Bollard   A strong post on a dock for holding a hawser fast

Bolt cutter   A heavy-duty mechanical shear for cutting heavy steel, chain, and wire

Bow   The front part of a ship; opposed to the stern

Bow pulpit   Steel rail around bowsprit platform to protect sailor from falling overboard

Bowsprit   A spar from which the foremost sail (jib) is attached projecting from the bow

Broke out   To unpack, to arise, to remove from storage

Butt blocks   A block of wood used in wooden boat construction to internally bridge over and connect where two ends of planks meet end to end

Cable   A chain or rope securing the anchor. Also, a British measure of distance—600 feet

Cable clamp   Clamp devised to bolt together two lengths of wire or wire rope

Caulk   To make a boat watertight by filling the seams or cracks with oakum, tar, or special puttylike caulking compound

Caulking cotton   Cotton strips used in caulking seams to make vessel watertight

Celestial navigation Position determination by observation of the sun, moon, stars, and planets

Certainement (French) Certainly, to be sure

Chafe check Inspection of worn or chafed areas of lines and sails

Chafe guard Canvas or other material to protect lines and sails from wear and chafe

Cleat An object to which a line is made fast

Clew The after lower corner of a fore-and-aft sail

Closing Ships approaching one another

Cockpit A sunken space toward the stern used by the steersman

Combers A large wave that rolls over or breaks

Come up Head into wind

Companionway Passage to the below-decks area of a vessel

Condenser Tanklike device through which passes cold seawater, which, in turn, cools hot refrigerant gas

Coordinates Latitude and longitude—position of vessel

Corona A crown of flowers in Polynesia

Cross bearings Bearings taken from objects of known position—i.e., lighthouse, point of land—where such bearings cross, fixes position of vessel

Cutter A single-masted sailing yacht carrying two headsails under normal wind conditions

Dan buoy Fiberglass man-overboard marker pole

Deadhead A watersoaked log floating in a verticle position just beneath the surface of the water

Dhows A single-masted vessel with a lateen sail, sharp prow, and raised deck at the stern, used in the Indian Ocean and Arabic countries, especially along coasts

Dielectric Nonconductor of electricity

Difficile (French) Difficult

Dismasted To remove or destroy the mast of a sailing vessel

Dock lines Mooring lines, ropes used to attach vessel to dock

Double head rig Two headsails, i.e., jib with forestaysail on separate stay behind it

Draw Sail begins to propel boat forward

Dugout Canoe hollowed from tree

Easting Making progress to the east

Ebb tide The outgoing or falling tide; opposed to flood tide

École (French) School

Engine intake Underwater aperture into which seawater is pumped, which, in turn, cools the engine

ETA Estimated time of arrival

Fair tide Tide running with the direction of the vessel

Fairwind Winds pushing a sailing vessel from behind

Fathom A measurement of depth equal to six feet

Felucca A narrow, lateen-rigged sailing vessel, chiefly of the Mediterranean area

Fender A pad, cushion of rope, or inflatable device hung over a ship's side to protect it in docking

Fender boards A board hung over the fenders to protect vessel's side against pilings, docks, or anything to which it is moored

Flaked To lay out a chain back and forth in an orderly manner in order to prevent pyramiding or entangling upon itself

Forced draft Full speed

Forereaching Making headway while hove to

Forestay Stainless steel wire running from the top of the mast to the end of the bowsprit to which the jib is fastened

Forestay eyebolt ¾″-diameter bolt bent into a closed circle to which the forestay is anchored

Forestaysail Second headsail behind the jib

Foretip Bowsprit—farthest point forward

Furl To wrap sail around furling spar

Furling line Rope controlling furling sails from cockpit

Furling tubes Stainless steel tube around which headsails are wrapped when furled

Garboards The planks adjoining the keel

Genoa forestaysail Large overlapping forestaysail

Genoa jib Large overlapping jib or headsail

Gunwale The upper edge of a boat's side

Halyard A rope used for hoisting a sail or a flag

Ham Amateur radio operator

Ham radio Amateur radio

Hank A cliplike piston device to fasten sail to wire stays

Harness Webbed straps fitting over the shoulders and around the waist of a sailor that are secured to the vessel to prevent falling overboard

Hauled out A vessel out of the water for maintenance and repairs

Hawser A large rope or small cable by which a ship is anchored, moored, or towed

Headstay See forestay

Heave to To stop forward movement by hauling in sail and heading into the wind

Heel, heeling To lay over off center as sailboat progresses to windward

Hove to Lying in head-to-wind position with sails aback—stopped

Jib Headsail—sail farthest forward

Jibe Turn the boat with stern through the wind

Jury rig Improvised, temporary, or emergency repair made out of whatever materials are available

Keel The main timber or steel piece extending along the entire length of the bottom of a boat or ship and supporting the frame

Kedge An anchor used for maneuvering or hauling a vessel off when she has gone aground

Ketch A fore-and-aft rigged sailing vessel with a mainmast toward the bow and a relatively tall mizzenmast, forward of the rudderpost, toward the stern; distinguished from yawl

Knot Aside from rope knots, a knot is a unit of speed of one nautical mile (6,076.12 feet) an hour

Landfall A sighting of land from a ship at sea

Lateen A triangular sail attached to a long yard suspended obliquely from a short mast

Lateen rig Having a lateen sail

Lavalava Wraparound skirt worn by both men and women

Lay off To turn with the wind

Lee The side or part sheltered or away from the wind

Lee of island Protection from wind and seas afforded by island with wind blowing against it, striking it on opposite, or windward, side

Lee shore Land in the direction toward which the wind blows

Leeward In the direction toward which the wind blows; opposed to windward

Light fee A charge for the use of navigational lights

Line A rope, i.e., heaving line, dock line

Log A device for determining the speed of and distance covered by a ship

Loom To appear, come in sight indistinctly, reflection in sky of lights below the horizon

Luff, luffed up Heading a sailboat into the wind

Lying ahull Drifting without any sail set in a storm

Magnaflux X ray of metal

Main Spanish Main—mainland

Main See mainsail

Mainsail In a fore-and-aft-rigged vessel, the large sail set from the mainmast

Mainsheet The sheet of a mainsail; line controlling the angle at which a mainsail is set

Marine railway Rail tracks extending into the water that support a cradled car used to haul vessel out of the water

Marlinspike seamanship The arts of the sailor involving rope and wire splicing, knot tying, etc.

Masthead The top or truck of the mast

Mayday Verbal distress call, i.e., S.O.S. in Morse code

Meltemi Strong northerly winds, especially found in the Aegean Sea

Mizzenmast The mast closest to the stern in a ship with two or three masts

Mizzen sail The sail set on the mizzenmast

Mooring bitt Any of the deck posts around which ropes or cables are wound and held fast

Motu Polynesian. A small islet or island

Muzzle Smother a falling sail

Outrigger A timber rigged out from the side of certain canoes to prevent tipping

Pandanus Malay pandanus same as screw pine, the leaves of which are used in many parts of the world for everything from basketweaving to roofing on grass huts

Pareu Wraparound skirt worn by both men and women

Paw paw Papaya fruit

Pay off Head off with the wind

Pilot A person who directs or steers ships into or out of harbor or through difficult waters

Pilot books A series of publications by the British Admiralty describing ports, facilities, routes, and all pertinent information to all of the sea lanes of the world

Piping up   Winds increasing

Pirogue   A canoe made by hollowing out a large log—any canoe-shaped boat

Plank   Horizontal section of teakwood 4″ x 1¼″ wooden planks making up the hull of the *Morning Star*

Planked   Act of applying planks

Planking   The horizontal planks used in the construction of a wooden vessel

Pod   A small group of animals, especially of seals and whales

Poles   Horizontal poles projecting from the mast

Port   The left-hand side of a ship as one faces forward, toward the bow; opposed to starboard

Porthole   Window of ship

Pour   (French) For, on account of; on behalf of; for the sake of; in the direction of; as regards; as for; in order; although

Q flag   Yellow quarantine flag required to be displayed until a ship has been cleared into a foreign port

Quarter   The after part of a ship's side—either port or starboard—the sections of a ship lying midway between her midships and her stern

Quartering   Seas or wind coming over after part of a ship's side

Radio patch   An amateur radio communication wherein one telephoned party can communicate a radio message directly to another telephoned party

Rafted, rafted up   Vessels tied up alongside one another

Ratlines   A ladderlike affair of wood or rope fastened into the rigging, used to climb up and down

Reach, beam   A point of sailing with the wind directly off the beam

Reach, broad   A point of sailing with the wind abaft the beam but not so far astern as to make the vessel running before the wind with the wind dead astern

Reach, close   A point of sailing with the wind forward of the beam but not so far as to make the vessel close hauled

Reef   To shorten sail, usually preliminary to heavy weather. A line or ridge of rock or coral lying at or near the surface of the water

Reefing spar   The two stainless steel spars upon which the headsails are secured, which, when rolled, will shorten or furl sail

Reef points   The means to tie down a reefed or shortened sail

Rig   The various wires, stays, and shrouds that support the masts of a sailing vessel

Rigging: standing, running   Standing rigging support wires permanently in place; running rigging; sheets, halyards, topping lifts,
downhauls, etc.

Rogue sea   A sea larger and often coming from another direction
than that of the seas preceding it

Rolling anchorage   An anchorage where the ocean swell causes a
vessel to roll

Run   To sail with the wind behind the yacht

Safety harness   See Harness

Sailing directions   A set of pilot books containing all pertinent data
re sections of the world, the seas, weather, and the ports, bays, and
anchorages in the world

Schooner   A ship with two or more masts rigged fore and aft, the
mainmast being as tall or taller than the foremast

Sea cock   A valve below the waterline in the hull of a ship used to
control the intake of seawater

Sea dye marker   A yellow stain that spreads over the surface of the
sea to enable searchers from the air to spot a man or object in the
sea

Seams   The space between the planking of a wooden vessel; on a
sail, the stitching that holds two cloths together

Sea room   Ample space at sea to allow maneuverability of sailing
vessel

Servopendulum rudder   See Servorudder

Servorudder   The airfoil section of a self-steering vane that is in the
water and is actuated by the power of the vessel's movement
through the water—moves side to side in a pendulum motion

Shackles   Any of several devices used in fastening or coupling

Shark repellent   A dark chemical that spreads over the sea; theoret-
ically to repel sharks

Sheet   A rope attached to a lower corner of a sail; it is shortened or
slackened to control the set of the sail

Sheet bend   A knot to tie the ends of ropes together

Shroud—upper, lower   Any of a set of ropes or wires stretched from
a ship's side to a masthead to offset lateral strain on the mast

Sights   Sextant observations of the heavenly bodies

S'il vous plaît   (French) If you please

Slatting   Lying becalmed with sails empty of wind snapping with
the motion of the vessel

Sleepers or railroad tie   Wooden cross section upon which railroad
tracks are laid

Slipway   A slope into the sea fitted with rails or skids, used for hauling a vessel out of the water

Slog   To make way with great effort, difficult sail to windward

Sloop   A fore-and-aft rigged, single-masted sailing vessel with a mainsail and a jib, and, sometimes, a spinnaker for racing

Spar   Any pole—as a mast, yard, boom, or gaff—supporting or extending a sail of a ship

Speak ship   Two ships meeting on the high seas coming close to exchange greetings with one another

Spinnaker   A large triangular, baggy headsail used when running before the wind

Spitfire jib   Small storm jib or headsail

Squall   A brief, violent wind, usually with rain or snow

Starboard   The right-hand side of a ship as one faces forward; toward the bow; opposed to port

Staysail boom   A wooden boom upon which the forestaysail is stretched along its foot

Storm jib   A small, strong jib used in heavy weather; the foremost sail on the vessel

Storm trysail   A small, strong sail set in place of the mainsail but not attached to the boom. Used in heavy weather

Strike sail   To drop sails

Strobe light   Electronic flashing brilliant light

Sulu   Wraparound skirt worn by both men and women

Swab   A mop for cleaning decks, floors, etc.

Swage   A kind of tool for bending or shaping metal

Swage fitting   A pressed-on fitting in the shape of a fork or an eye that is used to terminate the wire rigging on a sailboat

Swell   Long waves, the crests of which do not break

Tack   See Tacking, to tack

Tacking, to tack   A series of zigzag movements in a course against the wind

Taffrail   The rail around the stern of a ship

Telephone patch   See Radio patch

Teredo worms   A long, wormlike bivalve; marine mollusks that bore into and destroy submerged wood as of ships, pilings, etc.; shipworm

Through-hull fittings   Any device that penetrates the hull of a vessel; See Sea cock

Topsides   That part of a ship's side that is above water when she is afloat

Trades   See Tradewinds

Tradewinds   A wind that blows steadily toward the equator from the northeast in the tropics north of the equator and from the southeast in the tropics south of the equator

Travail   (French) Labor, work, industry, toil, trouble, pains, travail, childbirth, task, job

Très   (French) Very; most; very much

Trough   Small canyon or valley between large waves

Truck of mast   A small wooden block or disk with holes for halyards at the top of a mast

Turnbuckle   A metal sleeve with opposite internal threads at each end for the threaded ends of two rods or for ringbolts forming a coupling that can be turned—used to tauten or slacken rigging—British: bottlescrew

Turn of the bilge   The place on a vessel where the sides curve inward to meet the keel below

Twins   Two identical sails set well forward and poled out for sailing before the wind

Underwater epoxy putty   A two-part epoxy putty that can be molded and applied under water where it will harden—used for emergency repairs

Underway   Vessel moving through water; not at anchor or moored or aground

Un peu   (French) Little, not much; few, not many; not very

Vane   Wind vane, steering vane—a self-steering device actuated by wind and the power of the vessel's motion through the water. The wind turns a wind vane that through a series of gears turns an airfoil-shaped servorudder in the water, where the motion of the water causes the rudder to swing in a pendulum motion, transmitting this energy via ropes to the yacht's steering rudder

Vane line   A rope connecting the self-steering vane to the vessel's wheel or tiller

Veer   A change of wind; to shift clockwise. To change the direction of a ship by swinging its stern to the wind; wear ship. Opposite: wind backs counter clockwise

V.H.F.   Very high frequency short-range FM radio transmitter/ receiver

Vigia   A warning mark on a sea chart, i.e., "breakers reported"

Wake   The track or trail of disturbed water left in the water by a moving ship or boat

Windlass   An apparatus operated by hand or power for hoisting or hauling the anchor chain or ropes around its drum or cylinder

Windward   In the direction or side from which the wind blows; toward the wind, moving windward, on the side from which the wind blows; opposed to leeward

Wore or wear ship   To turn or bring a ship about by swinging its bow away from the wind; opposed to tack; coming about by having the stern turned through the wind

Yawl   A fore-and-aft rigged sailing vessel with a mainmast toward the bow and a much smaller mast set far aft, usually abaft the rudder post; distinguished from a ketch

The Track of the Ketch
Morning Star